CAPTIVE IN JAPAN

CAPTIVE IN JAPAN

VASILY GOLOVNIN

EDITED BY WILLIAM DE LANGE

First edition, 2020

Originally published as *Memoirs of a captivity in Japan*

Published by TOYO Press

Copyright © 2020 TOYO Press

ISBN 978-94-92722-256

Contents

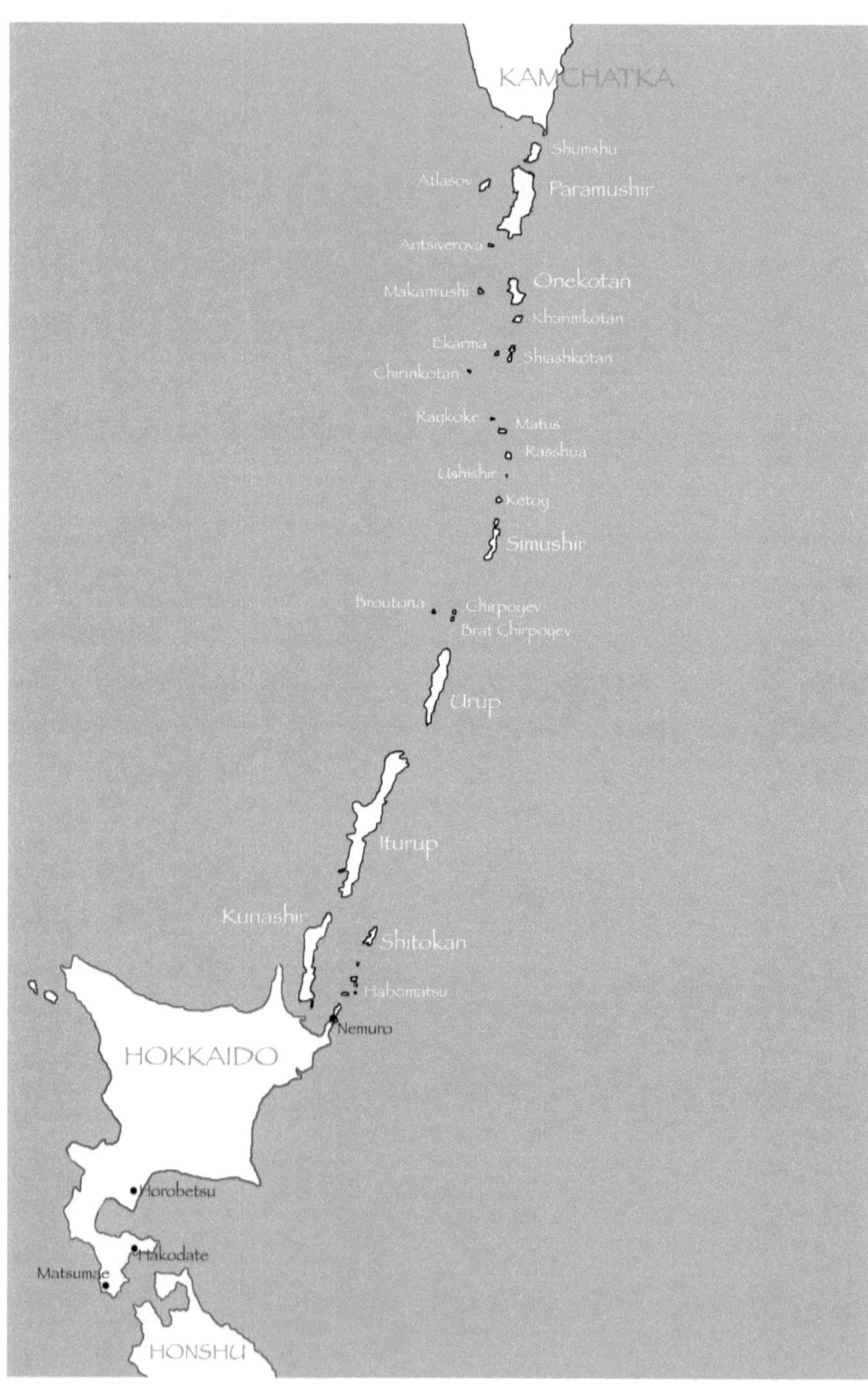

KAMCHATKA
Shumshu
Atlasov
Paramushir
Antsiverova
Makanrushi
Onekotan
Kharimkotan
Ekarma
Shiashkotan
Chirinkotan
Raykoke
Matus
Rasshua
Ushishir
Ketoy
Simushir
Broutona
Chirpoyev
Brat Chirpoyev
Urup
Iturup
Kunashir
Shitokan
Habomatsu
Nemuro
HOKKAIDO
Horobetsu
Hakodate
Matsumae
HONSHU

Departure

In April, 1811, I had the command of the imperial sloop of war, *Diana*, which then lay at Kamchatka, where I received an order from the minister of the marine, directing me to survey, in the most minute manner, the Southern Ainu and Shantar Islands, and the coast of Tartary, from the latitude 53° 38' north to Okhotsk.

The minister's dispatch referred to two papers, containing a copious detail of the instructions I was to follow, which had been forwarded by the Board of Admiralty, at the same time as his order. These papers, however, I did not receive. And according to the arrangements of the post office, they could not, as will appear from the following explanation, reach Kamchatka before autumn. In the course of the winter, three posts are dispatched from Okhotsk to Kamchatka. The last, which arrived at Petropawlowsk (the harbor of St. Peter and St. Paul) on the 20th of April, did not bring me the papers, and consequently they had not reached Okhotsk when the post left that place. But as the post departs only once a month from St. Petersburg for Okhotsk, the papers, if brought there by the next arrival, would have to be sent off to me one month after the departure of the third post. This too would be precisely the time when the snow melts, the rivers overflow their banks, and a complete interruption of communication takes place in these countries. It was, besides, impossible, on the re-opening of the navigation, to send the papers by sea from Okhotsk, as there was then no vessel in that harbor, all the transports having wintered in Kamchatka. To obtain the papers in course of the summer, there remained then no other means except that of sailing myself with the sloop to Okhotsk. The commander of that harbor, the captain of second rank, Minitzky, had indeed advised me to come to Okhotsk before the commencement of the expedition, as he, according to what he stated in his letter, presumed that the sloop must be in want of provisions and repairs, which could be obtained in that harbor. With respect to the latter, I observed no damage I could not repair with my own people. But as to the provisions, there was really a considerable deficiency, compared with the established rate of supply. I took, therefore, from the transport *Dionysius*, which had wintered at Petropawlowsk, what provisions remained on board that vessel. And I calculated that, with this addition to the stock of the *Diana*, I should be able to keep at sea for three months, without incurring any risk of short allowance.

I had thus no reason for going to Okhotsk before the commencement of the expedition, except that of obtaining possession of the two papers with my instructions, which had been forwarded by the Admiralty. This was, doubtless, a motive of considerable weight: the pleasure of His Imperial Majesty had, however, been fully made known to me by the order of the minister of the marine. I knew what coasts I had to explore, and that the result of my investigations ought to be detailed with the greatest accuracy. But in what particular manner, and to what degree of minuteness I was to execute the duty imposed on me, were circumstances respecting which the Admiralty dispatch would doubtless have served as an explanation and a guide. Though that dispatch could be regarded only as a supplement to the order I had already received, the papers referred to might contain directions, the want of which would expose me to the risk of leaving considerable chasms in my survey, both on account of the insufficiency of my personal experience, and of my being necessarily destitute of the extensive information which the Admiralty department possessed respecting the seas I had to visit. I deeply regretted that I had not received those papers along with the ministers order, and foresaw all the difficulties that might arise from the want of them. On the other hand, I perceived that the result of any endeavour to obtain them now would only be loss of time, injury to the public service, and the absolute impossibility of accomplishing anything that might compensate for so much expense and trouble. In a word, had I sailed to Okhotsk, the summer, and consequently the whole year, must have elapsed without the slightest advantage to the expedition. This opinion was grounded on the following considerations.

First—I reflected that, after calculating the season at which my passage to Okhotsk would be practicable, I had to add to that period the necessary time for laying in provisions, fresh water, wood, etc. for a long voyage from Okhotsk to the Kuril Islands. Consequently, with the greatest exertions, and most favorable wind, I could not have reached the place where my investigations were to commence until the month of July: the months of May and June would therefore have been completely lost.

Secondly—the state of the sloop, and in some measure that of the crew, rendered it absolutely necessary that we should pass the winter in a harbor, where the vessel might be cleansed and repaired; for, since my departure from Kronstadt, in the year 1807, no opportunity had occurred for taking out the ballast or stores, in order to see what repairs were requisite for the hull. And the ill-built storehouses of Petropawlowsk are insufficient for the accommodation of the garrison, and there are no buildings for other purposes. Thus, unless we went into port, the stores of every kind must have remained another winter in the vessel, where swarms of rats already made the greatest havoc among the provisions, sails, woollen cloth, casks, and everything within their reach.

Besides, the men were in want of clothes: their shoes and stockings were completely worn out, and they required to be entirely new clothed, which could not possibly be done without going into Okhotsk harbor. These circumstances required that I should winter in Okhotsk, which it was necessary I should enter by the latter end of September, or at the latest the beginning of October. There remained therefore only three months for the duty I had to execute, and these were (with the exception of July) the most unfavorable for the expedition.

All navigators who have sailed in the seas I had to traverse complain of the cloudy weather and excessively thick fogs, which prevented them from approaching the coasts, and consequently from making any observations upon them. In the foregoing year, when I returned from America to Kamchatka along the chain of the Kuril Islands, I was convinced by experience of the truth of this complaint. Besides the continual mists that arise from the water, and totally conceal the coasts and islands, navigators have to encounter other difficulties of a still greater and more dangerous description: the currents met with among the Aleutian and Kuril Islands run with extraordinary violence, and the depth of water, even in the neigh-borhood of these islands, is so great, that at a distance of only three miles from land no bottom can be found, after sounding with a line of one hundred and fifty or two hundred fathoms. In these seas, therefore, no reliance can be placed on the lead, which in general affords a certain indication of the proximity of land. I was perfectly aware of all these circumstances, and was consequently impressed with the necessity of choosing the most favorable time for the execution of my enterprise. For this purpose I perused the published accounts of the voyages of the most celebrated navigators, who have visited the quarter to which I was about to proceed, and from that perusal I collected the following information.

On the 9th of October, 1779 (N. S.), the English ships *Resolution* and *Discovery*, which, after the death of Captains James Cook and Charles Clerk, were commanded by Captain John Gore, sailed from the Bay of Awatska, with the view, in addition to the discoveries which were the object of their voyage, to explore the chain of the Kuril Islands. They succeeded in seeing only the first and second islands, namely, Shumshu and Paramushir; a violent westerly wind having prevented them from approaching the others, notwith-standing their most strenuous endeavours. The first land they had sight of, after these two islands, was the eastern coast of Japan, latitude 40° 05', which they descried on the 26th of October.

Captain Gore did not relinquish his plan of visiting the southern Kuril Islands, but violent storms prevented him from putting his design into exe-cution. He left the Bay of Awatska in the end of September (N. S.). Hence I inferred that the months of September and October are by no means favorable for nautical observations on the Kuril Islands.

In the middle of August, 1787, La Perouse sailed between the Peninsula of Sachalin and the Island of Hokkaido, through the strait which has since borne his name. Between Cape Aniwa and Cape Trou, on the Island of Iturup, which he descried on the 19th of August, he saw no other islands except the islands of Urup and Simushir between which he sailed. This strait he named La Boussole, after his own frigate. But the continued thick fogs prevented him from making further observations on the Kuril Islands, and he was compelled to abandon his design, and to direct his course to Kamchatka, which he did on the 1 st of September (O. S.).

Captain Gavril Andreyevich Sarychev, in his account of his voyage to the north-eastern parts of Siberia, on the *Frozen* and the *Eastern Oceans*, says that he sailed from the Bay of Awatska on the 6th of August, (O. S.) 1792, for the purpose of visiting the Korean Sea. He steered S. W. along the Kuril Islands, but owing to the thick fogs he did not discover land until the 20th. In latitude 47 28', he perceived what he supposed to be the Island of Simushir, and some others, but thick mists prevented him from observing them closely. And he was ultimately obliged to give up his design, and to return to Okhotsk. On his return he perceived the seventh island, and the peak of the twelfth, and further on, the southern coast of the second island, and the summits of the three volcanoes on the fifth. But they were almost constantly enveloped in mist, and he was consequently unable to fix their geographical situations.

In the year 1796, the English captain, William Robert Broughton, quitted Vulcan's Bay, on the southern side of Hokkaido and sailed along the eastern coast of the same island. He then passed between Kunashir and Iturup, the former of which he conceived to be a portion of Hokkaido. He continued his course along the north-western coast of the Island of Iturup, but of which he merely saw the first half, and the north-east extremity, without being aware that these were parts of one and the same island. He then sailed along the western coast of Urup and Simushir, and reached the Island Ketoy. From there he returned along the southern coasts of Urup, Iturup, and Kunashir, without being able to make any observations, though he anxiously wished to ascertain correctly the situation of islands as yet so imperfectly known. Fogs, violent winds and weather, upon the whole very unfavorable, prevented him from carrying his design into execution. Capt. Broughton's cruise among the southern Kuril Islands took place in the month of October.

Captain Adam Johann von Krusenstern, who, in the year 1805, returned to Kamchatka from Japan, was among the Kuril Islands during the latter end of May and beginning of June. On his passage to the Peninsula of Sachalin, he also sailed through these islands in the early part of July, and again, on his return, in the end of August (N. S.). This I learned from his atlas, which I obtained, along with some other charts, from the under-pilot Kuritzyn, who had commanded a vessel belonging to our Russian-American Company. But not having read the second part of Captain Krusenstern's

Voyage Round the World, I had no knowledge of the weather he had experienced among these Islands.

In addition to the information thus obtained from the above celebrated navigators, who served me as a council on the subject of my enterprise, I endeavored also to discover persons in Kamchatka, who had made voyages to the islands I was directed to examine, and questioned them with the greatest strictness on every point of importance. But what sort of information could I derive from men so ignorant in navigation, and, above all, so limited in their excursions, as the popes and pelt hunters of Kamchatka, who merely go to the nearest inhabited Ainu Island with the officers who collect tribute? They only knew that there were some bright days in summer, but how often and how long they continued, and particularly in what places they experienced that favorable weather, were circumstances of which they could give no account. It was merely during the passage and in the straits that they paid any attention to the changes of the wind: when once on the Kuril Islands, they cared little for the state of the atmosphere, or any meteorological phenomena. To make booty and collect the tribute were their sole objects.

An under-pilot, named Andrejeu, a man whose knowledge in his profession was not altogether despicable, and who had been at the Kuril Islands with Lieutenant Nikolai Aleksandrowich Khvostov,[1] on board one of the company's vessels during the beginning of June, assured me that the weather was then favorable. In the preceding year, I had sailed from Kamchatka to America in June, and returned in August and September. At both periods we had rough and hazy weather, and the horizon was constantly covered with heavy clouds. All, therefore, that has been stated respecting the weather in the Eastern Ocean, convinced me that fogs might be considered as proper to that sea, that they prevail there in all months without exception, though in some more frequently than in others, and that there

1 Nikolai Aleksandrowich Khvostov (1776–1809) was the captain of the Juno and entered the Russian-American Company, a state-sponsored chartered company formed largely on the basis of the United American Company, on the invitation of Nikolai Rezanov. In 1805–1804, Rezanov had led an unsuccessful mission to try and establish trade relations with Japan. Unable to establish trade by diplomatic means, in 1806, and without the sanction from the Russian government, Rezanov organized a military expedition consisting of two ships, the *Juno* under the command of Khvostov, and the *Avos* under the command of Gavrill Ivanovich Davydov.

was in no season good and clear weather for more than a week together. I perceived also that to survey so extensive a chain of islands and coast as was prescribed to me, would require an entire summer, from the beginning of May until October. Besides, it would be necessary to keep the land at all times as hard on board as possible, in order, as soon as the fog dispersed, to approach the coast more closely. It might therefore happen that a full investigation could not be completed in three years. On all these grounds and considerations, I felt convinced that it was necessary to proceed as speedily as possible to the execution of my mission.

I will now briefly state the plan I intended to follow. I resolved to sail direct from Kamchatka to the Nadezhda Strait, between the Islands Matus and Rasshua, and to regulate my chronometer according to their situation, in case I should find no opportunity for lunar observations. I then proposed to steer along the southern coasts of the Kuril Islands, and to commence my observations with the Island of Ketoy, which had not been seen by the Nadeschda, and so on with every island in succession until I arrived at Hokkaido; next to sail between the Islands Iturup and Hokkaido, and to explore the whole northern coasts of the latter, until I should reach La Perouse's Straits. From there, keeping the Peninsula of Sachalin in view, to steer to the spot (53° 38' latitude), from where my investigation of the Tartar coast was to commence; with which, as well as my observations on the Shantar Islands, I hoped to be ready towards the latter end of the summer.

Having thus determined on my plan, I immediately set about preparing everything for my departure. I opened for myself a passage through the ice, and on the 25th of April got the sloop out from Petropawlowsk to Avacha Bay. On the 4th of May we weighed anchor and put to sea.

On the 1 4th of May I reached Nadezhda Strait, the place, from where, according to the plan I had laid down, I was to commence my observations. I will not here detain the reader by giving an account of my cruise among the Kuril Islands, or the nature of my investigation, as I have devoted a particular work to that object.

It is sufficient to say, that previous to the 17th of June, the first day of our accidental communication with the Japanese, notwithstanding the impediments of thick fogs and violent irregular currents, we succeeded in making observations on the following islands: the 13th island of Rasshua (counting from the Kamchatka Peninsula), the 14th Ushishir, the 15th Ketoy, the 16th Simushir, the 17th the two Chirpoyevs and Broutona, and the western coast of the 18th Urup.

I think it proper, before I proceed, to describe the treatment we received from the Japanese, and the unfortunate occurrences that ensued, to state all I then knew respecting the political relations between Russia and Japan.

About thirty years ago, a Japanese merchantman was wrecked on the Aleutian Island Amchitka. The crew of the vessel, and the commander, whose name was Rodai, were saved, and taken to Irkutzk, where these unfortunate Japanese lived about ten years. At the end of that period, the Empress Catharine gave orders that they should be conveyed back to their native country, and that advantage should be taken of that opportunity to ascertain whether some commercial relations, beneficial to both countries, might not be established between Russia and Japan. The orders received on this occasion by General Ivan Peel, magistrate in chief of Siberia, are worthy of particular attention. He was expressly instructed to send as envoy to Japan a person of rather inferior rank, bearing presents in his own (General Peel's) name, as magistrate of a frontier province, but by no means in the name of the Empress.

It was further ordered that the commander of the vessel employed on this occasion should neither be a native of England nor Holland. In obedience to these instructions, Governor Peel appointed Lieutenant Adam Laxman envoy, who embarked on board the transport *Catharina*, commanded by the pilot Lowzov, and sailed in the autumn of 1792, from Okhotsk to Japan. Laxman landed on the northern coast of the Island of Hokkaido, and passed the winter in the little harbor of Nemuro. In the following summer, in con-formity with the desire of the Japanese, he entered Hakodate harbor, which is situated on the southern coast of Hokkaido, near the Straits of Tsuruga, from where he travelled by land to Matsumae, which is three day's journey to the west of Hakodate. Here he entered into negotiations with officers sent from the capital, in consequence of which the Japanese government issued a declaration to the following effect:

1st. Although the Japanese laws ordain that all foreigners who may land upon any part of the coasts of Japan, the Harbour of Nagasaki excepted, shall be seized and condemned to perpetual imprisonment, the penalties inflicted by the said laws shall not be enforced against the Russians in the present instance, as they were ignorant of the existence of such statutes, and have brought with them Japanese subjects whom they had saved on their own coasts. And they shall be permitted, without let or molestation, to return immediately to their native country, on this condition, that they never again approach any part of Japan, except Nagasaki, even though Japanese subjects should be driven on the coast of Russia, otherwise the law shall be executed in its fullest force.

2nd. The Japanese government returns thanks for the conveyance of its subjects to their native country. But at the same time informs the Russians that they may either leave them, or take them back again, as they shall think lit; for, according to the Japanese laws, such persons cannot be forcibly detained, since those laws declare that men belong to that country on which their destiny may cast them, and in which their lives have been protected.

3d. With regard to negotiations for commercial arrangements, the Japanese can admit of no relations of that sort anywhere except in the harbor of Nagasaki; for that reason they gave Laxman for the present merely a written certificate, on producing which a Russian vessel might enter that harbor, where would be found Japanese officers furnished with full powers to treat further with the Russians on this matter.

Having received this declaration, Laxman returned to Okhotsk in the autumn of 1793. From his account it appears that the Japanese treated the Russians with the greatest civility and courtesy, showed them every mark of honor in a way conformable to the customs of their country, maintained at their own expense the officers and crew during the whole time they remained on the Japanese coasts, provided them at their departure with provisions, for which they refused to accept of any payment, and made them various presents. He only regretted that, owing to the strict execution of the laws, the Japanese would never permit them to go freely about the town, but kept a constant watch upon them. I cannot divine why the Empress did not, immediately on Laxman's return, dispatch a vessel to Nagasaki: probably the commencement of the French Revolution, which, at that period, disturbed the peace of Europe, occasioned her to neglect this opportunity.

In the year 1803 the chamberlain Nokolai Resanov[2] was sent to Japan by the present reigning monarch. The public have learned the details of that expedition from Captain Krusenstern's narrative; from which I also collected my information on the same subject, having, as I have already observed, read the first volume before my departure from Kamchatka. I therefore knew that, in the declaration the Japanese government communicated to Resanov, it was notified that no Russian ship would be permitted to approach the coasts of Japan. And that in case the subjects of that country were driven by storms on the coasts of Russia, they were to be conveyed home in Dutch and not in Russian vessels. On his return to Kamchatka, Resanov sailed to America in one of the Russian-American Company's ships, commanded by Lieutenant Khvostov. He returned to Okhotsk with the same officer, and was travelling through Siberia on his way to St. Petersburg, when he fell ill and died. Khvostov put to sea again, and attacked the Japanese villages on the Kuril Islands. Further information on this subject may be found in Vice-Admiral Alexander Semyonovich Shishkov's preface to the voyages of Khvostov and Gavrill Ivanovich Davydov.[3] Were Resanov and Khvostov still alive, we should probably have ample explanations respecting the proceedings of the latter. But as it is, we ought, in obedience to the old rule, to say nothing but good of the dead! I must observe, however, that I have been informed our government was dissatisfied with the conduct of this officer.

Having received orders to visit the Southern Kuril Islands, and being aware that some of them were in the possession of the Japanese, I endeavored

2 Nocolai Resanov (1764–1807) was a Russian nobleman and statesman who promoted the project of Russian colonization of Alaska and California to three successive Tsars—Catherine the Great, Paul, and Aleksander I. In 1805–1804, Rezanov also led an unsuccessful mission to try and establish trade relations with Japan. Unable to establish trade by diplomatic means, in 1806, and without the sanction from the Russian government, he organized a military expedition consisting of two ships, the *Avos* under the command of Davydov, and the *Juno* under the command of Nikolai Aleksandrowich Khvostov.

3 Gavrill Ivanovich Davydov (1781–1809) was the captain of the *Avos* and entered the Russian-American Company, a state-sponsored chartered company formed largely on the basis of the United American Company, on the invitation of Rezanov.

to collect all the information in my power respecting Khvostov's proceedings in those seas. For this purpose I examined a pilot who had accompanied him on his cruise. And I was convinced by that man's declaration that the two attacks on the Japanese were unwarrantable, arbitrary acts. And that they had not the slightest ground for supposing the hostilities of two insignificant vessels authorized by the sovereign of a country, the power and greatness of which must have been known to them from the descriptions of their countrymen, who had lived many years in Russia. The account given by this pilot fully corresponded with what I had heard when I first arrived at Kamchatka, from an officer of the company, named Masnikov, who had been attached to Khvostov's expedition. But notwithstanding the opinion I had thus formed, I resolved, unless superior orders should otherwise direct, to hold no intercourse with the Japanese.

My determination was to sail without any flag in the neighborhood of the islands belonging to them, in order to avoid exciting either fear or doubt in the minds of this distrustful people. But Providence was pleased to ordain otherwise, and probably for the better.

Such, as far as I have above explained, was the state of the relations between Russia and Japan, at the time when the duty I had to perform required me to approach the coasts of those islands that are under the dominion of the Japanese. And I now proceed to the most important part of my narrative.

On the afternoon of the 17th of June we found ourselves very near the western coast of the northern extremity of the Island of Iturup, though we were not immediately aware that the land we saw formed a part of that island. On the contrary, that extremity appeared to us like a separate island; for the Bay of Sana, which extends very far in-land, resembles a channel. On Captain Broughton's chart this part of the coast is not defined, he not being certain whether the opening formed a strait or a bay. In order to remove all doubt, we approached within three Italian miles of the land. We soon descried several huts, and two large kayaks, in which were several persons sailing to and from the shore. Under the supposition that the island was peopled by Ainu, I dispatched Ensign Feodor Mur, accompanied by the under-pilot Nawitzky, in an armed boat of four oars, in order to make observations on the island, and whatever they could discover. I soon observed a kayak sailing towards them from the shore. And not knowing what kind of reception they might meet with from the natives, I immediately ran the sloop close in the shore, and, along with a midshipman named Jakuschkin, got on board another armed boat, of four oars also, to hasten to their assistance. In the meanwhile the kayak had come up to our first boat, and having put about, they both rowed towards the shore, which I likewise reached in a short time after them.

First Encounter

On stepping ashore, I saw to my astonishment that Mur was engaged in conversation with some Japanese. He informed me that some of our Ainu, belonging to the thirteenth island (Rasshua), who had been driven here by storms in the preceding summer, were still on this island. And that the Japanese having kept them prisoners for about a year, had at length resolved to liberate them, and send them home. These Ainu had been sent out by the Japanese to meet the boat, to enquire what induced us to approach their coasts, and likewise state to him that the Japanese were apprehensive of our designs, and to entreat that we would not set foot on shore.

I was exceedingly astonished at hearing this. And asked Mur, with great dissatisfaction, how he, after the Ainu had stated this to him, could dare, of his own accord, and without any order from me, to go on shore with a handful of men among a people so hostile to us, and why he had not immediately turned back and communicated to me what the Ainu had said to him. He justified himself by saying he was fearful I might have ascribed such conduct to cowardice, and have sent another officer to the island in his stead; adding, that such a disgrace would have been irretrievable, and would have rendered his life a burden to him. Though this reason was far from being valid, yet I was convinced that the rash conduct of this officer arose solely from want of reflection. I did not say another word to him on the subject.

Mur pointed out to me the Japanese commander, who was standing on the shore, at some distance from his tent. He was surrounded by about eighteen or twenty men, in full military dress, and armed with guns and swords. Each of these men held the butt ends of their muskets with the left hand, but without any kind of regularity: in the right they held two small lighted matches. I saluted the commander, after the manner of my own country, with a bow, which he returned, by raising his right hand to his forehead, and bending his whole body towards me. We conversed by means of two interpreters, namely, one of his soldiers, who understood the Ainu language, and one of our Ainu, who could speak a little Russian.

The Japanese chief, an assistant commissioner of Matsumae's magistrate office (*bugyōsho shirabeyaku no shitayaku*), whose name was Ishizaka Buhei, began by asking for what reason we had come among them? If with a view to trade with no base designs upon them, we might sail further along the coast, until we got behind the volcano, where Horobetsu, the most productive part of the island, was situated.

I replied that we wished to find a safe harbor for our ship, where we might procure a supply of wood and water, of which we were greatly in want; that upon this being obtained we would immediately leave their coasts; that they had besides nothing to fear from us, as our sloop was an Imperial ship, and not a merchantman. And that, in fact, we had not visited their islands with the intention of doing them any injury whatever.

Having listened attentively to my explanation, he said, "The Japanese cannot be entirely tranquil and free from apprehension on the appearance of a Russian ship, for some years ago Russian vessels twice attacked the Japanese villages, and carried off or burnt everything they found, without sparing the houses, temples, or provisions. Rice, which is brought from Japan to these islands, forms the principal food for the inhabitants. But the first attack having taken place late in autumn, when no vessels could be sent to sea to bring back a fresh supply for winter, and the second having followed early in spring, before the usual rice ships could arrive, these circumstances, joined to the destruction of their houses, and caused great distress to the Japanese, many of whom fell sacrifices to hunger and cold."

With such awkward interpreters as our Ainu were, it was not an easy matter to vindicate ourselves against so serious a charge. I tried to render my ideas quite intelligible to them, and begged that they would endeavour to restate what I said with the greatest exactness. I then asked the Japanese commander what number of ships and men his sovereign would send out against a people on whom he wished to make war.

He answered that he did not know. Would he send five or ten? I asked. "No, no," he replied, laughing, he would "fit out a great number, a very great number."

How then, I asked, can the Japanese believe that the emperor of Russia, the sovereign of so great and powerful a nation, would send only two small vessels to carry on war against the Japanese? This consideration ought to be sufficient to convince them that the vessels that attacked them were mere merchantmen, the crews of which were not in the service of the emperor of Russia, but of men whose only object was trade and pelt-hunting. The Japanese had been attacked and plundered without the authority, and without the knowledge of even the lowest Russian officer, but as soon as the offense became known, the affair was investigated, and the offenders punished conformably to our laws. As a proof that the Russian government had entertained no hostile intention, it was sufficient to mention, that after two successful attacks had been made, no ship had, for the space of five years, returned to these islands. Had, however, our monarch any reason or wish to make war on the Japanese, he would send every year large squadrons against them, until the object he had in view should be accomplished.

The Japanese chief, whose face now brightened up, assured me that he was glad to hear this from me; that he believed all I had stated, and was satisfied. He asked where the two men were whom Khvostov had carried off with him. I told him they had fled from Okhotsk in a boat, and had not since been heard of. Finally, he informed us that we could neither get wood nor good water at that part of the island (which we saw evidently enough), but that at Horobetsu, to the commander of which he would give me a letter, we might be supplied not only with wood and water, but also might procure rice and other provisions. Having returned thanks, I gave him and the other officers some presents, consisting of various European articles. He, in his turn, presented us with fresh fish, *sakana*, wild garlic, and a flask of *sake*, a Japanese beverage. He also treated us with this liquor, having first drank of it himself. Not to be behind-hand with him, I made him and his officers partake of some French brandy, after I had, according to Japanese custom, first tasted it myself to prove that I did not mean to give them anything injurious. They all smacked their lips, and appeared exceedingly well pleased with the brandy, of which they drank but little. Each, on receiving from me the cup out of which they drank, made a slight motion with the head, and lifted the left hand to the forehead. I took a match from one of them, to examine it. In returning it, I made it be understood, by signs, that I wished to cut off a piece, upon which they handed me a whole bundle.

I signified to the chief that I wished to see their tent, and he immediately conducted me to it. I found it very long, and covered with mats made of grass and straw. It was divided cross-ways into several apartments, each of which had a separate entrance from the south side. The light entered by the doors, for there were no windows. The apartment of the commander was in the eastern end. The floor was covered with very clean mats, on which we sat down, with our legs crossed under us. A large pan, with fire, was placed in the middle of the apartment. And a chest covered with a bear's skin, the rough side of which was outward, was brought in. The chief of the Japanese having now laid aside both his swords, and unbound his girdle, I perceived that he was disposed to entertain us in a regular manner. It was, however, dark, and the sloop was too near the land. I thanked him for his friendly reception, informed him I could not stop then, but would visit him another time, and left the tent to go on board the sloop.

Whilst I was conversing with the chief on the shore, an old man advanced towards me with demonstrations of the greatest respect: he was a *toion*, or chief of the hairy Ainu of this part of the island, of whom there were here about fifty individuals of both sexes. And they seemed to be so oppressed by the Japanese that they dared not move in their presence. They all sat crowded together, regarding their rulers with looks of terror. And whenever they had occasion to speak to them, they threw themselves upon their knees, with their open hands pressed closely upon their loins, their heads hanging downwards, and their whole bodies bent towards the ground. Our Ainu observed the same ceremony when they addressed themselves to us. In order to converse with them more fully, and without interruption, I invited them to come on board our vessel, if they could gain permission to do so. I at the same time desired them to assure the Japanese of our friendly disposition towards them, and that we entertained no intention of doing them harm. Our Ainu repeated my words, though I cannot of course be responsible for their accuracy of the translation. But the answer received amounted to this, that the Japanese were afraid of us, and that instead of believing that we had come to visit them with good intentions, they were convinced that we were disposed to do as much mischief as the Company's ships had formerly done. I was anxious to obtain further information on this subject, and I requested the Ainu to endeavour to make themselves acquainted with the real sentiments the Japanese entertained respecting us, and then to come on board our vessel.

At seven in the evening we returned to our sloop. And the Ainu arrived about an hour afterwards. Their party consisted of two men, two women, and a little girl, apparently four years old. The men spoke the Russian language so well, that we could understand each other without much difficulty. They brought along with them the letter from the Japanese chief to the commander at Horobetsu, which they assured us would sufficiently inform him of our pacific intentions. They likewise told us that as soon as we quitted the village, the Japanese dispatched a kayak with a similar intimation to Horobetsu: this we had ourselves observed. The letter was written on thick white paper, folded up in an envelope of about six inches and a half in length, and two and a quarter in breadth. This envelope was so formed that a piece of the paper, of a triangular shape, was left to fold down on one side, to which it closely adhered; the remaining part, or superior angle of this piece of paper, which was half an inch long, was folded down on the other side, to which it was also firmly attached, and was impressed with a stamp in black ink. The address was written on both sides. Our Ainu now informed us that the Japanese persisted in believing that plunder was the only motive that had induced us to visit their shores, and that the conduct of the crews of the Company's ships had excited their suspicions. Whenever they spoke of the violent proceedings of Khvostov, they usually said: "The Russians attacked us without cause, killed many of our I countrymen, took several prisoners, plundered us, and burnt all we possessed. They not only carried off our goods, but likewise all our rice and *sake*, and abandoned us to all the misery of hunger." Governed by this feeling, the Japanese were, as the Ainu informed us, convinced that we intended to commit some outrage on them, and had, some time before, removed all their property to the interior of the island. This vexed us exceedingly. The Japanese had, indeed, ample cause to suspect our designs, as they did not know the difference between a man-of-war and a merchant vessel.

Before our departure from Kamchatka, we foresaw, and frequently regretted, that the Japanese would inevitably blame the whole Russian nation for the unjust proceeding of Khvostov; for they possessed no means of making their complaints known to our government, and thereby discovering the guilty, and bringing them to punishment. The Ainu, however, consoled us, with the assurance that ill-will towards the Russians was by no means general among the Japanese, and that the apprehensions of the chief and his companions, with whom we had discoursed, were to be attributed solely to their excessive cowardice.

These Ainu also related to us their own adventures: they told us that in the preceding summer they had been driven by storms to that part of Japan. The Japanese immediately seized them, and threw them into prison. They asked them various questions concerning the attack of the Russian ships, to which they replied that the Ainu had no participation in the proceedings of the Russians, and that they had besides heard at Kamchatka that the commanders of those vessels were pelt hunters, and not imperial officers. The outrage was therefore to be attributed solely to them, and that the district commander had deposited the Japanese goods in the imperial warehouse, and had placed the officers themselves under confinement. The Ainu added that on receiving this intimation the Japanese were induced to think more favorably of them: they treated them with kindness, and at length gave orders for their liberation, having previously furnished them with rice, *sake*, tobacco, clothes, and other articles. Finally, they expected to sail to their native country with the first favorable wind.

Two glasses of brandy, with which I regaled each of the Ainu, seemed to inspire them with confidence, and they frequently mentioned, among other things, that they were in want of gunpowder to shoot with during the winter season, and that the Japanese had provided them with everything excepting powder. They mentioned this want of gunpowder so repeatedly, that I was convinced they were desirous of obtaining some from me, although they did not presume to ask it directly. And being confident that they wanted it only for hunting, I presented them with half a pound of fine English powder, some tobacco, glass beads and small earrings. It was now getting late, and I was compelled to break off my conversation with them. And after I had again requested that they would exert their endeavours to convince the Japanese of our peaceable and friendly intentions, they took leave of us about ten o'clock. Whilst these Ainu were on board our ship, I sent Ensign Filatov ashore, to exchange some leaf tobacco with the hairy Ainu for wild garlic and fresh fish. He soon returned, bringing along with him a considerable quantity, which I ordered to be reserved for such of our crew as were sick.

Not the slightest breeze blew during the whole night of the 18th of June, and we were consequently unable to quit the coast. Early in the morning we observed a kayak, with a flag, sailing towards our sloop. We concluded that the Japanese were about to pay us a visit, and proceeded to make preparations for their reception. To show that we expected them, I ordered the sails to be furled, though this was unnecessary, on account of the calm that prevailed. Towards eight o'clock the kayak had approached very near us. That which we supposed to be a flag, we now discovered was a white mat, and we recognized in the boat our friends the Ainu who had visited us on the preceding evening. They were accompanied by a young man named Alexei Maksimovich. The men wore long full Japanese gowns, with short wide sleeves, and made of thick cotton stuff of a blue color, striped with green. The women wore parka, made of the skins of birds with the feathers outward. And, by way of ornament, several rows of sea parrots' beaks strung together were suspended from the back part of their shoulders. They had thick cotton handkerchiefs rolled round their heads, whilst the men on the contrary were bare-headed. They all wore boots, such as are worn by the Russian peasantry, made of sea lion skin.

The chief came on board bare-footed. But before he either bowed or offered to address us, he drew on his boots. He then advanced, observing towards us the same ceremonies with which he had been accustomed to salute the Japanese. He appeared to be about fifty years of age, and extremely feeble. His little daughter was all the time on his back, wrapped in his cloak, and secured therein by a rope, which came round in front of his breast. By way of relief from the embarrassment this fastening occasioned, or when he resolved to move his arms with greater freedom, he lifted the rope to his forehead. On this account sometimes a broad strap was sewed to that part of the rope that touched the forehead. The men had stiff jet black hair and beards. Their hair was cut in the same way as that of the Russian carters. They had no artificial ornament either on the face or on any other part of the body. The women had a blue line drawn round their lips, from one-fifth to a quarter of an inch in thickness, and their hands were painted with the same color. They brought us presents, consisting of salmon trout and stock-fish, some fresh fish, and wild garlic. The fish I distributed among the crew, and the fresh fish and garlic were laid by for the sick.

Our first question related to the Japanese soldiers. I was informed that the chief, in consequence of having partaken too freely of the bottle of brandy I presented to him, had slept soundly the whole of the preceding evening and night. The others, on the contrary, had been under arms the whole time. Nothing could overcome the suspicions they entertained of us. And they threatened, in case we should attack them, to behead the Ainu, whom they regarded as Russian subjects. For this reason they had watched them closely the whole of the night, and had detained some of their companions as hostages. The Japanese themselves had now sent them to enquire more particularly respecting our motives in visiting them.

On this occasion the Ainu contradicted what they had formerly told us. According to the account they now gave, instead of having been driven by storms to the coast of Japan, they had sailed there for the purpose of trading, which they were permitted to do. The Japanese, in consequence of the outrages committed by the Russians, had seized them, as they before informed us, and had thrown them into prison. Having at length determined on liberating them, they furnished them with twenty bags of rice, *sake*, and tobacco, for their voyage. Previously to our arrival they had been detained by adverse winds. And the Japanese now threatened to imprison them again, and make their heads answer for our misconduct. Their party at first consisted of seven men, six women, and two children. But of these three men and three women had perished during their imprisonment in a small confined apartment. They did not know the Russian name of the disorder that had occasioned the death of their companions. But, from their description, it was probably scurvy, accompanied by great debility.

They declared that the Japanese had constantly shown the utmost care for their health, and had sent a physician to attend them. One of the Ainu had been afflicted with a swelling in his hands and cramp in the feet, in consequence of which the calves of his legs were drawn upwards and backwards towards his thighs. Veins were immediately opened by the Japanese surgeons in both his feet, and some time after in both his hands. Owing to the want of suitable expressions, these men could neither describe how, nor with what kind of instruments, the operations had been performed. Their companion recovered, and only regretted that, in consequence of his illness, his hands and feet had become considerably thinner than before. Our surgeon, M. Brandt, a man of very great experience in his profession, ascribed this last circumstance to some other cause.

Whilst relating what had occurred to them, the Ainu frequently became confused, and contradicted each other. At length they all entreated that I would keep them on board my vessel, and land them on their own island (the thirteenth island of Rasshua), where they declared they had resolved on returning. I asked them what would become of their companions, the two women and the child, who would remain in the power of the Japanese, upon which they all remained silent. But shortly afterwards they renewed their solicitations, protesting that they believed the Japanese would put them to death when they went on shore. On the preceding evening they had not mentioned a syllable about their determination of returning to their own island; they merely regretted not having sufficient gunpowder to enable them to shoot on Urup. To say that bad weather prevented their departure was a palpable falsehood. They were not aware that we had been cruising for some time in the neighborhood of the island, and were consequently acquainted with the state of the weather. There had been no violent winds for a considerable time, and the fogs were by no means so thick as to render it impossible to proceed from one island to another, particularly from Iturup to Urup, which are scarcely twenty-five kilometers distant from each other.

They had, besides, no reason to fear the fogs, since, as we observed, they had along with them a compass, which they seemed to value as dearly as their own eyes, for they would scarcely trust it out of their hands. This compass, which was fixed in a round case, was three inches in diameter. The card was divided into rhumbs, but without any degree, and colored.

Instead of glass it was covered with the kind of mica called Muscovy glass. The compass, with its case, was further secured by being placed within a box with a sliding lid. They pretended that they had got it in Kamchatka. When they came on board the ship, they carried it along with them, being fearful of leaving it in the kayak.

From all they related, the greater part of which is not worth repeating, we were able to form an idea of their situation. It appeared that as soon as the Japanese suspected we entertained an intention of attacking their village, they threatened to punish the Ainu for our acts, consequently these men had no less reason to fear us than the Japanese. For the sake of saving their heads they would willingly have remained with us, at the risk of sacrificing the two women and the child they had left on shore, and they accordingly entreated us to keep them on board. I endeavored to convince them that they had nothing to fear from the Japanese, against whom we entertained no hostile designs, and advised them to return to the island. I gave them four bottles of French brandy, as a present to the Japanese commanding officer, who, as I had learned, was extremely fond of that liquor.

When the Ainu were about to take leave of us, I proposed that one of the party should remain on board our sloop, that he might assist us in coming to a safe anchoring place off Urup. And likewise serve as our interpreter, in case we should land at Horobetsu. On hearing this, they all offered to continue with us. This, however, could not be permitted. And it was agreed that the Ainu Alexei should remain on board our sloop, and that the rest should return to the island. They were fully convinced that we intended to attack the Japanese. And one of the party assured us cannon were planted at Horobetsu, which would be fired upon the first Russian vessel that came within sight of the island. But, a few moments after this, another of the Ainu observed that there was only one piece of cannon on the island.

Towards noon the weather began to clear up, and a brisk south wind arose. I wished to take advantage of this gale for sailing towards the eastern coast of Urup. We therefore took leave of our guests, and steered under full sail in an easterly direction. We had not proceeded more than half a mile, or a kilometer, from the kayak, when we observed the Ainu raising their hands, beckoning us to return, and heard them calling loudly after us. *Can the kayak be sinking!* thought I, and immediately gave orders for the sloop to lie to.

They then rowed up to us, and merely repeated their dread of being massacred by the Japanese in the event of our committing any outrage upon them. We again found it necessary to summon all our powers of persuasion for the purpose of convincing and consoling them. And they, at length, agreed to return to the island, though not without some degree of apprehension, for they could not entirely divest themselves of the notions they had formed. I was much moved, on thus parting, for a second time, with these poor creatures. They repeatedly bade us farewell from the kayak, and promised, if the Japanese did not kill them, to catch fish, and gather wild garlic and fresh fish for us against our return.

From Iturup we sailed towards the eastern coast of Urup, in inspecting which we spent three days. We then wished to sail back to Horobetsu, but contrary winds prevented us from passing through the Straits of De Fries. we therefore steered in a southerly direction, along the eastern coast of Iturup, for the purpose of making observations on that island likewise. Meanwhile certain circumstances tended to confirm our Ainu shipmate Alexei in the belief that we really entertained the design of attacking the Japanese. When the wind was calm, and the weather clear and dry, I ordered the crew to perform their exercise on deck, and to practise firing with ball. Our Ainu was unable to conceal his astonishment when he beheld the men all under arms; some armed with blunderbusses, some with muskets, and others with pistols and pikes. We sought to persuade him that we ourselves had reason to apprehend an attack from the Japanese, and that we wished to hold ourselves in readiness for self-defense. But that if, on the contrary, they received us kindly, they need entertain no fear. He nodded his head as if he credited what we told him. But it was plain that, in his heart, he was far from being convinced of the truth of our statement. In the course of conversation, he would frequently disclose circumstances which he showed a disposition to conceal when questioned directly concerning them. For instance, he at first declared his ignorance of the way in which the Ainu trade with the Japanese. But some time after, whilst we were drinking tea, and discoursing on some other matters, he mentioned what the Japanese had given them in exchange for certain articles, without seeming to be aware that he was betraying what he before wished to keep a secret. I was well pleased to find that we could thus obtain from our guest all the information we desired, without either perplexing him or putting him in fear.

The facts thus communicated, as it were, accidentally, and of his own free will, without any questions being directly addressed to him, were doubtless more to be relied on than any which we might have wrung from him by inquisitorial interrogatories. That, under such circumstances, a wild ignorant Ainu should have stated many untruths would not have been surprising. Accordingly whenever I entered into conversation with him, I usually began by talking about common affairs, with the view of bringing him by degree to other subjects of discourse.

In this way I learned from him that previous to the attack made by the Company's ships, the Ainu had carried on a trade with the Japanese, as uninterrupted and regular as if it had been sanctioned by a duly ratified treaty. The Ainu brought to Japan bears' and seadogs' skins, eagles' wings and tails, and fox skins (the latter the Japanese seldom purchased, and never gave a high price for them). These articles they exchanged for rice, cotton manufactures, clothes (particularly nightdresses), tobacco pipes, domestic utensils of varnished wood, and other things. The Japanese sell their rice in large and small bags. The large bag is equal to three small ones, and, according to our Ainu's account, is so heavy, that a man can scarcely lift it. It may, perhaps, contain about 120 pounds. The barter was conducted according to a convention made by both parties, and without the least attempt at undue advantage on either side. The value of the merchandize scarcely ever varied. The Ainu usually received from the Japanese:

For the skin of a beaver that had attained its full growth, ten large bags of rice.

For a seadog's skin, seven small bags.

For ten eagles' tails, twenty small bags, or a silk dress.

For three eagles' tails, a cotton dress, lined with the same material, and wadded.

For ten eagles' wings, a bundle of leaf tobacco, which the Ainu are extremely fond of. They usually chew it. Some take it like snuff and others have learnt from the Japanese the custom of smoking with pipes, such as they use.

The Japanese give a high price for eagles' wings and tails, as they use the feathers for their arrows. They likewise set a high value on various European articles, which they purchase from the Ainu at a very dear rate; such as yellow and red cloth, and cloth of other colors, glass wares, strings of amber and glass beads, boots, hardware, etc. The yellow cloth is reserved for distinguished visitors. A piece of a suitable size is usually spread out where it is intended the guest shall seat himself. Cloths of other colors are made into wearing apparel. They ornament the seams of their boots with glass beads or pearls. But in other respects they wear them in the same way as we do.

the Russian-American Company purchased, in our presence, the rice that had been brought from Japan, paying for it at the rate of half a rouble the pound. They did not, however, consider the beaver skin to be worth more than fifty roubles. The Company would not have given the Ainu more than a hundred pounds of rice for a beaver skin.

Our guest, Alexei Maximovitsch, was no less communicative when our conversation happened to turn on the hunting trade, and how it enabled the Ainu to gain a livelihood. He complained that the number of beavers was constantly diminishing—a circumstance that appeared extremely probable. These animals have indeed become exceedingly scarce, both on the Aleutian Islands, and on those parts of the American coast that are visited by the Company's pelt hunters. The indefatigable perseverance of their pursuers has made them shun the human race, and they have retired towards the south, into the channels between the numerous islands on the north-west coast of America. In the summer season, when the sea is calm, and the Ainu can, without danger, sail from the coasts in their kayaks, they shoot the beavers with arrows. But in the winter they either shoot them from the shore, or catch them in nets, which they spread between the stones on which these animals sometimes station themselves.

They have three different methods of killing the dark-brown, grey, and red foxes. If they fall in with them accidentally, or in hunting, they shoot them in the usual way. But they also take them in the Kamchatka manner, by traps (namely, by placing in a trap some bait, which is no sooner touched by the fox than an iron weapon descends and kills him). Or they ensnare them with seagulls. They fasten a seagull in a place where they observe traces of the fox, and lay down around the gull snares formed of running loops; the hunter, in the meanwhile, remains on the watch to prevent the fox from gnawing the snare asunder. Whenever the seagull begins to flap its wings, the fox darts upon his prey, and is caught in a noose.

The ice fox is never seen on the Kuril Islands, and the inhabitants do not even know such an animal by name. When shown their skins at Kamchatka they called them white foxes. They shoot sea lions and seadogs. And catch eagles with seagulls, though not in the same way as they ensnare the foxes. They build a little shed, with an aperture at the top, and in the interior fasten a seagull. In a short time the eagle darts upon his prey, seizes it with his claws, and whilst he is endeavoring to carry it off or devour it, he is killed by the Ainu. It is only during the winter that the eagle inhabits the Kuril Islands. On the approach of summer these birds of prey take flight to Kamchatka, where they are then found in great numbers, because the streams which flow through that peninsula supply them with abundance of food. The Ainu hunt sea otters, sea lions, seadogs, and foxes, only for the sake of trade: to supply their domestic wants they catch different sorts of sea-fowl, such as geese, various kinds of ducks, &c, and likewise fish, which are by no means very plentiful in the Kuril Islands belonging to the Russians. On the coasts of the thirteenth and fourteenth islands namely, Rasshua and Ushishir, a fish is found which the inhabitants call seerbok: in size it resembles the *gorbusha* (a kind of salmon), and is of a red color. They are caught between the stones with hooks. The Ainu seldom go out to kill ducks and geese, as too great a quantity of powder and shot is expended on these birds. They catch in the nest—and with their hands—sea parrots, storm finches, and another kind of bird, which in their language is called *mauridor*. A man may catch thirty, forty, or even fifty of these birds in one day. The feathers are taken off with the skins, which are sewed together and made into parka, both for men and women. The fat is made into oil, and the Ainu smoke the flesh, and lay it by for provisions during the winter. Indeed, their chief sustenance consists of the flesh of these birds, together with wild garlic, fresh fish, and various kinds of sea plants. In addition to this, they frequently procure rice from the Japanese.

The Ainu who are under the dominion of the Russians have in general no beard. Those whom we found on Iturup had beards, but they had allowed them to grow in imitation of the hairy Ainu, who preserve their beards.

Alexei, therefore, in consequence of continuing on board with us, expressed a wish to have his beard removed, and was accordingly shaved. I besides gave him several articles of naval clothing that had belonged to seamen now deceased.

The inhabitants of Shumshu and Paramushir travel with dogs like the Kamtschatdales. On Rasshua and Ushishir they do not understand this art, but keep a number of dogs for hunting foxes. I did not before mention this sort of fox-hunting, because it is not general, and only practised by some of the Ainu on the Island of Rasshua. The inhabitants of Ushishir, on which there are no foxes, go in quest of these animals to other islands, where they cannot carry their dogs with them. In both islands they use dog skin for winter dress.

Alexei informed us that we might find a safe anchoring place near the Island of Kunashir (the twentieth in the chain of the Kuril Islands), and that it contained a fortified village, where we might be supplied with wood, water, rice, and fresh roots. Instead, therefore, of proceeding to Horobetsu, I resolved to sail straight to Kunashir. To this determination I was chiefly induced by the wish of closely examining the harbor of Kunashir, and the channel that separates that island from Hokkaido; this channel being as yet unknown to European navigators, and on many charts both islands being described as one connected piece of land. Even on Broughton's chart this uncertainty is not removed. Besides, I wished for other reasons to reach the village and anchoring place as speedily as possible. We found that the rats in the store room had consumed more than 120 pounds of biscuit, and about two-hundred pounds of malt. And as we knew not what havoc they might have made among the provisions that lay still lower in the hold, we judged it expedient to proceed with all possible haste to a place where, in case of necessity, we might procure a fresh stock.

Owing to adverse winds, fogs, and thick weather, we did not reach the straits between Hokkaido and Kunashir until the 4th of July. In the interim we cruised in the neighborhood of the Islands Iturup, Kunashir, and Shitokan, which we occasionally saw, though they were almost always veiled by mists. Towards evening we approached a long flat piece of land, forming the eastern side of the harbor of Kunashir. Our entering the harbor at so late an hour might probably have excited alarm among the Japanese. I therefore thought it advisable to cast anchor in the channel. During the whole of the night, we observed large fires burning on both the promontories of the bay, which were probably intended for signals.

On the following morning, the 5th of July, we sailed into the harbor. As we advanced, guns were twice fired at us from the castle. The shot, however, fell into the water without reaching our vessel. From this circumstance, we concluded that the Japanese on the Island of Iturup had not yet made known to those here our favorable intentions. And as the fortress and the bay were still enveloped in darkness, we again cast anchor. When the weather cleared up, we stood in towards the fortress, from which there was now no more firing; though the boat, which was ahead of us, and in which some of our crew were taking soundings, was within range of the guns. The works were hung round with white and black, or dark blue striped cloth, so that we could perceive neither walls nor palisades. Sentinels were posted in various places, and above them embrasures were painted, but in so rough a style, that even at a considerable distance we could perceive the deception (the poor Japanese powder created an uncommonly thick and black smoke).

Within the fortress we could only descry a few buildings, which stood upon an acclivity and overtopped the wail. Among these buildings the commander-in-chief's house was distinguished by numerous flags and weather cocks being fixed upon the roof. We likewise saw flags waving on other houses in the town, but not in such number. For this circumstance Alexei could not account, though he told us that the town was always so ornamented whenever a foreign vessel or any personage of distinction entered the harbor. We cast anchor at a distance of about two kilometers from the garrison. And the pilot's assistant, named Srednoy, four sailors, the Ainu, and myself, got on board a boat and rowed towards the shore. We had already come within fifty fathoms of the shore, when the Japanese unexpectedly began to fire their cannon upon us from different points. We immediately put about, and, as will readily be supposed, began to row off as quickly as possible. The first guns which were fired had nearly proved fatal to us, for the shot passed close to the boat. But afterwards they fired less frequently, and appeared to point their guns very badly.

On hearing the report of the first firing, Captain Lieutenant Pyotr Ivanovich Ricord,[1] the senior commandingofficer under me, immediately dispatched all the armed boats to our assistance. Fortunately we had no occasion for them, as not a single round touched us. Even when we were out of the reach of their shot, the Japanese did not cease firing, and we still heard the reports of their cannon after we had got on board the sloop. I was not a little indignant at this aggression. It appeared to me that none except the rudest barbarians would have been guilty of firing from the fortress upon a little boat, containing only seven men, when they could not but be aware that a single ball might have sent us all to the bottom. I at first thought I should be justified in taking vengeance on them, and had already ordered a cannon to be pointed at the castle, to convince the Japanese how powerfully our sloop was armed. But I soon reflected that the moment for vengeance would not be lost, and that without the consent of my government I should not be justified in resorting to hostile

---

1 Pyotr Ivanovich Ricord (1776–1855) would go on to become an admiral, scientist, diplomat, writer, shipbuilder, and statesman. He began his military career in the Baltic Fleet and first saw action on the coast of The Netherlands in 1799. Four years later he was sent as a volunteer to the British Fleet to study its maritime practices, making voyages to most of Britain's maritime dominions and taking part in Britain's wars with France and Spain.

proceedings. I therefore altered my intention, and stood off from the garrison.

A thought now suddenly came across my mind. I imagined that by means of signs I might make myself understood by the Japanese. For this purpose, on the 6th of July, I caused a cask to be sawed in two, and set both parts afloat in the water in front of the town. In the inside of one half of the cask were placed a glass containing fresh water, a piece of wood, and a handful of rice, to denote that we were in want of these articles; the other half contained a few *piastres*, a piece of yellow cloth, and some crystal beads and pearls, meaning thereby to intimate that we would give them either money or other articles in exchange for provisions. Upon this half of the cask we fixed a drawing of the harbor, the fortress, and the sloop; which was very skilfully executed by Ensign Mur. In this drawing the sloop's guns were very distinctly marked, but fixed in the ports with their tomkins in. But the guns of the garrison were represented as firing, and the balls flying over the sloop. By this means I wished, if possible, to make the Japanese sensible of their perfidy. No sooner had we set the cask afloat and rowed away, than the Japanese immediately seized it, and carried it into their fortress. On the following day we approached within gunshot of the castle, for the purpose of receiving an answer, having previously made every preparation for an engagement. But the Japanese did not seem to notice us. No one appeared near the works, which were still hung round with cloth.

I reflected seriously on all the circumstances that had occurred, and was convinced that I had a right to demand an answer of some sort or other from the Japanese. Our first intercourse with them had been purely accidental: the chief with whom we had communicated had voluntarily given us a letter to the commander-in-chief of a town, in order that we might be supplied not only with wood and water, but likewise with provisions. Relying on this assurance, we had sailed to Kunashir, and lost a fortnight, during which time we might have returned to Okhotsk. Our provisions having in the meanwhile greatly diminished, we hoped to obtain a fresh stock from the Japanese, who did not regard our proposal as worthy of an answer. In this critical situation, I requested that each officer should draw up a written declaration of his opinion respecting the course we ought to adopt. They all agreed that nothing but the utmost provocation could justify us in proceeding to hostilities, until the command of the monarch authorized us so to do. In this particular, the opinions of the officers coincided with my own, and we moved farther from the castle.

I now dispatched a well-armed boat, under the command of Captain-Lieutenant Ricord, to a fishing village on one side of the harbor, directing him to take the necessary quantity of wood, water, and rice, and to leave payment either in Spanish *piastres* or merchandize. I remained on board the sloop, which I kept under sail at a short distance from the shore, being fully resolved to obtain these articles by force, in case the Japanese should oppose the landing of Lieutenant Ricord. But neither soldiers nor any inhabitants were to be seen in the village. Here Lieutenant Ricord found only muddy rainwater. He carried off some wood, rice, and dried fish, and left behind him various European articles, which Alexei declared to be far more valuable than what he carried away. In the afternoon curiosity induced me to go ashore to try to discover the plans of the Japanese, and I was highly pleased to observe that all the articles Lieutenant Ricord had left were removed. The Japanese must, therefore, have visited the shore after his departure. And those who occupied the fortress would thus be convinced that plunder was not our object. There were two fishing villages on this side of the harbor, and we observed every necessary apparatus for fishing, salting, drying, and extracting oil. The Japanese nets are excessively large, and every article used by fishermen, such as boats, buckets, vats for the oil, etc. were all in astonishing good order.

On the 8th of July, 1811, we observed a cask floating before the town. I immediately weighed anchor in order to take it up. We found that it contained a little box wrapped up in several pieces of oilcloth. The box contained three papers, one of which was a Japanese letter, which we could not read, and the other two were drawings. Both these sketches represented the harbor, the castle, our sloop, the cask with a boat rowing towards it, and the rising sun, but with this difference, that in one the guns of the castle were firing, whilst in the other the muzzles of the cannon were turned backwards. We were a long time occupied in considering these hieroglyphics, and each explained them after his own way. But this will not be thought wonderful, as the same thing frequently happens among greater scholars. We all, however, agreed in one thing, namely, that the Japanese declined holding intercourse with us.

For my own part I interpreted these drawings in the following manner: I supposed the Japanese to mean that, though they had not fired upon us when they observed us sending off the cask, yet if we attempted to send out another, they would immediately fire upon it. We then got under weigh, and stood over to the mouth of a little river on the western side of the harbor, where we cast anchor. I now sent out some armed boats in quest of fresh water. The seamen continued at work all day on the shore without experiencing any opposition from the Japanese. They merely sent out some Ainu from the castle, who at the distance of about half a kilometer, observed the motions of our crew.

On the following morning, the 9th of July, our boats again went ashore. An Ainu immediately came out of the castle, and approached them with a very slow pace, and an air of extreme apprehension. In one hand he held a wooden crucifix, and with the other continually crossed himself as he advanced towards the shore. He had lived for several years among our Ainu on the Island of Rasshua, where he was known by the name of Koosma. There he had probably learnt to cross himself, and having observed that the Russians venerate the cross, he now ventured forth under its protection to meet us in the character of a flag of truce. Lieutenant Rudakov was the first who accosted him: he caressed him, and gave him various presents. But nothing could subdue the terror of the Ainu, who continued to tremble as if he had been seized with the shivering fit of an ague. I next approached him, but was unable to make myself understood, as Alexei was not along with us. The Ainu was so terrified that he would neither wait for him nor accompany us on board, and we did not think it prudent to detain him by force. He could scarcely speak ten words of Russian, yet I understood from his gesticulation that the commander-in-chief of the city expressed a wish that he and I should meet in boats, accompanied by an equal number of people on both sides, in order to hold a conference. I joyfully testified my willingness to accede to this proposal, and I gave the Ainu a string of beads. This present seemed to inspire him with so much boldness, that he ventured to ask me for a little tobacco. I happened to have none with me. but promised to bring him some the next time I came on shore. I then took leave of him, and put off with the boat.

Meanwhile the Japanese had placed another cask in front of the castle, but so close to the batteries that I deemed it imprudent to venture to take it away. Still nobody came out of the castle, though they beckoned to us with white fans to come on shore. I now began to suspect that I had misunderstood the Ainu. As we were preparing to row back again, we observed a boat put off from the shore. In this boat were several officers and an Ainu interpreter, and they immediately rowed towards us. They had many more men on board than we. But as we were well armed, I felt no reason to be afraid of them.

The conference began on their side, with an apology for having fired upon us when we first attempted to land. To justify this proceeding, they declared that their distrust had been excited in consequence of an outrage committed upon them some years before, by the crews of two Russian vessels, who had at first landed under pretense of the same motives which we professed. They perceived the difference between our conduct and that of their former visitors. Every suspicion had now vanished, and they declared their readiness to do all they could to serve us. I desired our interpreter, Alexei, to explain to them, that those ships were merchantmen; that the aggression had been made without the consent of our government, and that the owners of the vessels, both of whom were now no more, had suffered due punishment for their reprehensible proceedings. I sought to convince them of the truth of this assurance by the same method we had adopted with respect to the Japanese on the Island of Iturup. They replied that they believed all we had said, and rejoiced to hear that the Russians entertained such good dispositions towards them.

When I inquired whether they were satisfied with the payment they had received for the articles taken from the fishing village, they answered that what we had taken were mere trifles and that we had paid infinitely beyond their value. They moreover assured me that the commander-in-chief was ready to furnish us with anything their island afforded, and inquired what other articles we stood in need of. I requested to have ten bags of rice, some fresh fish and vegetables, for which I offered to give as many *piastres* as might be required. They invited me to land, in order to have an interview with the commander-in-chief. This, however, I declined doing, and promised to go on the following day, when the sloop would be nearer the shore. According to my promise, I had brought some tobacco for Koosma. But the Japanese officers did not think fit to allow the Ainu to receive my present. I wished to have had some further conversation on various subjects with the Japanese. But Alexei, who had recognized some of his old friends in the boat, was so fond of chattering with his countrymen, that he neglected to interpret my questions.

When we had parted from the Japanese, Alexei explained to us what his countrymen had communicated to him. They declared that the approach of our sloop had filled the Japanese with the utmost terror and consternation: they were convinced that we intended to attack them, and had accordingly removed all their property, with the greatest haste, to the forests. We had ourselves observed them driving loaded horses along the hills. The Ainu added that they fired on our sloop merely through fear, and when they observed our boat approaching the fishing village, they felt assured that we intended immediately to plunder and set fire to their habitations. When, however, we quitted the shore, they returned to inspect their houses, and finding everything in the same order as they had left it, and that we had left many valuable European articles behind in exchange for the rice, fish, and wood, which we had carried away, the joy of the Japanese knew no bounds, and all their apprehensions ceased. I was the more ready to believe that they had fired upon us merely through terror, since they probably suspected that we had a strong party concealed in the bottom of the boat. The boat was indeed in finitely too small for any such purpose, but then they might have been blinded by fear. They would not else have attacked a handful of men, who, as it were, threw themselves into their power. They might have waited on the shore, and have made us their prisoners whenever we landed. But Alexei had previously informed me that the very sight of a Russian inspired the Japanese with indescribable terror. They expressed great astonishment at the rapidity with which the Russians fired their guns, and the excellent order in which they fought, which they had witnessed during the attack made upon them by the Company's vessels.

On the morning of the 10th of July we filled our last cask with water; which business, and the state of the wind, did not permit us to approach the castle.

In the meanwhile the Japanese sent out a boat, and made signs that they wished to speak with us. We immediately rowed towards them, and, as we approached, I observed that the persons in the boat threw a cask into the water, and immediately put ashore. We found that this cask contained all the articles we had left in the village as payment for what we had taken, and likewise all that we had placed in the cask we had first sent off. I now put into it eighteen *piastres* and some East India silks, and was preparing to row on board, when the Japanese began to beckon us with white fans, and to make signs, indicating that they wished us to land. This invitation was given when we had no longer need of anything from them, and when we had obtained so abundant a supply of wood, water, and provisions, that we might have continued two months longer at sea, prosecuting our observations, and then have sailed back to Okhotsk.

I wished, however, to communicate with the Japanese for other reasons. I considered it my duty, as an officer in the service of the Emperor of Russia, to assure them, if possible, that our government had taken no part in the outrages committed on their coasts by the Company's vessels; that the directors of the Russian-American Company were not persons of great consideration in Russia, but even they had never sanctioned that illegal proceeding, which was wholly attributable to the captains of the vessels, and that his Imperial Majesty had ever entertained a wish to establish friendly compacts and commercial relations between Russia and Japan. I reflected that my duty to my native country required that I should, in such a case, lay aside all consideration of personal danger. I therefore ordered the sailors, of whom I took four with me, to conceal their arms, by wrapping sail-cloth about them, but to be careful to have them in readiness, in case of an attack. And we landed at a distance of from sixty to eighty fathoms from the gates of the castle. The Ainu Alexei, one of the sailors, and myself, stepped ashore. I ordered the rest to keep the boat afloat, not to permit any of the Japanese to get on board of it, and to keep their eyes constantly fixed upon me, in order to watch any signal I might make to them. We were met on the shore by an officer, two inferior officers, two privates, and upwards of ten Ainu. All the Japanese, though of different ranks, were dressed in costly silk garments, and were completely armed: each had a sword and poniard fastened in his girdle, but the Ainu, on the contrary, were without any arms.

I had only a sword by my side, but I had taken the precaution of concealing three pair of pistols in my pockets and my bosom. The officer received me with the utmost civility and politeness, and requested that I wouid wait on the shore for the commander-in-chief of the castle, who, he assured me, would soon come out to meet me. I asked him what we were to understand by their having sent back in the cask all the articles we had left in the fishing village. He replied, that they wished to return them, because they supposed we did not intend to have any further intercourse with them, and that in that case they durst take nothing. I immediately recollected that Laxman, in his narrative, mentioned that the Japanese would accept of no presents until the conclusion of the negociation, though it did not appear that they afterwards declined anything which he offered them. I therefore felt myself perfectly satisfied on this head.

I had not long to wait for the commander-in-chief: he soon appeared, completely armed, and accompanied by two soldiers, one of whom carried his long spear, and the other his cap or helmet, which was adorned with a figure of the moon. In other respects it somewhat resembled the crowns occasionally worn at nuptial ceremonies in Russia. It is scarcely possible to conceive anything more ludicrous than the manner in which the command-er-in-chief walked. His eyes were cast down and fixed upon the earth, his hands pressed close against his sides. He besides proceeded at so slow a pace that he scarcely extended one foot beyond the other, and kept his feet as wide apart as though a stream of water had been running betwixt them. I saluted him after the European fashion, upon which he raised his left hand towards his forehead, and bowed his head and his whole body towards the ground. Our conversation then commenced.

I apologized for having been compelled, by the most urgent necessity, to occasion them so much inconvenience. He expressed his regret that the ignorance of the Japanese respecting the object of our visit should have occasioned them to fire upon us, and inquired why, on first entering the harbor, we did not send out a boat to meet that which had been dispatched from the garrison, as we might thereby have prevented the occurrence of such disagreeable hostilities. I assured him that no boat had been seen by any of the crew on board our sloop, and imputed our not having perceived it to the darkness of the evening. I plainly saw that he was seeking to excuse his own conduct, and was at the same time asserting a direct falsehood; for when we entered the harbor, we could perceive every object around us with the utmost distinctness: not even the flight of a bird, and much less a boat proceeding from the shore, could have escaped our observation. He then asked whether I was the captain of the vessel, or whether it was commanded by some individual older than I, which question he repeated several times. He likewise asked where we were sailing to; why we had landed on their coasts, and where we next intended to proceed. Lest an explanation of the real object of our visit to their islands might create fear and suspicion, I informed him that we were sailing from the eastern extremity of our empire to St. Petersburgh; that contrary winds had considerably lengthened our voyage, and that, being greatly in want of fresh water and wood, we wished to enter some safe harbor to procure a supply of these articles. I added, that we had accidentally touched at the Island of Iturup, where we found a Japanese garrison, the commander of which had furnished us with a letter to Horobetsu, which I wished to have sent ashore. These were the reasons that had induced us to enter their harbor, and that we now wished to take the nearest course to Canton, for the purpose of procuring some articles from that place. Here he observed, that on landing at Iturup we had declared trade to be our object, but that we now told a very different story. I replied, that if he had been so informed, the mistake was to be ascribed to the Ainu, who spoke but little Russian, and, as in the Ainu language there were no words signifying money or purchase, they had been obliged to translate these terms by the words exchange or trade. He then asked what was our emperor's name, what was my name, whether I knew Resanov, who had been sent as ambassador to their islands, and whether there were any persons in St. Petersburg who could speak the Japanese language? To all these questions I returned suitable answers. I informed him of Resanov's death, and told him that there were several persons in Russia who could translate the Japanese language. He carefully noted down everything I said. He then invited me to partake of some tea, *sake*, and caviar, and to smoke tobacco. Everything was served upon separate dishes, and presented by different individuals, who were all armed with poniards and swords. But instead of going away after having handed us anything we wished for, they remained standing near, till at length we were surrounded by a formidable circle of armed men. Among the various articles I had brought ashore as presents to the commander-in-chief, were several bottles of French brandy. I accordingly asked him whether he would choose to taste this liquor, and ordered my sailors to draw a bottle, at the same time taking an opportunity of repeating the order I had previously given them, namely, to hold themselves in readiness.

To desire that the overplus of the Japanese should remove, or to show that I was in any way alarmed by their presence, was what I could not stoop to do. Besides, I thought it prudent not to let them suppose that I distrusted them. There was also no appearance of any intention to resort to violence on their part, notwithstanding that they might have done what they pleased with us, though certainly not without suffering some loss. We smoked, drank tea, and joked together. They were curious to know the Russian names of several things, and I in return asked the Japanese names. At last I stood up, and inquired when I should receive the promised provisions, what I should have to pay for the same, and held up a *piastre*, in order that the number of that coin, which they required, might be mentioned. To my great astonishment I was then informed, that the officer with whom I had been conversing was not the commander-in-chief of the fortress, and therefore could decide nothing on this point. He invited me to go into the castle with him, in order to make the necessary arrangements with the commander-in-chief myself. This I declined, on the pretense that I had already spent too much time with him, and that were I to comply with his desire, a suspicion would probably be excited on board of the sloop, which might give rise to hostilities. I offered at the same time to follow him into the fortress, provided that some persons of distinction among them went on board the sloop in my boat, as that would satisfy the officers with respect to my safety.

The proposal was no sooner made, than one of the Japanese left us, as if for the purpose of obtaining the commander-in-chief's consent. The answer was a refusal, accompanied with an assurance that the commander-in-chief would immediately come out to us. But soon after a messenger announced that he was gone to dinner, and could not yet come. I declined to wait any longer, but promised to bring the ship nearer the shore, and to visit the castle. The lieutenant commander-in-chief made no objection to my going. But on parting presented me with a flask of *sake* and some fresh fish, expressing regret that he had not more of the latter to give. He pointed to a large net that had been thrown, and requested that a boat might be sent on shore before the evening set in, as the whole draught should be given to us. He accepted from me a burning glass and a bottle of brandy, but would not permit the Ainu to take any tobacco from us. As a mark of friendship, he gave me a white fan, with which he said we were to beckon when we came on shore, as a signal of our being peaceably disposed.

During the interpretation of the Japanese officer's speech, Alexei talked frequently to me of the cross, but in so obscure and unintelligible a manner, that I could not comprehend him. It was not until we were again in the boat, and felt ourselves quite free, that he sufficiently collected himself to explain what he really meant. It was well known to the Japanese, he observed, that the Russians entertain the greatest veneration for the cross, and on that account he had wished me to cross myself, and signify that I made that sign in confirmation of our friendly disposition towards them. On hearing this I was exceedingly vexed that I had not been able to understand him before we left the shore.

Towards evening we stood in within gunshot of the castle and brought the sloop to anchor. It was now too late for me to think of entering on any conference. But I ordered Ensign Jakuschkin to go ashore with an armed boat, to deliver the letter we had brought from the Isle of Iturup, and to bring on board the fish that had been promised us. I further directed him to row to the place I had landed at, and not to leave the boat a single moment. He executed my orders with the greatest punctuality, and returned at twilight. The Japanese received him with much kindness, and sent us more than a hundred large fish on board. When they were informed that they might expect me in the morning, they expressed their hope that I would not fail, and their wish to see some of my officers along with me. I must confess that this invitation ought to have excited some degree of suspicion. But I was led into the error of disbelieving Jakuschkin. As an officer, this midshipman was zealous in the performance of his duty. But his curiosity was insatiable: he wished to be everywhere and to see everything with his own eyes. I, therefore, conjectured that it was not agreeable to him to see me go ashore by myself, and that he had invented this invitation in order that I might be induced to take him with me next day. What confirmed me in this notion was, that at the same moment he asked leave to make one of the party. this I had to refuse, as I had previously promised to take Ensign Mur and Khlebnikov, the pilot.

Next morning, July 11, at eight o'clock, I landed with the above-named officers, the ainu Alexei, and four seamen. I was so fully persuaded that we stood on a friendly footing with the Japanese, that I had not ordered the seamen to arm themselves. The officers, three in number, including myself, had each a sword, in addition to which Khlebnikov brought with him a pocket pistol, more for the purpose of making a signal in the case of a fog, than for defense. On passing the cask we had sent on shore, we looked into it, and found all the things we had placed there unremoved. I again recollected what had happened to Laxman, and ascribed this circumstance to the Japanese practice of accepting no presents while a negociation was pending. At last we landed close to the fortress. The three officers whom I had seen the day before, came out to meet us, and begged that we would wait a little until everything was prepared for our reception in the castle. Wishing by my confidence in the Japanese to extinguish any suspicion they might yet entertain, I ordered the boat to be hauled up on the shore until it was half out of the water, and left one sailor with it. The other seamen I directed to follow us, carrying seats, and the presents which I destined for the Japanese. We walked from ten to fifteen minutes on the shore, during which time I conversed with the officer. I made inquiries respecting the coast of Hokkaido, of which we had a view, and the trade between their island and the peninsula of Japan. I remarked, however, that he answered my questions with reluctance. Finally, we proceeded to the castle.

On entering the castle gate, I was astonished at the number of men I saw assembled there. Of soldiers alone, I observed from three to four hundred, armed with muskets, bows and arrows, and spears, sitting in a circle, in an open space to the right of the gate. On the left a countless multitude of Ainu surrounded a tent of striped cotton cloth, erected about thirty paces from the gate. I never could have supposed this small insignificant place capable of containing so many men, and concluded that they must have been collected from all the neighboring garrisons since we appeared in the harbor.

We were soon introduced into the tent, on a seat opposite to the entrance of which the commander-in-chief, a commissioner of Matsumae's Magistrate office (*bugyōsho shihai shirabeyaku*), Nasa Sezaemon Masatatsu, had placed himself. He wore a rich silk dress, with a complete suit of armour, and had two swords under his girdle. A long cord of white silk passed over his shoulder. At one end of this cord was a tassel of the same material, and at the other a steel baton, which he held in his hand, and which was doubtless the symbol of his authority. His armour bearers, one holding a spear, another a musket, and a third his helmet, sat behind him on the floor. The helmet resembled that of the second in command, with this difference, that instead of the figure of the moon, it bore the image of the sun. This officer now sat on the left of the commander-in-chief, on a seat somewhat lower than that of his superior; he too had his armour bearers behind him. Four officers were sitting cross-legged on the floor on each side of the tent: they wore black armour, and had each two swords. On our entrance Masatatsu and his lieutenant both rose up. We saluted them in our own manner, and they returned the compliment. They invited us to sit down on a bench placed directly opposite to themselves, but we chose to use the seats we had brought with us. Our sailors seated themselves on the bench behind us.

After the introductory civilities were concluded, they entertained us with tea without sugar, in cups which, according to the Japanese fashion, were only half filled; the cups had no saucers, but were handed to us on small trays made of varnished wood. Before they gave us the tea, they asked whether we would prefer anything else. Pipes and tobacco were afterwards brought to us, and the conference commenced. They desired to know our names and rank, the name of our ship, from where we came, where we were bound, why we had visited them, what had induced Russian ships to attack their villages, and further, whether we knew Resanov, and where he now was? Our answers to these questions were conformable to the statements we had previously made, and were written down by the lieutenant.

We were next told that to enable them to prepare the proper quantity of provisions we wanted, it was necessary they should know the exact number of our crew. Ridiculous as this question was, they had an object in putting it. On our part we thought it advisable to make our force appear more considerable than it was, and therefore doubled it, calling it one hundred and two men. Alexei could neither understand nor express this number. And I was obliged to make an equal number of marks with a black-lead pencil on paper, which the Japanese counted off. We were further asked whether we had any other ships of the size of the *Diana* in their seas. We answered that we had many in Okhotsk, Kamchatka, and America. Among their questions were several of a very insignificant nature, relative to our dress, customs, etc. They also carefully examined the presents I had brought for the commander-in-chief, among which were maps of the globe, ivory-handled knives, burning-glasses, and *piastres*, with which I intended to pay the Japanese for a supply of provisions, as soon as I could ascertain the number they required.

While the conference was going on, Mur observed, that naked swords had been distributed among the soldiers who were sitting in the open space. He immediately mentioned this to me. But I supposed that a sword or two might have been accidentally out of their sheaths. And I asked him, with a smile, whether he had not made a mistake, as the Japanese always carry swords, and could at present have no reason for drawing them. This remark appeared to satisfy him. But circumstances soon occurred that roused all our suspicion, and convinced us that some mischief was intended against us. The lieutenant having withdrawn for a short time as if to make some arrangement, returned and whispered to the commander-in-chief, who immediately rose up to go away. We got up also to take our leave. And I repeated my question respecting the price of provisions, and also asked whether he intended to supply us with any. On hearing this he sat down, invited us to do the same, and, though it was early in the day, ordered dinner to be served up.

We accepted his invitation, and waited with impatience to see what would next occur, as it now appeared we were caught in a snare from which it would be difficult to escape. But the kind behavior of the Japanese, and their assurances that we had nothing to fear, again tranquillized us, and induced us to abandon our suspicions of their treachery. They entertained us with rice, fish in a green sauce, and other savory dishes, the ingredients composing which we did not know. They also gave us *sake*. After we had dined, Masatatsu was again about to withdraw. I now declared that we could wait no longer, but must return immediately on board. On hearing this he once more sat down, and having intimated that he could not supply us with anything without an order from the magistrate (*bugyō*) of Matsumae, under whose jurisdiction he was, proposed that one of us should remain in the castle as a hostage, until a decision should be returned by that commander on the report he was about to transmit to him.

The Japanese now began to throw off the mask. I desired to be informed what time would be occupied in sending the report to Matsumae and obtaining an answer; he replied a fortnight. I felt, however, that it would be dishonourable to leave an officer behind me as a hostage. There was, besides, no knowing when such an affair would be brought to a conclusion with a people like the Japanese. It was probable that when the report reached Matsumae the commander of that island would say he could do nothing without the authority of the general government: thus I perhaps should have to wait until winter for a decisive answer. I therefore stated that I could not wait so long without consulting the officers who remained on board the *Diana*, and that I would leave no officer as a hostage, upon which we rose to go away.

Masatatsu, who had hitherto conversed in a soft and gentle voice, now altered his tone, spoke loud and with warmth. He frequently mentioned "Resanoto" (Rcsanov) and "Nicola Sandrejetsch" (Nikolai Aleksandrowich, meaning Khvostov the captain of the Company's ship) and struck several times on his sword. In this manner he made a long speech, of which the terrified Alexei interpreted to us only the following sentence: "The commissioner says that if he lets a single one of us out of the castle his own bowels will be ript up." This was brief and decisive! We instantly made all the haste we could to escape. The Japanese did not venture to close upon us, but set up a loud cry and threw oars and large pieces of wood at us to knock us down. On our reaching the gate they fired several times on us, but without effect, though one of their balls whistled past the head of Khlebnikov. We now found that they had succeeded in detaining Mur, the sailor Makarov, and our Ainu Alexei, in the castle. We ran to our landing place. But on arriving there, perceived with horror that the tide had ebbed above five fathoms, and left the strand quite dry. As the Japanese saw that it was impossible for us to get the boat afloat, and had previously ascertained that it contained no arms, they became confident, advanced against us with drawn swords, which they held in both hands, muskets and spears, and surrounded us beside the boat. I cast a look upon the boat, and said to myself, *It must be so; our last refuge is lost; our fate is unavoidable!*—I surrendered. The Japanese seized me by the arms and conducted me to the castle, into which my unfortunate companions were also conveyed. On the way thither a soldier struck me several times on the shoulder with a small iron bar, but one of the officers said something to him, accompanied with a look of displeasure, and he immediately discontinued.

We were carried into the same tent in which we had held the conference, but neither of the commanders with whom we had communicated were now there. The first thing done was to tie our hands slightly behind our backs, and conduct us into an extensive but low building, which resembled a barrack, and which was situated on the opposite side the tent towards the shore. Here we were all, except Makarov, (whom we had not seen since our separation) placed on our knees, and bound in the crudest manner, with cords about the thickness of a finger: and yet this was not enough; another binding with smaller cords followed, which was still more painful.

The Japanese are exceedingly expert at this work. And it would appear that they conform to some precise regulation in binding their prisoners, for we were all tied exactly in the same manner. There were the same number of knots and nooses, and all at equal distances, on the cords with which each of us was bound. There were loops round our breasts and necks; our elbows almost touched each other, and our hands were firmly bound together. From these fastenings proceeded a long cord, the end of which was held by a Japanese, and which on the slightest attempt to escape required only to be drawn to make the elbows come in contact, with the greatest pain, and to tighten the noose about the neck to such a degree as to produce strangulation. Besides all this, they tied our legs in two places, above the knees and above the ankles. They then passed ropes from our necks over the cross beams of the building, and drew them so tight that we found it impossible to move.

Their next operation was searching our pockets, out of which they took everything, and then proceeded very tranquilly to smoke tobacco. While they were binding us, the lieutenant showed himself twice, and pointed to his mouth, to intimate perhaps that it was intended to feed us, not to kill us.

We passed an hour in this melancholy and painful situation, without being able to form any idea of what was to be done with us. We indeed supposed, when the ropes were passed over the cross beams, that we were about to be hanged. I never so totally despised death as at that moment, and I wished with all my heart that the murder we anticipated might be perpetrated without delay. We once fancied that we should be carried to the outside of the castle, and hung up within sight of our countrymen. And in our state of despair this notion was in some measure consolatory. I was persuaded that if we were butchered in so inhuman a manner before the eyes of our friends and shipmates, their hatred of the Japanese would be further augmented, and their desire of vengeance rendered more ardent. And that when they carried back the news of this massacre to Russia, the same feelings would be excited in the hearts of our monarch and his people. We should then, in dying, have had the satisfaction to reflect that our death would be avenged, and the Japanese be taught to repent their crime, or even to deplore our fate. At last, they removed the cords from above the ankles, and loosened a little those above the knees, and led us from the castle, first into a field, and then into a wood. We were bound so fast, that a child, without the least risk, could have led us where he pleased. The Japanese did not think so lightly of the business. Each was led with a cord, by a particular conductor, and had also an armed soldier walking by his side. In this manner we moved onward, one behind the other.

On ascending a hill, we saw our ship under sail. This sight lacerated my heart, when Khlebnikov, who was immediately behind me, exclaimed "Wasily Michailovitsch! Take a last look of our *Diana!*" It seemed as though a deadly poison had been running through my veins. *Good heaven!* I thought, *how much do these words comprehend! Take a last look of Russia, of Europe—we belong now to another world! We are not dead, but all is lost and dead to us. Never more shall we know what is passing in our country, in Europe, or in any part of the world!* I felt all the terrors of my situation.

When we had walked the distance of two kilometers, we heard a cannonade. We could easily distinguish the firing of our sloop, from that of the castle. But the strong garrison of the Japanese, and the thick earthen wall that formed their fortification, did not permit us to expect any fortunate result from the contest. We were afraid lest the *Diana* might catch fire or run aground, and the whole crew fall into the hands of the Japanese. In this case the knowledge of our dreadful fate would never reach Russia. What I most dreaded was that the attachment Lieutenant Ricord and the other officers entertained for me would induce them to overlook every danger, and to land with the crew, in order to storm the garrison. They might, I feared, make the attempt, as they were not aware how greatly the strength of the garrison exceeded that of the sloop's crew; which, officers, seamen, and servants, amounted only to fifty-one men. This idea troubled me the more, as we could learn nothing of the fate of the *Diana*.

I was so tightly bound, particularly about the neck, that before we had travelled six or seven kilometers, I could scarcely breathe. My companions told me that my face was swollen and discolored. I was almost blind, and could not speak without the greatest difficulty. We made signs to the Japanese, and requested them, through Alexei, to loosen the cord a little, but the cannonade so frightened them, that they paid no attention to our remonstrances. They only urged us to move faster, and kept constantly looking behind them. Life now appeared a heavy burden to me, and I resolved in case we should have to pass a river, to make a sudden jump into the water, and thus terminate a painful existence. I soon saw that it would not be easy to execute this purpose, as the Japanese always held us fast by the arms when we had occasion to cross even a little brook. I fell at length senseless on the ground. When I recovered, I found the Japanese sprinkling me with water, and the blood flowing from my mouth and nose. My unfortunate companions, Mur and Khlebnikov, were, with tears in their eyes, begging the Japanese to loosen the cords with which I was bound. They at last, with the greatest difficulty, prevailed on them to comply. I then found myself much eased, and was soon able to make an effort to proceed.

After completing a journey of about ten kilometers, we arrived at a small village, situated on the straits that divide this island from the island of Hokkaido. We were conducted into a house, where boiled rice was offered us, but we felt no desire to taste food of any kind. On our declining to eat, we were taken into another apartment, in which we were laid down close to the walls, so as not to touch each other. The ropes by which we had been led were attached to iron hooks, driven into the wall for that purpose. Our boots were pulled off, and our legs tied as before in two places. When the Japanese had disposed of us in this way, they sat down in the middle of the room round a chafing dish, and drank tea and smoked. Any man might have slept tranquilly beside lions, had they been bound as fast as we were, the Japanese, however, never thought themselves secure. The cords with which we were tied were inspected every quarter of an hour. At this moment we regarded them as the rudest barbarians on the face of the earth, but subsequent events proved that there are worthy men among them. And we were afterwards rendered more comfortable, indeed as much so as men could be under such circumstances.

The sailor Makarov, who had been separated from us in the castle, but who now joined us, related that as soon as the Japanese seized him, they took him to a barrack, were the soldiers treated him with *sake* and boiled rice, and that he ate everything that was offered to him with the keenest appetite. They then bound his hands, and conveyed him out of the fort. But when they had taken him a short distance he was unbound. In this way they conducted him to the village, where he was again tied. He was allowed to rest on the way, and one of the soldiers gave him a drought of *sake* out of his flask.

In this situation we remained the whole of the night. Even now, the bare reflection of that moment fills me with horror. My own fate was not my first consideration. I would willingly have made any sacrifice to release my unfortunate companions from their bondage, for I alone had been the cause of their misfortune. In the meantime, the generous conduct of my two officers, Mur and Khlebnikov, made a deep impression upon me. Instead of casting the slightest reflection on my rash confidence in the Japanese, they endeavored to console me, and reproached some of the sailors when they began to murmur, and to ascribe their misfortune to my want of prudence. I can, however, declare that no murmurs ever caused me to feel the slightest dissatisfaction towards those men. They had, indeed, ample reason for complaint, but while they bewailed their distressed situation, they observed such respect towards me, that I felt their complaints most severely. Our misfortune had placed us all on a footing of equality. Every hope of returning to Russia had vanished, and consequently men in their situation might have been expected to let loose their tongues against me in revenge for what they suffered. But our sailors were incapable of such conduct.

Notwithstanding the excessive and almost insupportable pain the bandages had occasioned in my wrists and every joint in my body, yet severe anguish of mind rendered me, for the moment, regardless of all bodily suffering. Every attempt at moving my position, or even turning my head, was accompanied by the most indescribable agony. I frequently prayed for death as the greatest of blessings.

We observed that the captain of our guard repeatedly received scraps of paper, which he read and handed to those about him. On reading those papers, they discoursed in a very low tone of voice, and with the utmost caution. Though we understood not a single word of Japanese, they nevertheless seemed fearful lest we should comprehend what they said. I desired Alexei to attend to their conversation, and to endeavour to make us acquainted with it. He told me that the Japanese had received these papers from the garrison, and that they were talking of our sloop, and the Russians. But this was all he could collect from their discourse.

At the approach of twilight, our guards began to bestir themselves, and seemed to be preparing a journey. About midnight a broad plank was brought in, to the four corners of which ropes were attached. These ropes were fastened at the top, and slung across a pole, the ends of which were laid on men's shoulders. And thus the whole was suspended. The Japanese placed me upon this plank, and immediately bore me away. We now concluded that we were to be separated forever, and that we could entertain no hope of seeing each other again. Our farewell was like the parting of friends at the hour of death.

The sailors wept aloud as they bade me adieu, and my heart was wrung on leaving them. I was conveyed to the seaside, and placed in a large boat, with a mat beneath me. In a few moments Mur was likewise brought to the shore in the same way as I had been, and placed in the boat beside me. This was indeed an unexpected happiness. I was so overjoyed, that for a few moments I experienced a diminution of my torment. Mur was soon followed by Khlebnikov, and the sailors Simanov and Vassiliev; the rest were placed in another boat. A soldier under arms was stationed between each of us. After we were covered over with mats, the boats were rowed from the shore.

The Japanese sat beside us without either saying a word, or taking the slightest notice of our complaints; except a young man, about twenty years of age, who spoke the Ainu language, and who kept constantly singing and mocking us while he assisted in rowing the boat. He counterfeited the sound of our voices, when anguish both of body and mind forced us to offer up supplications to heaven, or to break forth in bitter lamentations.

At break of day, on the 12th of July, 1811, we landed near a little village (Shibetsu), on the coast of the Island of Hokkaido. Here we were removed into other boats, which were drawn with ropes along the shore in a south-easterly direction. In this way we were dragged the whole of that day and the following night. There was no halting, except at certain fixed places, where the men, who were employed in the dragging, and who came from the neighboring villages, were relieved. The whole coast was, indeed, thickly strewed with buildings and habitations of various kinds. Between every third or fourth kilometer we observed populous villages, in all of which extensive fisheries appeared to be carried on.

The methods adopted by the Japanese in this branch of industry are in many respects singular. We frequently passed by at the moment when they were drawing their large nets out of the water, filled with an incalculable number of fish. The best fish in these parts are of the salmon species, and are likewise caught at Kamchatka.

The Japanese frequently offered us stewed rice and broiled fish. And when any one of our party expressed a wish to partake of these dishes, they lifted the food to his mouth with two or three pieces of sticks, which were used by them instead of forks.

The Japanese even carried their attention to us so far, that some of them stood constantly near us with boughs of shrubs in their hands to drive off the gnats and flies. We were not a little surprised at this inconsistent conduct; for, notwithstanding their excessive care to protect us from the flies, they showed the utmost indifference to our complaints, and never offered to ease our sufferings by loosening the cords with which we were bound. We had, indeed, but little kindness to expect from them. To suffer us to pine away our lives in everlasting imprisonment, instead of putting us to death, was, in their opinion, the greatest act of mercy they could show us. The bare thought of never again enjoying liberty, was to me a thousand times more dreadful than death. But even on the brink of an abyss man seldom abandons hope, and we now sought consolation in her smiles. We might some time or other find an opportunity of escaping. The Japanese, who were cautious, in consequence of our vessel being still in the neighborhood of their coasts, might, one day or other, be induced to loosen our bonds, without reflecting on what despair might force us to attempt. We might even find an opportunity of getting possession of a boat, in which we could proceed to the Tartar coast. From thence, under pretense of shipwreck, we might easily obtain a conveyance to Peking, and, with the consent of the Chinese government, it would be no difficult matter to gain permission to proceed to Kyakhta. Thus we pictured our return to Russia, our dear native country. But these pleasing reveries quickly vanished. And we recognized the truth of the Russian proverb, which says, *It is easy to think, but not so easy to do.*

That the Japanese would not keep us eternally bound with ropes, was indeed no improbable supposition. Yet what would avail us the freedom of our hands and feet, since that freedom would doubtless only be enjoyed within four high walls, and behind an iron grating. Where then was the coast of Tartary, where Kyakhta? With this reflection the last ray of hope became extinct, and our souls were filled with the blackest despair. I frequently thought that had shipwreck, or any other misfortune, thrown me into the hands of the Japanese, I would never have murmured at my fate, but have borne my sad imprisonment with resignation. I should then have cheerfully entered the fortress, willing to render myself useful to the Japanese, and regarding them as friends. Or, had I, who was the sole cause of the misfortune, been the only one to suffer from it, I should not at least have been tormented by self-reproach. But seven of my crew were likewise doomed to pay the forfeit of my imprudence.

My companions sought to banish these feelings of remorse from my mind. Mur, who perceived that I was harassed with vexation at having been over-reached by the Japanese, referred to several historical examples, to prove that men of higher rank than myself, such as Cook, Paul Antoine Fleuriot de Langle, Prince Pavel Dmitriyevich Tsitsianov, and others, had become the victims of similar accidents. Yet I thought their fate far preferable to my own. They suddenly perished, whilst I was doomed to live, the cause and the witness of the sufferings of my companions. To the honor of Khlebnikov, I must declare that he manifested more resignation than any of our party. He never murmured, but consoled himself with the reflection, that no human wisdom or foresight could have averted a misfortune, to which, in his opinion, we had been doomed by all-governing fate. I, on my part, entertained very different notions of predestination. In my opinion, such men as are to blame for their own misfortunes, are as a warning to others, justly visited with the pain of repentance and sorrow. But, on the contrary, those whom fate has plunged into a state of misery, which no earthly wisdom or foresight could have averted, can have no remorse, and therefore bear their destiny with calmness.

At break of day, on the 13 th of July, we stopped to breakfast at a little village, the inhabitants of which immediately collected on the shore to look at us. A grey-haired man of very venerable appearance begged that our guards would allow him to furnish us with a breakfast and some *sake*. This permission was granted, and the old man stood near the boats during the whole time of the repast, to see that we wanted for nothing. The expression on his face plainly showed that he sincerely pitied us. This trait of benevolence and sympathy for our misfortunes, in an utter stranger, afforded us no little consolation. We now began to entertain a better opinion of the Japanese and no longer regarded them in so barbarous a light as their former conduct seemed to justify.

When we had finished our breakfast, the boats were again dragged along the shore. The weather was calm and serene; the thick clouds, which before obscured the horizon, had now dispersed. All the neighboring hills and coasts, including Kunashir, and the banks girding its fatal harbor, lay full before us, brightened by the gleam of the morning. But our *Diana* had disappeared. Indeed, to have beheld her would only have increased our affliction. An hour or two before sunrise we stopped in front of some huts, which were inhabited by Ainu. Here the Japanese, assisted by the Ainu, pulled the boats ashore, without desiring either us or our guards to get out, and having dragged us through several thickets and a little wood, they proceeded to ascend a hill, and as they advanced cleared the road out with hatchets and other implements. We were utterly unable to divine what could have induced them to drag boats of such extraordinary size up an acclivity. We suspected that they had caught a glimpse of the *Diana*, and were consequently fearful of being deprived of their booty. But we soon discovered the real cause, for when the boats had reached the summit of the hill, which was tolerably high, they dragged them down the other side into a little stream, which had very much the appearance of an artificial canal. We travelled in this manner by land in the boats about the distance of three or four kilometers. During this journey Vassiliev began to bleed at the nose as profusely as if he had had a vein opened. We begged that the cords that passed round his throat might be loosened. But the Japanese paid no regard to our entreaties, and proceeded to insert cotton in his nostrils. But observing that this did not diminish the effusion of blood, they slackened the cords, though in a very slight degree. This cruelty again effaced the good impression their conduct, a short time before, had made upon our minds, and confirmed us in our first opinion, that they were the most unfeeling of barbarians.

When our boat was dragged into the stream, and fairly afloat, our guards began to treat us somewhat more kindly, probably because they now no longer feared an attack from our sloop. They endeavored to explain to us by signs, that in the course of eight or ten days we would reach Matsumae, where, after our case should be investigated by their superior authorities, we would be set at liberty, and permitted to return to Russia. Though we could not place full faith in this assurance, we did not entirely discredit it, and a faint ray of hope again beamed upon us.

The stream emptied itself into a large lake, which communicated with several others. Our boats sailed slowly along this lake the whole of that night, and the day following. When we arrived at places where the water was shallow, the Ainu jumped out of the boat, and dragged it. It rained violently the whole night, and the Japanese covered us over with mats. These were, however, so frequently tossed off, that we found it necessary, every other moment, to request that they would lay them straight again. One of the soldiers, who stood near Khlebnikov, was an extremely kind-hearted man, and was always ready to do anything to serve us. The attention of the rest was, on the contrary, only manifested towards us during the day.

They were always displeased if we disturbed them at night. We were completely soaked with rain. One of the guards struck Mur for troubling him so frequently. But, for this act of insolence, he was immediately reprimanded by the rest.

At midnight, we stopped before a small village or town, to relieve the rowers. Large fires were burning near the shore, by the light of which we discovered a number of Japanese soldiers and Ainu drawn up rank and file. The former were in their military dresses, wearing armour, and bearing muskets; the latter were armed with bows and arrows. Their chief stood in front, clothed in a rich silken garment, and holding in one hand a symbol of his power, which somewhat resembled a balance. The captain of our guard advanced towards him with testimonials of the highest respect. And, kneeling down with his head inclined towards the earth, he continued a long time engaged in relating something to him, probably giving him an account of our seizure. The chief then came on board our boat, and inspected each of us with a lantern. I entreated that he would order our guards to loosen the cords with which we were bound. The guards immediately comprehended us, and interpreted our request. Instead of returning an answer, the chief began to laugh, muttering something between his teeth, and stepped ashore. Our boats now quitted the shore, and rowed off.

On the night of the 15th, we suddenly stopped before a large fire, which had been kindled on the shore. There our guards unbound our feet, and conducted us to the fire. After we had warmed ourselves we ascended a high hill, and entered a large empty building, which had probably served as a store house, and in which there was no aperture except the door. There our conductors laid us down, provided us with covering, and having again bound our feet in the same way as before, presented us with boiled rice and fish. The Japanese now began to drink tea, and smoke tobacco, and seemed to give themselves no further concern about us.

On the 15th, it rained violently the whole day; we, therefore, remained where we were, and, indeed, scarcely ever altered our positions. Three times, in the course of the day, the Japanese gave us boiled rice, fish, and a kind of soup made of mushrooms.

On the morning of the 16th, the sky became serene, and our guards made preparations to depart. The bandages above our ankles were now removed, but those above our knees were merely loosened so as to enable us to walk: our boots were then drawn on, and we were conducted into the open air. We were now asked whether we preferred walking, or being carried in litters. We all chose to walk, except Alexei, who complained of excessive pain in his feet. The Japanese officer took a considerable time to determine on the order of our procession. He at length disposed of us in the following manner: two Japanese from the neighboring village proceeded first, walking side by side, and carrying staves of red wood, very handsomely carved: their office was to direct our course. These were relieved, on entering the next district, by two new guides, carrying staves of the same description. The guides were followed by three soldiers. Next came my turn, with a soldier on one hand, and on the other an attendant, who, with a twig, kept the gnats and flies from fixing upon me. Behind me was a conductor, who held together the ends of the ropes with which I was bound. We were followed by a party of Ainu, carrying my litter. And after them another party, who were destined to relieve the others when they became fatigued. Next came Mur, guarded in the same manner as I was; after him Khlebnikov; then the sailors, one after the other. And last of all Alexei. The whole retinue was closed by three soldiers, and a number of Japanese and Ainu servants, carrying provisions, and the baggage of our escort. The party must have amounted to between one hundred and fifty and two hundred men. Each individual had a wooden tablet suspended from his girdle, on which was an inscription, stating with which of us he was stationed, and what were the duties of his office. The officer had all this marked down on a list of their names.

The Japanese frequently halted to rest on the way, and always offered us boiled rice, salt fish, dried herrings, and mushrooms: tea, without sugar, was our only drink. About noon they entered a tolerably spacious and neat country house, for the purpose of dining. The owner of this house, who was a young man, furnished us himself with provisions and *sake*. He ordered beds to be prepared for us, and entreated that we would rest there for the night. To this our conductors gave their assent. But we expressed a wish to proceed on our journey. The excessive pain of our arms induced us to wish as quickly as possible to arrive at our journey's end; for, if we could place confidence in the assurance of the Japanese, we were to be unbound on reaching Hakodate.

In the afternoon we proceeded at a very rapid pace, as our guards wished to reach the town of Akkeshi before night. We were likewise equally anxious to advance, since they assured us, that, on arriving there, we should be unbound for a while, and that a surgeon would be directed to dress the sores the tying of the ropes had occasioned on our arms and legs. The weather was fine, but excessively warm. We almost fainted with fatigue, and were scarcely able to advance another step. To seat ourselves comfortably in the litters was impossible, for they were so small, that it was necessary, when we tried to use them, to contract the body. As our hands were bound, we were unable to change the position in which we happened to be placed without assistance. We experienced the utmost pain in every part of the body. Unfortunately too, our road lay along a foot-path that crossed a forest, and as the Ainu advanced with great rapidity, our litters frequently came in contact with the trunks of the tree. This occasioned an insupportable shock, and after an experiment of ten minutes duration, we were usually obliged to get out of our litters and to proceed on foot.

A short time before sunset we reached a little stream, where two boats were waiting for us. This stream, we were informed, communicated with the harbor upon which Akkeshi was built, and where we soon expected to arrive. Mur, myself, and two sailors, were placed in one of the boats, and Khlebnikov and the rest of our party in the other. The boats were hung round with matting, so that, excepting the sky, every external object was screened from our sight. Men in a situation like ours are naturally inclined to notice mere trifles, and try, if possible, to derive consolation from every occurrence. We, accordingly, regarded this circumstance in a favorable point of view, and concluded that the distrust of the Japanese had induced them to veil the bay and seaport from our observation, to prevent us from acquiring further knowledge of that part of their coast. If so, thought we, our guards are right in supposing that our imprisonment will not last forever, and that sooner or later we shall obtain our freedom: why else should they conceal from us an object, the sight of which, if we were to be imprisoned for life, we could never turn to their disadvantage? This thought revived our hopes, so that we almost forgot our misery, and were as cheerful as though the period of our liberation had already approached.

In the meanwhile our boats reached the bay. Our flattering anticipations were now at their height, when one of the soldiers suddenly tore down part of the matting, and by a sign gave us to understand that we might rise and take a view of the city and bay. Heavens! we were in a moment plunged from the highest pinnacle of hope into the deepest despair. The idea of regaining our freedom seemed all a dream: the Japanese, said we, conceal nothing from us; there is, therefore, little ground for supposing that they will liberate us of their own accord. Though this circumstance tended greatly to depress our spirits, yet hope never completely forsook us. We soon recollected that a Russian transport had entered the same bay twenty years before. And that, consequently, the Japanese could have no reason to conceal from us that with which the Russians had long since been acquainted. We should, however, have enjoyed much greater consolation of mind, had the soldier left the mat standing, the use of which was probably to keep off the flies, and not to deprive us of a view of the bay and city.

It was night when we entered Akkeshi. A detachment of soldiers came out to meet us, and conducted us to the castle, which was hung round with striped cotton cloth. We were shown into a neat house, the interior of which was remarkably clean, and adorned with paintings after the Japanese taste. We all entered a large apartment, to the walls of which planks with iron hooks were affixed, and to these hooks the ends of our ropes were fastened. Our guards besides supplied us with beds and cotton coverlets, and gave us some supper, they then bound our feet as before, and in this situation we remained until next morning.

On the 17th of July we rested in Akkeshi. In the morning our hands were unbound for a few minutes, and rags were rolled round the parts on which the skin was broken. We were utterly unable to place our hands in their natural position. And when the Japanese forced them asunder, the pain was excruciating, and far more severe than when they bound them together again. We received food three times every day, and were provided with cotton wadded nightgowns to throw over our own clothes, in order to protect us from the cold and rain.

On the morning of the 18th, we passed over to a village on the south side of the bay, where we breakfasted, and then proceeded on our journey in the manner before described. Our litters were still carried behind us, and we might have lain down if we had wished. Our conductors, for the most part, proceeded on foot, though they occasionally, by way of relaxation, for a short time mounted packhorses.

During the whole journey, the Japanese uniformly observed the same regulations. At daybreak we prepared for our departure, breakfasted, and then set out. Our conductors frequently stopped in villages to rest, or to drink tea and smoke tobacco. At noon we dined. Having rested for one hour after dinner, we again proceeded, and an hour or two before sunset we halted for the night, usually in a village furnished with a small garrison. These night-quarters, when we first entered, were generally hung round with striped cotton cloth. We were always conducted to a neat house, and placed altogether in one apartment, where our guards never failed to fasten us to iron hooks fixed into the walls.

When we arrived at the station where we were to pass the night, we were always conducted to the front of the house belonging to the person possessing the highest authority in the place. We were there seated on benches covered with mats, and he came out to inspect us. We were then taken to the house allotted for our lodging; on entering which our boots and stockings were pulled off, and our feet bathed with warm water, in which there was a solution of salt. We were regularly provided with meals three times a day; namely, breakfast in the morning before we set out on our journey, dinner about noon, and supper in the evening, in our night-quarters. There was little variety in our diet. It consisted usually of boiled rice instead of bread, two pieces of pickled radish for seasoning, broth made of radishes or various wild roots and herbs, a kind of noodle, and a piece of broiled or boiled fish. Sometimes they gave us stewed mushrooms, and each a hard-boiled egg. There was no limitation as to quantity; everyone ate as much as he pleased. Our general beverage was very indifferent tea, without sugar. They seldom gave us *sake*. Our guards fared as we did. And I suppose the expense of their provisions, as well as our's, was defrayed by the government, for at each station the senior among our conductors paid for everything.

On the 19th, we implored the Japanese to untie our hands, in order that we might better arrange the pieces of cloth that had been wrapped about them, and which had become so hard with blood and purulent matter, that the friction produced by the slightest movement caused extreme pain. In consequence of our solicitations, they sat down in a circle, and held a council. After some deliberation, it was resolved to grant our request. But under the condition that we should be again searched, and every article of metal taken from us. This had been already done in the castle, but the Japanese thought it necessary to repeat the precaution. We readily complied, and they hastened to relieve us from our torment. I had in the under part of my dress a key, which they did not discover in their search, and I showed it them when my hands were free. This threw them into a dreadful alarm, and they began to search me over again. Their caution, however, or rather their fear, would not allow all our hands to be loose at once, but only two at a time, and merely for the space of fifteen minutes. They then changed the cloth bandages, and tied our hands as before.

This day an officer, who had been dispatched from Kunashir, came up with us, and took the command of our guard. He treated us with great kindness. And, on the following day (the 20th) ordered our hands to be unbound, leaving the elbows tied.

We were now, for the first time since our imprisonment, able to use our hands in taking food. And the motion of walking was much easier to us. When we had to be ferried over in boats from one point of land to another, our hands were re-bound. But these passages were short, and seldom occurred. The Japanese exercised so much precaution, that they would scarcely ever allow us to go near the water in our march. When we wished to approach it, as walking on the soft sand eased our feet, it was with great difficulty they could be induced to grant our request, and then always walked between us and the water, even when there was not room to do so without wetting themselves. They were not only thus vigilant in preserving us from the commission of suicide, but also in guarding us against everything they thought might injure our health. They took care that our feet should never be wet, and we were all carried, sailors as well as officers, over the shallowest pools or streamlets we had to cross. In the course of our journey, we often met with raspberries and strawberries, which, at first, they would not allow us to pluck, as they conceived them to be unfavorable to the health. We asserted, however, that quite the contrary opinion prevailed in Russia, and were at last permitted to refresh ourselves with the fruit.

We passed the 21st and 22nd in a village which, though but small, had a garrison and a commandant. The rain had raised a river to such a height as to prevent us from prosecuting our journey. There was in this village a professor of the medical art, who was ordered to do something to remove the effects of the severe binding we had undergone. For this purpose he employed a powder which very much resembled white ceruse, and which he strewed on the wounds. To the swellings and indurations on the hands and fingers he applied white plaster, the ingredients of which I could not discover. We soon experienced great ease from the operation of his medicaments, a sufficiency of which for use during our journey was provided.

We could now sleep tranquilly and walk with ease. When we were fatigued, we reposed in our litters, in which we found it practicable to remain without experiencing any particular pain. The behavior of the Japanese was more and more kind. At every station the person first in authority in the village always visited us, remained some hours with us, and made frequent inquiries relative to Laxman and the Russians who accompanied him, whom some of the Japanese still recollected. They also often mentioned Resanov. They praised the former, and held out the hope to us that the Japanese government would not condemn us to perpetual imprisonment, but would, in due time, set us free. It struck us as very remarkable that none of the Japanese who conversed with us alluded in the most distant manner to the conduct of Khvostov, though they spoke much of other Russians whose names were known to them, and frequently mentioned the Japanese who had lived in Russia, and who, they said, were exceedingly well satisfied with their reception and treatment in our country. We knew not to what cause this forbearance was to be attributed; whether to a wish not to throw us in despair by reminding us of the conduct of our countrymen, for which we had no reason to expect a kind return, or from an equally delicate desire to avoid questions which might make us blush for offenses in which we had no share.

In every village, on our arrival and departure, we were surrounded with crowds of both sexes, young and old, whom curiosity to see us drew together. And yet on these occasions we never experienced the slightest insult or offense. All, particularly the women, contemplated us with an air of pity and compassion. If we asked for drink, they were emulous to supply us. Many asked permission of our guards to entertain us, and on their request being granted, brought us *sake*, comfits, fruits, or other delicacies. On one occasion the chief of a village treated us with good tea and sugar. They often inquired respecting an European nation called "Oranda," and a country to which they gave the name of "Kabo." We assured them that we knew of no such people or countries in Europe; upon which they expressed surprise, and testified distrust at our answer. Sometime after we learned that the Japanese called Holland, Oranda, and the Cape of Good hope, Kabo. Our not understanding them was owing to the stupidity of our interpreter Alexei. We regretted excessively having given the Japanese cause to suspect that we concealed from them any information we possessed. We now entertained a very good opinion of them, and were persuaded that nothing but the inhuman conduct of our countrymen could have induced them to treat us with cruelty. Without having received any satisfactory explanation of that affair, they now began to show kindness towards us. We felt certain that they would immediately liberate us, could we only convince them that our government had no share in the proceedings of the Russian vessel. We began therefore to look upon our liberation as an event that might possibly take place, and flattered ourselves with the hope of, one day or other, returning to our native country. But a fresh difficulty arose.

Alexei, with whom we had frequent opportunities of conversing in the course of our journeys, as well as in the night quarters, informed us that about ten years ago some Kamptschatdale priests had conveyed a party of Ainu, in a kayak, from the Island of Rasshua to Iturup, which is under the dominion of the Japanese, for the purpose of converting the hairy Ainu to Christianity, or, as Alexei expressed himself, "to teach their people our faith." When we inquired what instruction the missionaries had sent to them, he replied: "The missionaries gave us a great many copper images of saints, and written prayers, with pictures, and desired us to show them to the hairy Ainu, and to tell them that the images represented the Russian God. And that, if they hung them about their necks, they would live long and happily, would never suffer sickness, and would hereafter exist in another world." He further added that the missionaries received a fox skin from the Ainu, in return for every image or prayer. On arriving at Iturup they were however seized by the Japanese, who took from them the images and prayer books. On being asked what these things meant, and why they had brought them thither, they candidly replied that the images represented the Russian God, and that they had been sent by the Russians to convert the inhabitants of Iturup to the Russian faith. The Japanese placed a strict watch over them, but they were fortunate enough one night to effect their escape, and to reach the shore, where they found a boat, in which they rowed off. They were immediately pursued by the Japanese, but a thick fog concealed them, and they reached their island in safety.

This information made a melancholy impression upon us. *Heavens!* thought I, *we are doubtless destined to be punished for the faults of others.* Though we were convinced of the good intentions of our monarch towards Japan, and felt conscious of our own innocence, yet we could not exculpate ourselves to a people who possessed such strong evidence against us. Even though we had proved to them that Khvostov had acted without the knowledge of the Russian government, how could we ever hope to persuade them, that obscure and ignorant missionaries had, to the disgrace of the Christian religion, transported images of saints and prayerbooks to a foreign land, for the sole purpose of serving their own interested views. We never could have convinced the Japanese that this had taken place without the authority of our government. I asked Alexei whether he had informed them of the missionaries having exchanged the images and books for fox skins. "No," he replied, "we were afraid to mention that"—Singular fatality! The Ainu had concealed the only circumstance that might have served for our justification.

There appeared now no possibility of recovering our freedom with the consent of the Japanese, and flight we regarded as our only resource. I communicated my design to my companions; first to the officers, and then to the seamen. But how was our plan to be executed. We knew only of one doubtful and uncertain means: on arriving at our night quarters, the Japanese always consigned us to the care of two or three inhabitants of the village, who had scarcely any arms about them, and who usually seated themselves in the middle of the room, and entered into conversation with each other, without paying any attention to us. The soldiers themselves were accustomed to lay their swords down in a particular spot, at a short distance from us, to undress and wash themselves in bathing tubs. Having thrown on their night dress, they would stretch themselves before the fire to smoke tobacco. Fires were never kindled in our rooms till dusk. Two of the sailors, Simanov and Makarov, and myself, were so loosely bound, that we could with ease draw the ropes down from our elbows. As we lay very closely together, we might, in the darkness of the evening, have freed our own hands and likewise have liberated our companions, who were faster bound than we. This might have been done without difficulty; though our shoulders ached excessively, and our hands were much swollen. Yet in a case of necessity we could have managed to make use of them. We had only to wait until we should arrive at a village on the coast where boats were stationed, and when a smart breeze should be blowing from the land. We might then watch an opportunity for seizing the swords of our guards, and hastening to the shore. So daring an attempt would have overwhelmed the Japanese with terror; their well-known cowardice would have deprived them of presence of mind. Whilst they would be engaged in searching for their arms, we might have reached a boat, and have cut the ropes that fastened it to the shore. Before they could have got on board their boats, the wind would probably have driven us to some distance. And it even appeared doubtful whether they would venture to attack us in the open sea, particularly if the waves were in the slightest degree rough. We therefore hoped, assisted by the compass, with which the Japanese boats are always furnished, to reach the coast of Kamchatka.

This project, however, did not appear altogether practicable. In the first place we never might find a favorable opportunity for its execution. Secondly, the sailors might not all resolve, as we did, to prefer death to imprisonment, and in our situation we had no control over them. The Ainu themselves, who, we observed, hated the Japanese, held out to us another means of escape. Many of these Ainu, when unobserved by the Japanese, had given our sailors to understand, by means of signs, that they might loosen their ropes and escape into the woods. But whether they were inclined to assist us, or whether we were ourselves to break from our bondage, and to seek safety by flight, we knew not. We could only make ourselves understood through Alexei, to whom we dared not communicate our design, lest he should betray us; for owing to the ill treatment which he declared his countrymen had experienced from the pelt hunters, we had reason to suspect that he was much more partial to the Japanese than to the Russians. We suspended our decision for the present, but resolved to be on the watch for a favorable opportunity.

Meanwhile, the Japanese continued to treat us with increasing kindness. Alexei having informed them that the drawing they had found in the cask was executed by Mur, they earnestly requested that he would make a sketch of a Russian ship. He of course supposed he should only be required to make one drawing, and set to work with great alacrity, though he could merely obtain permission to have the ropes that bound his arms slackened in a very slight degree. Having finished his task, the Japanese one after the other requested that he would draw a ship for each of them. He was tormented by their importunities, and Khlebnikov undertook to assist him. I knew nothing of drawing, and they therefore requested that I would write something upon their fans. They always requested these favors very courteously and intreated us to make sketches and inscriptions, not merely for themselves, but for their friends. They sometimes brought us ten or more fans at once, in order that we might inscribe upon them the Russian alphabet, or the Japanese alphabet with the corresponding Russian characters; our numerals, names, a song, or anything we might fancy. They quickly observed that Mur and Khlebnikov wrote better than I, and consequently they never applied to me, except when they were fully employed. Our sailors were likewise requested to write. And the Japanese expressed surprise when they excused themselves on the score of inability. They considered a specimen of Russian writing as great a curiosity as an inscription in Japanese would be looked upon in Europe, and showed us a fan upon which were inscribed four lines of a popular Russian song, signed by a person named Babikov, who, it appeared, had visited Japan along with Laxman. Though these lines must have been written twenty years before we saw them, yet the fan was as clean and fresh as if perfectly new. The owner kept it wrapped up in a sheet of paper, and set so much value upon it, that he would scarcely suffer it to be opened. In the course of our journey we must have made inscriptions on at least a hundred fans and sheets of paper for the Japanese. They never obliged us to write, but always requested us to do so with much politeness, and constantly thanked us by raising the writing to their foreheads and bending their bodies. In return they usually gave us some refreshment, or presented us with tobacco for smoking.

When the Japanese occasionally unbound our hands, they took care to hold our pipes for us whilst we smoked, fearing that we might by some means or other convert the pipe into an instrument of suicide. But of this they soon became weary and, after a consultation, they resolved to permit us to hold our own pipes, on condition of our fastening to the mouth-pieces a wooden ball the size of a hen's egg. We laughed at this, and explained to them that it would be a much easier matter to choke ourselves with this ball than with the mere pipe. They then smiled at their own apprehensions, and told us, through Alexei, that their laws required that they should watch their prisoners strictly, and use every precaution to prevent them from committing self-destruction.

The curiosity of the Japanese was carried to so great a length, that, at every station at which we halted, we were requested to tell our names, our ages, how many relations we had, where our clothes had been manufactured, etc. Our answers were always set down in writing. They frequently requested the sailors, as well as the two officers and myself, to tell them Russian words, and the names of various things, and they thus formed little vocabularies for themselves. This surprised me very much, and we suspected that they were not induced to question us so closely from mere curiosity, but that they had received orders to that effect from the government. We accordingly became more circumspect in our answers.

The 29th and 30th of July we spent in one place. The Japanese at first told us that they could not proceed on account of the illness of some of the soldiers. But the commandant of the village afterwards informed us, that a deficiency of the requisite number of men prevented him from sending us forward, and that we should continue our journey as soon as he could obtain a reinforcement. From these different accounts we concluded that they were deceiving us, and that our delay was occasioned by some cause they did not wish to explain. This proved to be the fact. Alexei learned from some Ainu that the place of abode which was preparing for us at Hakodate, where we were proceeding, was not yet completed, and that three officers had been dispatched from that city to meet us, and to give orders for stopping our march. These officers soon made their appearance, and informed us, that they had been sent to meet us by Ōshima Eijirō, the deputy magistrate (*tsume-ginmiyaku*) of Hakodate, for the purpose of conducting us to that city, and seeing that we were provided with everything we stood in need of.

The eldest of these officers, who was named Yamada Gooiso, showed great attention to us, and during the journey constantly marched by our side. We now received food of a quality superior to that with which we had before been supplied. Gooiso assured us that when we reached Hakodate we should inhabit a fine house, which had been prepared for our reception; that we should enjoy our liberty, and be maintained in an expensive style; and that the most distinguished inhabitants of the place would seek our acquaintance, and invite us to their houses. But when we reflected that we were bound with ropes like the basest criminals, we strongly suspected Gooiso said all this only with a view to console us. Yet our guards informed us that whenever any of their most distinguished officers were arrested, they were always bound with ropes, even before they were proved to be guilty. Considering then that the customs of the Japanese were totally unlike those of Europe, it was not improbable that persons of rank might associate with us, and Gooiso treated us with so much kindness that we felt inclined to place faith in what he said rather than in our own conclusions.

Besides our three new conductors, another individual was added to our escort. He was an officer in the service of the *daimyō* of the fiefdom of Nanbu (Morioka). As a mark of distinction, a spear with a horse's tail was carried after him. All the rest treated him with the highest respect, and were entirely under his control. His whole duty appeared to consist in keeping a watchful eye over us. Our expenses were defrayed by the three *bakufu* soldiers who had been sent to Hakodate to meet us. One of Gooiso's companions was a very intelligent young man. He was extremely agreeable in conversation, and treated us with the utmost attention and politeness. The other, who was a man advanced in life, seldom spoke to us, was seized with an immoderate fit of laughter whenever he looked upon us, and listened with great attention during our conversations with each other. From this last circumstance we concluded that he must have been one of those Japanese who had lived in Russia. And as he probably understood our language, had been sent for the purpose of collecting information from our discourse. We were confirmed in this suspicion when we recollected, that in one of the villages at which we had stopped, the commandant's secretary privately informed us that there were persons in Matsumae who understood the Russian language, though our conductors had never even hinted this to us.

After Gooiso became our conductor we experienced very different treatment. When we made a halt, the sailors were not suffered to sit upon the same bench with us, as our mats were considerably better than theirs. And whenever the situation permitted it, the officers had a particular apartment assigned to them. With regard to our food, however, no difference whatever was observed.

As we were proceeding on our journey, on the 7th of August, we met an officer from Matsumae, who was on his way to Kunashir, to inquire into every circumstance relative to us. When his suite came within sight, we received orders to turn back, at which we were very well pleased. We supposed that the magistrate of Matsumae had dispatched this officer for the purpose of ascertaining exactly the events that had passed at Kunashir and, if our friendly intentions were made manifest, to give orders for removing us to the Russian Kuril Islands that very summer. But our hopes proved unfounded, for we were informed that we must proceed to the nearest village, where the officer wished to have an interview with us. He, however, soon changed his mind, and expressed a wish to hold a conference with us on the road. We found him seated in a little hut, accompanied by two other officers, and with some persons of his suite. We were directed to seat ourselves opposite to him, on a plank, which was supported by two logs of wood, and covered over with mats. He asked us our names and ages, and inquired whether we were in good health. All the questions and answers that passed between us were written down by one of his officers, who acted as a secretary. He then wished us a pleasant journey, and desired us to proceed.

We now ascended an eminence, from the summit of which we beheld a vast plain, and the city of Hakodate at some distance before us. On descending the other side of this hill, we reached our last night's quarters, the village of Ono, which was the largest, and, from its situation, by far the most beautiful of any we had hitherto seen. It lies in the centre of a valley, which is about twenty-five or thirty kilometers in circumference, and is surrounded on three of its sides by high hills, which serve to shelter it against the cold winds. The harbor of Hakodate and the Straits of Tsuruga lie to the south of the village. The valley is intersected by numerous rivulets and small streams. The village is, as it were, built within a garden, for every house is surrounded by a piece of cultivated ground, which is planted with kitchen roots and oriental tree. Besides the culinary vegetables common in Europe, we also observed apple, pear, and peach tree. And, in a regular order, hemp, tobacco, and rice. Ono is about seven kilometers distant from Hakodate.

With regard to the extensive population of Japan, and the remarkable industry of the inhabitants, it may not be superfluous to observe, that during our journey along the coast, which extended to the distance of full one thousand and twenty kilometers, we beheld populous villages on every bay and creek we got sight of. During the summer some of the people reside in leaf huts, built between these villages. The whole population is employed in catching, salting, and drying fish. They likewise gather a kind of seaweed, which grows in great abundance on the coast, and which the Russians in these seas call sea cabbage. This weed they spread out upon the sand to dry. They then collect it together in heaps, resembling haycocks, and cover it over with matting, until the time arrives for loading the vessels, which carry it to the harbor of Japan.

Everything produced by the sea is considered eatable by the Japanese: fish, marine animals of every description, sea-plants, and weeds, are all made to contribute towards their support. A vast number of individuals gain a livelihood by selling, among the numerous population of Japan, the articles of food they collect upon the coasts.

The boundary between the Ainu and Japanese villages lies about one hundred and fifty or two hundred kilometers distant from Hakodate. The two divisions are separated by a beautiful little stream, which, at the time of our arrival, was so swollen by heavy rains, that it was not without considerable difficulty we succeeded in fording it. The Ainu villages are generally small, consisting of huts without either kitchen-gardens or orchards, and, upon the whole, present an appearance of poverty. The only structures deserve to be called houses are those inhabited by the Japanese civil and military officers. They are built in a neat style, kept clean, and have kitchen gardens and orchards attached to them. The Japanese villages, on the other hand, present a very different aspect. They are large, have regular streets, and the houses, which are all of wood, are very neatly built. Every house has a kitchen garden, and many are furnished with orchards. The cleanliness that prevails in the streets and houses is truly astonishing. The inhabitants are extremely lively, and content and cheerfulness are painted on every face. And it cannot be said that the personal appearance of the Ainu is the opposite of all this. The Hokkaido Ainu are generally tall and strongly built, very active, and far more handsome and manly than the Russian Ainu, or those who inhabit Iturup and Kunashir.

On the morning of the 8th of August, our conductors made preparation for a formal entrance into the city. They put on new clothes, and armed themselves with coats of mail and helmets. Our breakfast was much better than usual, consisting of a fowl, excellently cooked in a kind of green sauce, which is reckoned a great delicacy among the Japanese. But we did not promise ourselves any good fortune from this circumstance. We always observed that the Japanese treated us very kindly whenever they were about to communicate to us any unwelcome piece of news. It was even so in the present instance. We had no sooner finished our breakfast, than the Nambu soldiers, who had accompanied us from Kunashir, formally declared to us, through Alexei and their Ainu interpreter, that, to their great regret, they were compelled to conduct us into the city bound in the same manner as when we left Kunashir. They accordingly set to work without further preamble. But Gooiso, his companions, and the Nambu officer, who had recently joined us, opposed the tying of our hands behind us. The soldiers, in a respectful manner, made their counter representations, and a discussion ensued, which lasted upwards of a quarter of an hour. The soldiers frequently mentioned the commander-in-chief of Kunashir, and apparently insisted on executing his commands, which were, that we should be conducted into Hakodate bound as we had left Kunashir. Gooiso immediately dispatched a messenger to Hakodate. And, after we had advanced two or three kilometers beyond Ono, an order arrived for unbinding our hands, which was immediately obeyed. When we came within three kilometers of the city, we halted, and stepped into a little hut, to wait for further orders respecting our entrance.

In the meanwhile a vast number of individuals, of both sexes, old and young, came from Hakodate, to see us. We observed several men on horseback in silken dresses, which, as well as the rich harnessing of their horses, proved that they were persons of rank. In the afternoon the procession began to move with great pomp. Both sides of the road were crowded with spectators, yet everyone behaved with the utmost decorum. I particularly marked their faces, and never once observed a malicious look, or any signs of hatred towards us, and none showed the least disposition to insult us by mockery and derision.

We, at length, entered the city, where the concourse of people was so immense, that our guards had great difficulty in clearing a passage for us. Having proceeded to the distance of half a kilometer along a narrow street, we turned down a cross street on our left, which led us into the open fields. Here, upon a rising ground, we first beheld the building which was destined to be our prison. The very sight of it filled me with horror. We saw only the long roof. But that sufficiently enabled us to form a notion of the extent of the edifice. A high wooden enclosure or fence, which was of great strength, and which was well provided with chevaux-de-frise, concealed the body of the building. This wooden fence was surrounded by an earthen wall, somewhat lower, which, on this occasion, was hung with striped cloth. There was a guardhouse near the gate, in which several officers were seated. Along the path leading to our prison soldiers were stationed in full military dresses: they stood at the distance of two fathoms from each other, and were armed in various ways; some with muskets, some with bows and arrows, and others with spears, etc. A party of officers were stationed in front of the building. On arriving at the gate we were received by an officer, to whom a list of our escort had previously been handed, and we were then conducted into a sort of court or yard. Here our future gloomy and horror-stirring residence presented itself fully to our view. It was a large dark building, resembling a barn, and within it were apartments formed of strong thick spars of wood, which, excepting the difference of size, looked exactly like birdcages. The darkness, however, did not permit us to observe the whole at once.

The Japanese placed us in a row near the fence, and began to consult with each other respecting the way in which they should dispose of us. We remained for half an hour in a state of fearful anxiety. At length, Mur and I were asked which of the sailors we wished should remain with us. We were overjoyed at this question, and inquired whether Khlebnikov might be with us. But this the Japanese objected to, and informed us that they thought it improper to leave private sailors without an officer, who would teach them, by his example and advice, to bear unavoidable misfortunes; adding, that the men might otherwise lose courage, and become the victims of despair. Upon this they conducted me, followed by Mur and Skajev, along one side of the building, the rest of our companions being conveyed round to the other. Our eyes were bathed in tears at this separation, which we apprehended was to be eternal.

I was led into a passage or lobby in the building, where my boots were drawn off, and the ropes with which I was bound removed. I was then directed to enter a small apartment, which was divided from the passage by wooden palisades. I now looked around me in quest of Mur and Skajev. But how great was my astonishment to find that I could neither see nor hear them! The Japanese, without saying a word, closed the door of my apartment, and quitted the lobby, the door of which they likewise closed after them. I was now alone. The thought of being separated from my companions, perhaps separated forever, completely overpowered me, and, overwhelmed with despair, I threw myself upon the ground.

I remained for some time in a state of insensibility. At length, having raised my eyes, I observed at the window a man, who beckoned on me to approach him. I complied with his wish. And reaching his hand through the railing, he presented me with two little sweet cakes; at the same time entreating me, by signs, to eat them quickly, as a punishment awaited him if he should be observed. At that moment I loathed the very sight of food. But I made an effort to eat the cakes, lest a refusal might have given offense to my kind visitor. His face now brightened up, and he left the window with a promise to bring me more at a future time. I thanked him as well as I was able. I was greatly astonished that a man, who from his dress apparently belonged to the very lowest class, should be actuated by so powerful a feeling of benevolence, as to hazard his own safety for the sake of conveying comfort to an unfortunate stranger.

My guards now brought me some food. But I felt not the least inclination to partake of it, and sent it all away. In this state I remained until evening. I sometimes threw myself on the floor, or upon a bench, and occasionally walked about the apartment, meditating on some means of effecting my escape. With this view, I attentively inspected the construction of my cage. It was six feet in length and breadth, and about eight feet in height. It was divided from the lobby by wooden palisades of a tolerable thickness, and the door was fastened by a lock. There were two windows, secured externally by strong wooden gratings and in the inside furnished with paper screens, which I could open and shut at pleasure. One window faced the wall of a building about two feet distant from that in which I was confined.

And the other looked towards the southern side of the fence surrounding our prison. From this window I had a view of the neighboring hills and fields, part of the straits of Tsuruga, and the opposite Japanese coast. In the interior of the chamber stood a wooden bench, which was so small that I could not stretch myself upon it. And three or four mats lay in one corner on the floor. The place contained no other furniture.

Having fully considered the situation of my prison, I was convinced, that with a common knife I could, in three hours, cut the grating that covered the window, through it get into the yard, and that, favored by the darkness of the night, I might, with the utmost ease, cross the wooden fence and the wall. But how was a knife to be procured, since we were not entrusted even with the possession of a needle. And though I had succeeded in recovering my liberty, what could I have done alone? My flight might perhaps induce the Japanese to wreak their vengeance on my unhappy companions. The very thought of what might be their situation so distressed me that, though I had possessed the means of effecting my escape, and a boat had been in readiness on the shore, with an easterly wind to blow me to the Tartar coast, I could not have taken advantage of the opportunity. Accordingly I abandoned every idea of attempting to escape alone.

At the approach of night the attendants brought me a new wadded cotton quilt, and a large wadded nightdress. But the latter was so old and dirty, that I could not allow myself to put it on, and I threw it into a corner. During the night patrols hourly walked round the wooden hedge, making a noise like the sound of rattles; and the guards in the interior frequently came into the lobby with lights, apparently for the purpose of watching me.

Early in the morning, when everything around me was silent, I suddenly heard the sound of voices discoursing in the Russian language. I instantly sprang from the bench on which I was lying, and ran to the window that looked towards the wall of the neighboring building, from where I distinctly heard Mur in conversation with Skajev. I was transported at this unexpected discovery, and thanked heaven that my companions were not doomed to solitary imprisonment, but at least enjoyed the consolation arising from mutual condolence. I moreover hoped we might one time or other gain an opportunity of communicating our designs to each other, and of escaping together. I burned with impatience to let them know I was near them. But

I feared lest the sound of my voice might give rise to suspicion. In the meanwhile the soldiers and attendants began to move about the prison, and their noise prevented me from hearing anything farther. One of my guards now brought me cold and warm water for washing and suffered the door to stand open whilst he remained with me. But as soon as I had finished washing he went out, and closed it after him. My breakfast was then sent in to me, but I was unable to eat a morsel.

About noon an officer appeared in the lobby, accompanied by a new Ainu interpreter, by a physician, a man about fifty years of age, and by Alexei. They discoursed with me through the palisades. The officer asked whether I found myself well. And pointing to the physician, whose name was Gotō, he said had been sent by the magistrate of Matsumae for the express purpose of superintending our health. Whilst the Japanese were discoursing together, I had an opportunity of learning from Alexei that Khlebnikov and Simanov were shut up together, as were also Makarov and Vassiliev, but that he, like myself, was imprisoned alone. He added that their dungeons were without windows, and excessively filthy. At twelve o'clock my dinner was brought in, but I refused it. The guard then opened the door, muttered something to himself in ill humor, and laying down the dinner, went out and closed the door behind him. I was, however, unable to taste food.

In the evening the same officer returned with the interpreters, Wechara and Alexei, and informed me that Ōshima Eijirō, the deputy magistrate of the city, fearing that time might hang heavily upon me whilst I was alone, wished to know which of the sailors I should like to have along with me. On my replying that I had no preference, he observed that I must make choice of one, since such was the wish of Ōshima Eijirō. I then requested that they might be sent to me by turns, and that Makarov might be permitted to come first. He was instantly conducted to me. I endeavored to persuade Alexei to request that the Japanese would send him to keep company with Vassiliev in Makarov's absence. But this he refused to do, which made me somewhat doubt his good intentions towards us. On this occasion, I learnt that the officer who had visited me was a person of the highest rank in the city, next to the deputy magistrate. I asked him whether the Japanese intended to keep us always separately confined? "No," answered he, "you will hereafter live all altogether, and be sent back to your native country."

"Shall we soon be confined in one place?" I continued. "Not very soon," he replied. Men in a situation like our's eagerly catch at every word, and form conclusions from all they hear. Had he answered "soon," I should have looked upon all he had said as mere groundless consolation, but I now firmly believed every word he had uttered.

When the Japanese officer had departed, I turned towards Makarov. He was much astonished at the excellence of my apartment, and viewed with the greatest joy the objects that were to be seen from the window: my dungeon appeared to him a paradise when compared with those in which Khlebnikov, Simanov, Wassiijefl and Alexei, were confined. His description of them filled me with horror. He told me that they were shut up in small cages, built of thick wooden palings, which were placed near each other in the middle of a large room, so that there were passages on every side. Instead of doors, the only entrance to them was by small apertures, through which the prisoners were obliged to creep. Not a ray of the sun could penetrate these dismal abodes, which were left almost constantly in complete darkness.

What I had heard from the Japanese officer, together with my conversation with Makarov, in some measure contributed to ease my mind, and in the evening I ate a little supper, which was the first food I had tasted in Hakodate. Here, however, our meals were much worse than those with which we had been furnished on our journey. In the evening our attendants brought us two round cushions, in form resembling our sofa-cushions, covered with cotton cloth and stuffed with hempseed.

On the morning of the 10th of August 1811, the interpreter Uebara Kumajirō[1] informed me that the deputy magistrate had signified his wish to see me that day, and that we would all be required to appear before him in the afternoon. At the appointed hour, we were conducted one after the other into the yard of the prison. Here a rope was bound round each of our waists, the end of which was held by one of the Japanese. Our hands however remained free. We were placed beside each other in a row. The officer, who had been sent to conduct us, was occupied for a quarter of an

---

1 Uebara Kumajirō was a native of Matsumae and originally active as an interpreter in the ainu language in the eastern part of what was then still called Ezo. After 1807, when the region came under direct jusrisdiction of the *bakufu*, he was attached to the magistrate's office (*bugyōsho*) at Matsumae.

hour in arranging the procession, which at length started in the following order—First, two grey-haired men in the common Japanese dress, bearing staffs, to the ends of which lance-headed axes were affixed. They were followed by three Nambu soldiers with swords in their girdles. I proceeded next, with a *bakufu* soldier marching by my side, and a Japanese behind me, who held the rope with which I was bound. Mur, Khlebnikov, the sailors, and Alexei, followed in the same order, and the procession was closed by three Nambu soldiers.

We were conducted, at a slow pace, through a long street, which extended from one end of the city to the other. The windows of the houses were crowded with spectators. Here we observed, for the first time, that all the houses had shops attached to them, which were all stocked with various kinds of merchandize. From this street we turned to the left, and ascended a rising ground, on which a castle was situated, surrounded by palisades and an earthen wall. We entered by a gate into a large courtyard, in the centre of which we observed a brass cannon, mounted on a two-wheeled carriage of very bad construction. A narrow path led us from this yard into another, where a party of imperial soldiers were stationed. They were seated on mats, and were armed with muskets and bows and arrows. We were then conducted into a space, between two buildings, and directed to seat ourselves on a bench covered with matting. The sailors and Alexei seated themselves on mats spread out upon the ground. There we waited for a considerable time. In the meanwhile we were presented with pipes, excellent tobacco, and some fine green tea and brown sugar, with which we were regaled in the name of Ōshima Eijirō. This proved a great luxury to those among us who were fond of smoking, for since our arrival in Hakodate neither pipes nor tobacco had been sent to us.

Here we had leisure and opportunity to converse with each other. Khlebnikov described the place in which he was confined in a manner corresponding with the account previously given by Makarov. Mur he said had an apartment similar to mine, with two windows, from which he had a view of several objects.

After waiting more than an hour, I was called into the adjoining building by my name, "Captain Choworin!" (for so the Japanese pronounced my name.) Two soldiers, one on each side, conducted me through a large gate, which was shut immediately after us, into an extensive hall. Here I was delivered over to other soldiers. This hall resembled a shed, or barn, as one half of it had no ceiling. And instead of being planked, or paved, had a kind of flooring made with small stones strewed on the ground. The other half of the floor rose three feet from the ground, and was covered with curiously worked straw mats. The hall was from eight to ten fathoms long, of an equal breadth, and eighteen feet high. It was divided from the adjoining chambers by moveable screens, very neatly painted. There were only two or three apertures for windows, which had wooden frames, with paper instead of panes of glass, and which admitted an obscure, gloomy light. On the right side of that part where the floor was elevated, there hung against the wall, at the height of four feet, several kinds of irons for securing prisoners, ropes, and various instruments of punishment. These were the only ornaments of this hall, which at first sight I conceived to be a place of execution, or torture. Ōshima Eijirō sat on the floor, in the middle of the elevated platform. Behind him were two secretaries, with paper and ink-stands before them. On the left of the deputy magistrate sat the officer nearest him in authority, and, on his right, the third in command. There was, besides, an officer of inferior rank on each side next to these commanders. They all sat at the distance of two paces from each other, with their legs folded under them. They were in the ordinary black dress of the Japanese, with daggers in their girdles. But each had, also, a large sword lying on his left side. Two sentinels without any arms sat one on each side, on planks, at the corners of the raised flooring. The interpreter, Kumajirō, sat on its edge.

The soldiers who received me when I entered the hall conducted me to the front of the elevation, or platform, I have described, and were about to make me sit down on the stones. But the commandant said something to them, and they allowed me to stand. Mur was next brought in, and placed on my right. Khlebnikov followed, and was placed next to Mur. The sailors were then introduced one after the other, and placed in a row behind us. At last came Alexei, who was made to sit down in the same line with us, and near to Khlebnikov.

When we were all in the order in which they wished us to be placed, the interpreter, by desire of the deputy magistrate, pointed to him, and informed us that he was the chief person in authority in the town. We bowed to him, upon which he nodded with his head, and cast down his eyes. After these compliments had passed, he drew from his bosom a paper, to which he referred while he examined us. I was first asked my name and family name, what was my rank, and to what country I belonged. Both secretaries wrote down my answers. The same questions were put to Mur, Khlebnikov, and all the sailors in succession. Other questions followed in the same order; namely, how old we were, whether our fathers and mothers were living, what was the name of the father of each of us, whether we had brothers and what number of them, whether we were married and had children, in what towns we were born, how many days journey the places of our birth were distant from St. Petersburg, what was the business of each on board of the ship, what we did when on land, and whether the force then entrusted to us was great? All our answers were written down as before. When we had answered the question respecting our birthplace, the Japanese asked how it happened that we should all serve on board the same ship, though we were from different towns. We replied that we did not serve the towns in which we were born, but the whole country and the emperor, and that it was a matter of indifference to us whether we were employed on board the same or different ships, provided they were Russian. The secretaries did not fail to note down this explanation also.

The question that, according to Alexei's interpretation, related to the number of men we commanded on land, gave us, in the result, considerable trouble. The Japanese wished to know exactly how many men were under the orders of each of us. When we stated the number was very different at different times, and depended on circumstances, they still asked what rule was established with respect to these circumstances. In order to get over the difficulty, we made a comparison between our rank and the rank of the army, telling them that a major commanded a battalion, a captain a company. We now believed the affair ended, but I shall have occasion hereafter to notice the vexation we experienced in consequence of these answers.

The next questions related to the names of our ships, their burthen, and the number of cannon they carried. At length Ōshima Eijirō desired to be informed whether some change of religion had not taken place in Russia, as Laxman wore a long tail, and had thick hair, which he covered all over with flour, whereas we had our hair cut quite short, and did not put any flour on our heads. On our telling them that with us there was no connexion between religion and the form of the hair, they laughed out loud, and expressed no little surprise that there should be no express law on this point, though they carefully wrote down our answer.

Finally, they required that we would relate to them, and trace out on the chart, where we had been since our departure from Petersburg. For this purpose they produced a chart that had been drawn after the globe constructed by the Russian Academy, in the time of Empress Catherine. I showed them our course, and then mentioned the chart I had destined as a present for the commandant of Kunashir, remarking that it was better than the one before me, and had part of our voyage marked upon it. The Japanese replied that they had received no chart from Kunashir, but that they would show it to us as soon as they received it. In the meantime the present chart would do for the information they wanted. They not only desired to know every direction in which we had shaped our course, and the period occupied in our navigation, but also the precise time we had spent at each place into which we had put. Our answers and explanations on this, as on all the former topics, were written down. The interpreter being always previously asked whether what we said was correctly translated. As our interpreter was far from being well versed in the languages he had to explain, and the Japanese required the greatest precision in the answers to their questions, this examination lasted several hours. At last Eijirō dismissed us, informing us that, if it should be necessary, we would be brought there again, but that, in the meantime, we had no occasion to be uneasy—we should be used well.

Twilight had commenced when we left the castle, from which we were reconducted in the same order in which we had arrived. The number of spectators was much greater on our return, which perhaps was owing to the labours of the day being finished. On entering our prison we were distributed as before, and to each was given, by order of Eijirō, a cotton night gown and some *sake*. During our absence the Japanese had thrown the passages between Mur's place of imprisonment and mine into one, and formed a space in the middle for the guard, from which a sentinel could see through the railings what either of us might be about. All hope of flight was thus annihilated, though on the other hand, we obtained the advantage of communicating with each other. I spoke to Mur, but not in a direct manner, for I turned towards Makarov, and seemed to be addressing him. Mur did the same to Skajev. This singular mode of conversation lasted only a few days; for having an opportunity to ask the commander of the officers (*kanjō kumigashira*) whether we might converse with each other, he replied, "Speak what you please, and as openly as you please." After this permission we might have talked freely, but we took care to say nothing injurious of the Japanese, lest some person who understood Russian might be within hearing. We were besides afraid to speak much in a language unknown to our guards, as these suspicious people would certainly have reported our doing so to their superiors, and thus have excited new doubts respecting us.

Eighteen days had elapsed since our first audience with the deputy magistrate. And he had neither required us to attend again, nor intimated what was to be done with us. When we questioned the Japanese on these points, their usual answer was that they knew nothing of what was intended. During this time we were regularly visited every morning and evening by the city officers (*kanjō*) who happened to be on duty. They brought along with them the physician and the interpreter, and inquired respecting our health, and whether we wanted anything. Notwithstanding all this attention, the food with which they supplied us was very indifferent. They gave us chiefly a very insipid soup, made of radishes. Mur was seized with a complaint in his breast, for which the physician ordered him to drink a decoction from several roots and herbs. With respect to diet, he merely advised him to eat as much as possible of whatever was brought to him. Mur took this opportunity of remonstrating against his bad fare, and alleged that the medicine could not operate to advantage with such food. Upon hearing this, the commander, whose name was Odachi Kōeki, inquired what the Russians ate when they were sick. Whatever the physician prescribes, replied Mur, which is commonly soup made of fowls or chickens. Odachi Kōeki then inquired very particularly in what way this soup was prepared by the Russians, observing, that the Japanese could cook it also. Mur described it very minutely, and the Japanese officer wrote down his description. It appeared that this was done either from mere curiosity, or for sport, for the chicken soup was never after mentioned, but the old dish was still served up.

This officer was the only Japanese who jested with us. He once promised us beef, butter, and milk, as we told him that the Russians were fond of such food. But some days after he excused himself by saying, with a laugh, that the cows were grazing in the fields. Another time he gave us *sake*, and expressed a wish that I would order the seamen to sing and dance, for, he said, when Laxman was in Japan he had seen a Russian dance, with which he was much pleased. I observed to him that in our situation nothing could induce us to sing and dance, upon which he replied, "Right, right. In such a situation the Japanese also would feel but little inclination to sing or dance."

Besides the orderly officers who visited us at fixed periods, the interpreter Uebara Kumajirō, and the physician Gotō, usually spent about six hours in our company daily. They placed various objects before us, and asked the Russian names of them, which they wrote down each in a separate vocabulary. When the one was with us, the other was with Khlebnikov. The physician possessed considerable knowledge in geography: he had a very fine globe, made in imitation of a European one, and several manuscript maps of the Japanese possessions, which he often showed us. He explained everything respecting which we asked for information, and added his own personal observations on the places known to him.

The chief trouble which the Japanese, both officers and soldiers, who did duty as guards, gave us, arose from their requests to write on their fans and pieces of paper. But as they always solicited the favor with great courtesy, and never failed to return thanks with very humble reverences, we never refused it. Some imposed so far on our complaisance as to bring us ten or twenty fans at a time. These tedious labours fell chiefly on Mur and Khlebnikov, as their hand-writing was very fine. The former wrote more than seventy sheets of paper for one of the soldiers. And from their unceasing applications we at length concluded that they must have sold these manuscripts as articles worthy of being preserved in cabinets of curiosities. This task was the more laborious, as the officers were always desired to give a translation of what was written. When we translated anything for them, they carried it to Khlebnikov, to compare his translation with ours. And if he wrote anything, they brought it for the same reason to us. In this way Khlebnikov was once involved in an embarrassment of no slight nature. One of the officers had, for the third time, asked me to write him something in Russian. In the irritation of the moment I wrote the following words:

> The Russians who may hereafter come in force to this place are hereby informed that the Japanese, in a treacherous and cowardly manner, seized seven of their countrymen. And, without any cause, imprisoned and kept them languishing in dungeons like the vilest criminals. These unfortunate Russians request that you will take a just vengeance on this faithless people.

When the officer asked what this piece of writing meant, I told him it was a Russian song, and desired him to show it to the next Russians who might come there. He went immediately with it to Khlebnikov, who was at first greatly puzzled what to say. But at last thought of telling him that it was a very old song, which could not be easily translated, and thus got over the difficulty.

On the 25th of August, Odachi Kōeki, the deputy-commandant, whom we now seldom saw, and that only on extraordinary occasions, came to us, followed by a large train, and caused mats to be spread in the passage before my apartment. I waited with impatience to see what was to follow. At last, four or five men appeared, bearing on their shoulders my chest, which used to stand in the cabin of our vessel; the portmanteaus of Mur and Khlebnikov, and some bundles. I was thunderstruck at the sight of these things. How could the Japanese have got possession of them? Had they taken the *Diana*, or had she been wrecked on the coast? With much effort, and in broken accents, I answered their questions respecting the ownership of these articles. We soon learned that the *Diana* had sent them on shore before leaving Kunashir. That information tranquillized me. *Now*, thought I, *my companions will return to Russia, and our fate will not remain unknown.*

After the Japanese had written down what I said respecting these things, they proceeded to question my companions. The articles consisted of some clothes and linen, which my successor in command, Lieutenant Ricord, thought necessary to send on shore, and which ultimately proved of great use to us, though at first the Japanese would not deliver any of them.

This day was doubly memorable to me. First, on account of the great surprise and alarm the appearance of our baggage occasioned. And secondly, because the want of paper and ink, or anything on which I could note down the events in which we were interested, induced me to fall on the following singular method of keeping a journal. When anything happened that was agreeable to us, I tied a knot on a white thread, which I drew out of the frill of my shirt: when any unpleasant event occurred, I made a memorandum of it by tying a knot on a thread of black silk, taken out of my neck handkerchief. With regard to other circumstances which, though remarkable, had occasioned us neither joy nor sorrow, I recorded them by knots on a thread of green silk, which I extracted from the lining of my uniform coat. Often did I count over these knots, and recall to my mind the events they served to denote.

About this time the soldiers told Mur, as a secret, that we should not remain much longer in Hakodate. This appeared to us very improbable, as from everything we had observed, we were persuaded that we were likely to continue a long time in our present quarters. In the first place, the Japanese had given us new wadded nightgowns, which they use for sleeping in instead of coverlets, but which they seldom carry with them on journies. Secondly, we had learned that soon after our arrival, they had constructed sentry boxes at different parts of the fence surrounding our prison, and had besides made several changes in the internal arrangements of the building.

On the morning of the 28th of August, we were, for the second time, carried before the deputy magistrate, Ōshima Eijirō, in the same order and in the some manner as on the former occasion. We were seated in the same place in the castle, and conducted, as before, into the court hall. The number of the officers was the same, except that Eijirō was not seated when we first entered, but after about ten minutes he came forth from behind a screen. After he had taken his place, he drew some sheets of manuscript from his bosom, and laid them before him. Having read over our names, he ordered the interpreter to inform us that our former examination had been sent to the magistrate (*bugyō*) of Matsumae, who had given orders for the strictest investigation of our case. It was therefore required that we should circum-stantially and truly answer all the questions that might now be put to us, and neither conceal nor misrepresent anything whatever. We replied that we had no reason to conceal anything from the Japanese, and would readily give them every information in our power.

The questions were chiefly a repetition of the former, but they were put with so little regard to order or connection that we could with great difficulty recollect the manner in which they followed each other. There were besides so many new questions, and they were altogether so numerous, that it was impossible to retain them, as we had no ink and paper wherewith to make memorandums. In general these queries related to the conduct of Resanov, on his return from Japan, and the attacks made by Khvostov's ships on their villages.

In our answers we gave an account of Resanov's arrival at Kamchatka, his subsequent voyage to the Russian-American Company's factories and California, his return to Okhotsk, and his death at Krasnojarsk, on his way to Petersburg. "I have heard," I observed, "that our sovereign was very much dissatisfied with the proceedings of Resanov in Japan: but that, on the other hand, Resanov had represented the conduct of the Japanese as having been bad towards him. The vessels which committed the depredations complained of were merchantmen, and their crews were not in the emperor's service. The attacks originated with the individuals themselves, whose only object must have been plunder, as they believed that the complaints of the Japanese never could reach our government. And the Japanese had themselves to blame for the prevalence of that impression, as they had declared to Resanov that they would have nothing to do with the Russians. The two Japanese who had been carried off were set at liberty on their arrival at Okhotsk. But they fled from that place in a boat. And it was not known what had become of them. Everything had been taken from the Japanese was put under sequestration by the Russian commandant of Okhotsk. The ships were embargoed, and the captains imprisoned, though they afterwards got out of prison: the investigation of their offense still proceeded, but in the meantime they died."

The Japanese desired us to state their names. And were much surprised when we called them Khvostov and Davydov. They immediately asked whether these were the same persons who had been known to them under the names of "Nicola Sandrijetsch" (Nicolai Alexandrovitsch) and "Govrilo

Ivanotsch" (Gavrilo Ivanovitsch). We, on our part, were no less surprised to find that the Japanese knew the christian names of these persons and not their surnames. And at first concluded that they must have learnt them from the two men who fled to the island of Iturup, to avoid the threatened vengeance of Khvostov. But in that case the Japanese must have known their surnames also. We were perfectly well acquainted with them, though we did not choose to say so. And merely observed, that we knew them only by the names of Khvostov and Davydov. We feared lest the Japanese might have been informed of our custom of using the christian names, in speaking of persons of distinction and intimate friends. Had they suspected that we knew anything of Khvostov and Davidov, there would have been no end to their interrogatories: they would have inquired who were their parents, where they had been born, how old they were, what kind of characters they bore, what professions they followed, and a thousand other things. In order to rid ourselves of so tedious and tormenting an examination, we said that we knew them only by report. Though the Japanese did not absolutely deny our assertion, yet they were far from giving credit to what we said, and seemed still to retain their first notion, that Nicolai Alexandrovitsch and Khvostov were not the same individual.

They eagerly inquired why, after the first attack had been made upon them, a second had been permitted. We replied that we knew nothing of this matter, but supposed that this expedition had either been kept a secret from the commandant of Kamchatka, or that he had been informed that such proceedings had been adopted in consequence of an order from the government, with which he was unacquainted, and that without making further inquiries he had given credit to this account. But the Japanese were not to be satisfied with this: they suspected that some of our party had been attached to the expedition, or had at least been in Kamchatka at the period of its departure. They accordingly questioned us with the utmost minuteness respecting our voyage from Kronstadt to the harbor of St. Peter and St. Paul, and compared the time of our arrival there with the period at which their coasts had been plundered.

From what fell from them, they seemed likewise to suspect that we had not sailed from Petersburg until after Resanov had arrived there, and had informed the government of the failure of the embassy. They inquired for what reason we had been sent to so distant a place. And asked many questions that appeared to us extremely ludicrous, considering the advanced state of the science of navigation in Europe; such as, how could we possibly remain so long at sea, without getting a fresh supply of provisions and wood and water from some harbor—how the Russians could build such large vessels, in which they were enabled to sail about in the open ocean for so long a time——for what reason had we cannon and arms on board with us—why we sailed in the middle of the ocean instead of steering along the coast from Petersburg to Kamchatka. The real object of our mission, namely, the survey and description of unknown coasts, as I have before observed, we thought it prudent to conceal, in order to avoid creating suspicion. We said therefore, that we were proceeding to Kamchatka with government stores, which were wanted at that place.

Whilst they were thus interrogating us respecting our voyage, they did not fail to inquire, under the semblance of mere curiosity, the distances between Kamchatka and Okhotsk, Okhotsk and Irkutzk, and Irkutzk and St. Petersburg. And what time the post or travellers usually occupied in proceeding from one place to the other. But we plainly perceived that the real object of all their inquiries was to ascertain whether Resanov had arrived at Petersburg before our departure. For the same motive they questioned us respecting the return of the vessel in which Resanov had been sent to them, and whether it was true that it sailed back to Petersburg without him, and that he had remained in Kamchatka, and gone in another ship to America.

In consequence of the smallness of the territory of Japan, and its separation from the rest of the world, every communication with foreigners interests the whole country, and is regarded as a great and important, event, which ought to be handed down to the latest posterity. The Japanese were, therefore, of opinion, that not only Russia, but all Europe, must be informed of Khvostov's attack. For this reason, they did not credit what we told them, and insinuated that we could, if we pleased, give them more minute information concerning the property that had been taken from them, their countrymen who were carried off, etc. Their doubts and extraordinary questions so irritated us, that we sometimes asked them how they could suppose, that an insignificant spot like Japan, the existence of which was not even known to many of the inhabitants of Europe, could engross the attention of every enlightened nation. Or that each minute circumstance attending the plundering of a few of their villages by two obscure merchant vessels must necessarily bge well known; adding, that they ought to be satisfied with our assurance, that the attack was made upon them contrary to the will of the emperor. At this they usually laughed, instead of feeling in the least offended.

They are endowed with a most extraordinary degree of patience. Every question was twice or thrice repeated, and the interpreter was incessantly desired to note everything down with the utmost exactness: indeed, they were frequently occupied for more than an hour about a single question. But they never testified the slightest dissatisfaction. And, as usual, by way of relaxation, frequently put questions of an apparently trifling nature; such, for example, as, "Whose office is it on board the Russian vessels to foretell the state of the wind and weather?" When we replied that this task was not allotted to any particular officer, but that it was part of the duty of the commander of the ship, they were not a little astonished; for, with them, a boat never puts to sea without having a prophet of the weather on board.

Our examination lasted until evening: we were, however, permitted to partake of refreshments at two different times. Our repast was brought to us by our attendants, and consisted of boiled rice, and herrings dried in the open air. And, by way of dessert, a tea-cup full of *sake*, which is the wine of the Japanese. We were likewise regaled with tobacco for smoking, and tea with sugar, which in Japan is regarded as a high luxury. In the evening we quitted the castle, and returned to our prison, where we found everything just as we had left it.

On the following morning, the 29th of August, we were again conducted into the presence of Deputy Magistrate Ōshima Eijirō, being escorted and introduced in exactly the same form as before. When we had entered the hall, and the magistrate had taken his place, he drew from his bosom several pieces of paper, which he delivered to Odachi Kōeki. The latter handed them to the officers who were sitting near him, and they in turn gave them to Kumajirō, who unfolded one of them, and, by order of the commander, gave it to us to read. We immediately cast our eyes on the signatures of the officers whom we had left behind us on board the *Diana*. This unexpected sight plunged us into the deepest distress. We reflected on our former situation, and that in which we then were, and concluded that this letter was probably the last farewell of friends with whom we had served so long, and whom we should probably never see again: we were unable to repress our tears. Mur was most of all affected; he threw himself upon his knees, pressed the letter to his lips, and wept bitterly. The Japanese observed us with great attention: they scarcely ever turned their eyes from us. And all, except Odachi Kōeki, seemed deeply moved. Some even shed tears, which they endeavored to conceal. But Odachi Kōeki laughed at our emotion. The contents of the letter was as follows:

> Heaven knows whether these lines will ever reach you, or whether you are still alive—At first, all the officers on board resolved to adopt pacific measures to obtain your liberation. But whilst we were deliberating what course to pursue, a ball passed over us, and fell into the water, at a considerable distance astern of the sloop. I immediately gave orders to return the fire of the castle. But what was to be done? How were we to act? Our guns were so light that they could be of little service to us; the shallowness of the water prevented us from approaching nearer to the land. And the small number of our crew precluded all idea of debarkation.
>
> We, therefore, wish to inform you that we have adopted the last resource. We will sail back to Okhotsk, and if the number of our crew be increased will return, and never quit the coasts of Japan until we have obtained your liberation, or sacrifice our lives for our beloved captain and faithful friends. Should the Japanese permit you to answer this letter, pray write to us. We are bound to obey all the orders of our commander. Every man on board the sloop is ready to lay down his life for your sake.
>
> Until death, Your's faithfully, Peter Ricord, Ilja Rudakov, etc.

Having read this letter several times over, the Japanese desired us to translate it. We complied with their order, though we judged it prudent not to give a faithful explanation of many of the passages it contained.

According to our translation, the firing from the sloop was merely an act of self-defense, and not done with a view to injure the Japanese, who had fired from their castle: the small calibre of the guns we construed into a deficiency of shot. And we made it appear that the idea of landing proceeded merely from a wish to surround us, and prevent the Japanese from carrying us off, but that for this purpose there were too few men on board the sloop, Instead of saying anything about the obtaining of a reinforcement at Okhotsk, we explained that part of the letter by saying, that our friends had returned to request permission to proceed against the Japanese, as they could not attack them without the consent of the Russian government.

Upwards of an hour elapsed before we could render everything clear and satisfactory to the Japanese. They then asked me what answer I should send to that letter, provided I were permitted to write. I replied, that I should advise the officers on board the sloop not to proceed to any act of violence, but to return immediately to Russia, to inform our government of the circumstance.

As the letter furnished no ground for further interrogatories, they proceeded to other subjects, many of which had been discussed at large on the preceding day. They examined us as before, without either regularity or connexion, and frequently referred to matters of the most trifling nature. The principal questions put to us had for their object to ascertain whether we were acquainted with what had passed on the embassies of Laxman and Resanov. In particular they asked, why we had approached their coasts, since the Japanese had prohibited the Russians to do so, and had informed Resanov that their laws required them to burn all foreign vessels, excepting such as entered the harbor of Nagasaki, and to place their crews in eternal imprisonment.

We answered, that all we knew respecting the embassy of Laxman, and the answer given to him, as well as those afterwards received by Resanov, were communicated to us merely by public report. We had indeed heard, that the Japanese would not permit Russian vessels to enter their harbors for the purpose of trading, but that we never imagined this prohibition extended to vessels the crews of which were suffering from want, as the rudest and most barbarous nations never withheld assistance from suffering navigators, or refused them a place of refuge. Want of provisions, I added, had alone compelled us to land on their shores. That some Japanese officers whom we accidentally met with had furnished us with a letter, and had assured us that their countrymen in Horobetsu would afford us assistance; contrary winds had, however, obliged us to put into Kunashir, where we had endeavored, by every possible means, to convince the Japanese of our distressed situation and our peaceable intentions, and that the remainder of our story was known to them.

They, however, expressed a wish that we should relate to them in succession every circumstance that had occurred to us since our first communication with their countrymen on the island of Iturup, up to the moment we were made prisoners at Kunashir. On this occasion we observed the dissimulation of the Japanese: they pretended that all we said was entirely new to them, and affected particular surprise that the commander of Kunashir should not immediately have returned the cask and the goods sent ashore. They asked where we were sailing when we experienced a want of provisions, and required us to point out the spot upon the map. We complied with their wish, and explained the object of our voyage in a way corresponding with what we had previously stated.

They asked us several questions totally unconnected with the main object. For example, concerning the inhabitants of Denmark, England, and other countries we had visited; in what parts of Russia ships were built; what kind of wood was used in constructing them, and, how quickly they could be completed, etc. Under pretense of mere curiosity, they asked us the extent of our land and sea forces. We thought it advisable to give an exaggerated account of both. We increased the number of fortresses and their garrisons in Siberia, and distributed at pleasure numerous fleets in the harbors of the coast of Okhotsk, in Kamchatka, and on the northwestern coast of America. Among other things, we accidentally said that there was a considerable naval force in the harbor of St. Peter and Paul. And when the Japanese inquired how many ships were there, unfortunately for ourselves, as will hereafter appear, we fixed upon the number seven.

The conference lasted until evening. We were frequently taken out of the hall for relaxation or refreshment. And *sake*, tobacco, and tea, were brought into the courtyard to us. In the evening we were re-conducted to the place of our confinement, with the usual ceremonies.

On the two following days we underwent no examination. But we observed that the Japanese treated us much more kindly than before. They provided the sailors with warm water, and permitted them to wash their own and our linen in the lobby. They gave us several articles from the trunks, which had been sent ashore, and at our request furnished the sailors with a change of linen. A large pail was filled with warm water, in which we were directed to wash our hands and face. Several of the orderly officers, by whom we were visited at certain hours, regaled us with good tea, sugar, fruit, *sake*, etc. One in particular, named Ogasawara Kaemon, was extremely kind, and never quitted us without saying something consolatory, and even giving us a present. We afterwards learnt that his brother had been lost on board of a vessel some time before. The idea that he might probably be doomed to suffer a fate similar to ours, in some distant land, induced him to sympathize with us, and pay particular attention to our wants.

Notwithstanding all this good fortune, we learnt from the Japanese a piece of news, which again plunged us into despair. On the morning of the 31st of August, during the usual visit of the orderly officers, the physician, and interpreter, the latter said something to Mur, which I did not distinctly understand, and at the same time delivered a paper to him. Mur glanced over the paper, laughed, and said it was all a fraud. But, immediately turning to me, he exclaimed, in a faltering voice, and with great agitation, "Vasily Michailovitsch! hear this," and read as follows:

In the year 1806, the 12th (24) of October, Lieutenant Khvostov, commander of the frigate *Juno*, distributed to the chief of the villages on the western coast of the Bay of Aniva a silver medal and ribbond of Vladimir, as a token of the Russian Emperor, Alexander I. having taken possession of the Island of Sachalin, and placed its inhabitants under his gracious protection. I therefore request the commanders of all vessels, either Russian or foreign, which may hereafter visit Japan, to regard the said chief as a Russian subject.

Signed Khvostov, Lieutenant of the Russian Fleet

Our embarrassment may easily be conceived. How could we now hope that the Japanese would give credit to anything we told them. We knew that their government was extremely cautious and circumspect with regard to all public proceedings; that the execution of all measures was watched with the utmost care and attention; that every misdemeanor was punished with severity, and even with cruelty, and that they judged of the laws of other countries by those of their own. Could we expect by mere words to convince such a government that an obscure individual like Khvostov would, without any authority, have had the audacity to issue a proclamation, declaring that a country under the dominion of a foreign state was to become a dependency of the crown of Russia; to distribute among a half barbarous people medals bearing the likeness of his sovereign, and to describe a mere merchantman as a Russian frigate.

This document had convinced the Japanese that Khvostov had fulfilled the orders of our monarch; they of course could regard us only as spies, who wished to impose on their credulity, by attributing the attack made upon them to the hardihood of so inconsiderable a person as the commander of a private ship, while our real object was to reconnoitre their coasts and garrisons.

Though this unexpected occurrence threw us into the utmost distress, we did not lose courage: we boldly declared to the Japanese that they might instantly put us to death, if they disbelieved what we stated. We told them that we entertained no fear of death; that the truth would sooner or later come to light; that then they would reproach themselves for their distrust, and lament our fate when it would be too late, and that we only regretted they should entertain such an opinion of our government. We asked them how they could suppose that the monarch of a great and powerful empire like Russia, should find it necessary to send a handful of men to burn and pillage villages, for the sake of placing a desert country under his dominion. And by what means—by distributing medals bearing his likeness, and proclamations signed by the captain of a merchant vessel, among people who were unable to form any notion of the meaning of these things. To suppose this would be equally ridiculous, as to lay to the charge of the emperor of Japan any similar proceedings, which might be committed by Japanese vessels on our Kuril Islands.

The Japanese listened to our explanation with the utmost attention: and answered yes to all our observations. They, however, seemed to smile within themselves, and to place but little reliance on anything we said. They wished to be informed of the precise meaning of the paper, from where Khvostov had brought the medals, and whether he was really the same individual as Nicolai Alexandroivitsch. Whilst we translated the proclamation, we found it necessary to assure the Japanese, that a Russian frigate signified a merchantman, as well as a ship of war in the Russian navy. For the ribbon of Vladimir we substituted the words striped ribbon, for we well knew the disposition of our interrogators. Had we called the thing by its right name, we should have been tormented with questions for five or six hours at least. We must have told them who created the order, and for what purpose it had been instituted; who Vladimir was, at what period he reigned, by what deeds he had distinguished himself, why the order had been named after him; whether there were any other orders of knighthood in Russia, and what privileges were attached to them; in a word, we must have related to them the history and the statutes of all our orders. The word striped, however, at once removed all these difficulties. With regard to the medals, we told them that in Russia none were permitted to wear medals except those who received them from the hands of the emperor: that silver medals were distributed as rewards to soldiers who had distinguished themselves in battle, and that they were usually sold after the death of the possessor. We knew not whether Khvostov had purchased these medals, or whether he had procured them from some of his seamen, who might have received them whilst they were in the imperial service. We moreover assured them, that the vessel by which they had been attacked, was commanded by Lieutenant Khvostov, who was in the service of the Russian-American Company, and that he was perhaps the same person who had been known to them by the name of Nicola Sandrejetsch.

Having given these answers, the Japanese suffered us to depart. But on the following morning, the 1 st of September, we were again carried before the magistrate with the usual ceremony. It rained, and an attendant walked by the side of each of us, holding umbrellas over our heads.

This was a mark of attention the Japanese never failed to observe whenever they brought us out in rainy weather. We were again interrogated concerning Khvostov's proclamation and the medals he had distributed, and our explanation was the same as that which we had given on the preceding day. They inquired what was meant by the drawings of flags, which were made at the bottom of the letter. We replied that one of those drawings represented the flag borne by the imperial ships of war, and that the other was merely the flag of a merchant vessel: for what reason they had been sketched on the paper in question we knew not, but supposed that Khvostov wished by this means to mark the difference between a Russian ship of war and a merchantman. The Japanese, however, entertained a very different opinion: they asked us whether both the flags were not borne by imperial vessels, and whether the one was not hoisted to indicate hostile intentions, and the other to show that a vessel was proceeding for the purpose of trade. We assured them that in Europe ships of war were never in the habit of trading. They then inquired why Khvostov had hoisted the flag of war when he visited their coasts. We replied that in so remote a part of the world, where his conduct could not be observed, he had presumed to display the standard, which is only unfurled in the presence of our emperor. On making this unthinking reply, we were tormented with questions for full two hours: they inquired respecting the shape and size of the flag, what were the figures and colors it exhibited, on what occasions it was displayed, whether the emperor frequently inspected the fleets, etc.

During their inquiries respecting Khvostov's proclamation, the Japanese frequently asked us questions on other particulars. And seemed greatly alarmed about two small copper plates which we had left behind us at Iturup and Kunashir; on the former island, we gave one of these plates to the Japanese commander himself, and we left the other behind us in a village in Kunashir. On these plates was the following Latin inscription, as also the same in Russian:

Navis. Imperialls. Russica. *Diana*. An. Dom. 1811.

We stated that we left these tablets upon every island that we passed through, even on those which were uninhabited, where we hung them upon the tree, that, in case of shipwreck, it might be known where we had been, and, consequently, near what place the misfortune had occurred. But the Japanese were far from being satisfied with this story. In the first place, they wished to know the meaning of the inscription, and required that we should explain every individual word: they set down each word as we translated it, hoping by this means to detect us in some inconsistency. They then observed that they had heard from the Dutch in Nagasaki that Europeans left such tablets on islands they wished to subject to their dominion, and inquired whether we entertained that intention. We replied that in such a case Europeans would use a very different inscription. But this did not seem to satisfy them: we plainly saw that they did not believe us, and that they even doubted whether we had given them a correct translation of the inscription.

During the whole day, the Japanese were occupied in examining us concerning Khvostov's proclamation and our tablets. According to custom, they put many ridiculous questions to us; such as, how many ships of war and merchantmen are there in Russia, and the whole of Europe; what number of harbors are there in Russia, and in other countries. It was late in the evening when we were sent back to the castle.

When we were conducted from the Hall of Justice into the courtyard, for the purpose of partaking of refreshment, we found opportunities of discoursing and communicating our thoughts to each other. Our situation was, indeed, none of the best, and we looked upon it as next to impossible to make it appear that Khvostov's proclamation was a spurious document. The Japanese, of course, could only look upon us as spies. In that case, death, or what was still more dreadful, eternal imprisonment awaited us. Flight was our only resource: but how was that to be effected. We were confined separately, and therefore could not escape all at once. In despair, we often contemplated the possibility of forcing our way through the guard, which conducted us in the evening from the castle: but, besides our strong escort, we were always surrounded by a multitude of spectators, so immense, that all chance of escape was hopeless. There remained, then, no alternative, but to wait until we should be all confined together, and then to deliberate, in concert, on the means of our deliverance.

The second or third day after, while the civil officer, the physician, and the interpreter, were paying their usual morning visit to Mur, and making inquiries respecting Russian words, Alexei walked several times through the passage, close to the palisades of my apartment, looked at me, then at the Japanese attendants, and appeared to have some secret to communicate to me. When I spoke to him, he did not answer. At last, seizing a favorable opportunity, he cast some paper, rolled up, through the palisades. I immediately placed my foot upon it, and remained standing in that position till the Japanese left us. On taking it up, I found wrapt up within several pieces of paper, an iron nail, and a card, on which some words were scratched with the nail. The writing was by Khlebnikov. But, though it consisted of several lines, I could only make out the following words: "God—hope—the Kamchatka district commander, Lamakin—Alexei, the Ainu—be cautious," and a few others. I could not comprehend what this card meant. If Khlebnikov had written anything respecting our present situation, what connexion could this Lamakin, of whom I knew nothing, have with it. I was afraid that confinement had bereaved him of his understanding, and the idea gave me great pain.

In the evening, when Alexei again came to us, I asked him whether Khlebnikov had not lost his senses, and what was meant by the words on the card, which I could not decipher. "You will soon know," he replied, and immediately departed, leaving us in a state of painful uncertainty. I communicated everything to Mur, but could not gain an opportunity of sending the card to him: he was equally unable to comprehend what part this Lamakin was playing between the Japanese and us.

On the 4th of September, we were again conducted to the castle: we had to wait in the courtyard until the magistrate gave orders for our entrance. And, in the meanwhile, we were indulged with the permission of smoking tobacco. Here we had an opportunity of conversing together. And Khlebnikov communicated to us a secret, with which Alexei had acquainted him. He told us, that Alexei and some of his countrymen had, about a year before, been seized by the Japanese. And, on being asked for what reason they had visited Japan, instead of the romantic story they had related to us on board the *Diana*, the Ainu replied, they had been sent by the Kamchatka district commander, to inspect the Japanese villages and garrisons. On being asked what was the object of their examination, they had answered that in the following year, seven vessels from the harbor of Petropawlowsk would visit the Japanese Islands, four proceeding to Hokkaido, and three to Iturup, with the same design with which Khvostov had approached them. The Ainu said this with the view of averting danger from themselves, by making the

Japanese believe they had been forced to come among them by the Russians. And Alexei had entreated Khlebnikov to persuade us to declare that they had really been dispatched by Lamakin.

Our situation may be easily imagined. The arrival of the Ainu for the purpose of converting Japanese subjects to the Christian Faith, Khvostov's attack, the medals, and proclamations, and, finally, the declaration of the Ainu, all tended to convince the Japanese that we sought to deceive them. Our only means of exculpation was to assure them that if the Emperor of Russia had wished to declare war against the Japanese, he would have sent more than two ships for that purpose. It was to be feared, however, that the Japanese might attribute the trifling character of the enterprise to ill-digested plans on the part of our government, or to deficiency of means in the Russian provinces opposite their coasts; descriptions of the state of which must have been given to them by their countrymen, who had travelled through Siberia to Petersburg. But Alexei was the most formidable proof against us. I have already observed, that he wished us to confirm the tale he and his countrymen had invented; that is to say, to criminate ourselves, and to do all we could to justify him, who was alone guilty. We were persuaded that he would insist on the truth of his assertion, and endeavour, by all the means in his power, to fix the offense on us. But to have apparently assented to his request would have emboldened him. And knowing that a severe punishment awaited him on his return to Russia, he would, of course, place every obstacle in the way of our liberation. Besides, we could not, for evident reasons, consent to bear testimony to the truth of his false declaration; we therefore told him, in as friendly a manner as possible, that we could in no way comply with his wish. And that all solicitation for that purpose would be fruitless. To this Alexei made no reply, and we now began to regard him as a dangerous and irreconcilable enemy.

When we were again conducted into the presence of the magistrate, he asked whether it was true that the Kamchatka district commander had sent Ainu to inspect the Japanese villages and fortifications. We replied that we had never heard of such a proceeding, and that we looked upon it as impossible, upon which they addressed themselves to Alexei. But we could neither understand their questions nor his answers. After having asked us many trifling questions, they conducted us back to our prison. Alexei however was detained, and remained a long time behind us. When he at length joined us in the prison, we asked him about what the Japanese had been discoursing with him. He answered drily, "About my old affair." After this he was twice carried alone before the magistrate, but he always refused to tell us what had passed between the Japanese and him.

Among a number of silly questions put to us in our last examination, I shall mention one, as it led to an explanation that shows the severe character of the Japanese morality and the strictness of their laws. They asked us why we had carried off wood and rice from the coast without the consent of the owners of those articles. We replied that they had doubtless been informed by the report of the Commandant of Kunashir that we had employed every means of making ourselves understood. He, however, had ordered all the troops to retire into the garrison; the villages on the coast were deserted, and whenever we attempted to approach the castle, cannon were fired upon us. The hope the letter of the Japanese officer at Iturup afforded of obtaining through it a supply of every article we stood in need of, induced us to neglect sailing back to the Russian coast, which we should have immediately done had we not received that letter. During the long period our vessel had remained at sea, our stock of provisions had become exhausted. And for this reason, having no other object in holding intercourse with the Japanese, we carried off a small quantity of rice and wood, in payment for which we left various European articles behind us. That we had moreover deposited silver coins in the cask. And that when a correspondence was opened on the part of the Japanese, we ourselves proceeded to the castle to pay such price as they might fix upon the articles we had carried away. We were now asked whether any law existed in Europe, which, under such circumstances, would authorize us to seize the property of strangers. I replied that there was indeed no particular law to that effect. But that if a man in a state of starvation chanced to meet with deserted habitations, and took from thence what was necessary to support his existence, he would not be declared guilty under any European law; particularly if he left behind him articles equal in value to those he took away. With us, replied the Japanese, it is very different; our laws ordain that a man must sooner die of hunger, than touch, without the consent of the owner, a single grain of rice that does not belong to him.

To the honor of the Japanese, I must observe that they always questioned us with the utmost civility and politeness: they frequently laughed with an air of good humor, and endeavored to render our examinations more like discourse between intimate friends than formal and official investigations.

On the 5th of September we were conducted to the magistrate of Hakodate, for the last time. The whole of the forenoon was occupied in asking us questions we had previously answered, and very minute inquiries were made respecting the seven Japanese who had been saved on the coast of Kamchatka. We described to them the spot on which the vessel had been wrecked, mentioned the time at which the event had taken place, how many individuals had been saved, and that they were at Nischny Kamchatka at the period of our departure. Mur had seen them there, though the dread of being tormented by a thousand questions deterred him from saying so.

In the afternoon we sat a long time in the courtyard, drinking tea and smoking tobacco. The interpreter Kumajirō went continually backwards and forwards, asking us Russian words, which he wrote down. We were at length conducted into the hall. Here one of the officers, a grey-haired man, apparently about seventy years of age, who in Laxman's time had been employed in compiling a Russian dictionary, unrolled a large sheet of paper, filled with Japanese characters, which he began to read in a style very much resembled singing. We were totally unable to comprehend the first ten or twenty words. But we at length discovered that he fancied he was reading Russian, and from some of the words conjectured that the paper contained an account of our affair, translated into Russian. We could not refrain from laughing, and told the Japanese that we understood only a few words here and there: upon which they all laughed heartily, not excepting the translator, who laid the paper aside. The magistrate now took leave of us, and we left the castle.

The Japanese, particularly those who were appointed our guards, continued to treat us with increasing kindness. They even several times permitted Mur to go out of his chamber for the purpose of warming himself at the fire in the lobby. On these occasions he sometimes stepped up to my palisades, when we found an opportunity of making communications to each other that we could not speak aloud, as several of our guards, who had been in Russia, understood something of our language.

With respect to our food, however, it was no better than before, though we many times sent it away without tasting it. One day Mur made an effort to speak Japanese to Kumajirō, and told him that we had been treated like dogs: he contrived to make himself intelligible, and Kumajirō told him he ought not to vex himself on that head, and at the same time advised him to speak with more caution in future; observing, that if his complaint had been heard by any except himself, it might have been attended with serious consequences.

In the meanwhile we continued in the utmost uncertainty with respect to the way in which the Japanese government might regard our answers and declarations, and how it was intended to dispose of us. A severe destiny seemed indeed to await us, for celestial phenomena conspired with an unfortunate concurrence of earthly events to produce unfavorable impressions against us. About this time a comet made its appearance. We wished to know whether the Japanese had any notion of the nature of that heavenly body, and put some questions to them on the subject. From the answers of those with whom we conversed, it was evident that they knew nothing about comets, except that they were seldom visible. We then wished to ascertain whether the Japanese, like other Asiatic nations, regarded comets as the usual forerunners of unfortunate events; for, had this been the case, it was possible that their superstition might have had favorable consequences for us: they might, perhaps, have regarded the comet as the harbinger of Heaven's vengeance for their unjust and cruel conduct towards us. But when we inquired whether they did not regard these planets as prognosticating certain events, they replied, to our no small mortification, that the same year (1807) in which Khvostov had visited them, a comet, similar to that which appeared on our arrival, was visible in the heavens.

On the 13 th of September, the officer next in rank to the magistrate told us that he had received orders, on the approach of the cold weather, to provide us with some warm clothing, from the trunks that had been sent on shore from the sloop at Kunashir, and asked us what we were accustomed to wear. At my request, I was immediately furnished with my mantle, a warm waistcoat, a shirt, a cap, some stockings, and pocket handkerchief. And my companions received whatever articles they required.

I have already observed that the Japanese agreed to let the sailors be with us by turns. On the 31st of August Vassiliev was sent to Mur, and Skajev was shut up alone. But on the 23d of September, Makarov, who had before been with me, was relieved by Skajev. The latter communicated to me two unexpected pieces of information. First, that Simanov, through some oversight of the Japanese, had gained possession of a large knife. It appeared that he had fastened this knife, by a leather strap, to one of the buttonholes of his jacket, which is a custom among our sailors, lest they should lose their knives when using them on the masts or yards. This jacket had been sent from the sloop, and was given to him, although the strap could scarcely fail to be noticed. We were much astonished that this strap should have escaped the rigid and circumspect vigilance of the Japanese; particularly when they carried their caution so far as not to allow us to have a pair of scissors to cut our nails with. And we were obliged to thrust our hands through the palisades to get the soldiers to perform that office for us. We were never once suffered to have needles in our possession. And our clothes were always mended by the guards who attended us. I was overjoyed at this accident, as I hoped that, in course of time, the knife might be made useful to us. And I took the first opportunity of desiring Simanov to preserve it like a treasure. Secondly, Skajev informed me that the soldiers had been hinting something about our departure for Matsumae, and that the old litters were already brought into the courtyard. On the following morning this story was confirmed by the Japanese officers themselves, who formally acquainted us that we must hold ourselves in readiness for a journey.

In the evening we were each furnished with a cloak, made of varnished cotton-cloth, a straw hat with a round brim, a pair of Japanese stockings, and straw shoes, which the Japanese wear for travelling.

On the evening of the 26th of September we were informed that on the following morning, if the weather proved fair, we should set out on our journey. At break of day, on the 27th, preparations were accordingly commenced, and several of the officers came to bid us a formal adieu. They entered our little apartments and, with the assistance of the interpreter, said that they had come to bid us farewell, to wish us good health, a safe journey, and a speedy termination of the difficulties in which we were involved. In the meanwhile we had each a rope tied round the waist. We were then led into the courtyard, and placed side by side: a soldier was stationed beside each as a guard, and a superintendent or conductor held the rope. These travelling regulations in no way corresponded with the politeness the Japanese had, a short while before, manifested in taking leave of us. We were almost tempted to believe that their conduct was all mockery. But it was highly improbable that all the officers of the city, the commander-in-chief included, should have combined together to pass a joke upon us. By degree, however, we became accustomed to the singular habits of this people.

About midday we set out on our journey. We were conducted in the same order as in our former march, only that in addition to the litters horses were introduced into the procession, bearing our quilts and nightdresses, instead of saddles. In the road through which we passed, at the distance of about a hundred fathoms from the prison, we met with a detachment of infantry under arms. It was a clear and warm day, and a vast number of spectators had accordingly assembled, many of whom accompanied us to the distance of three kilometers. Our escort consisted of one officer, from twelve to sixteen soldiers, two superintendents, and a considerable number of individuals, whose business was to carry the litters, lead the horses, etc. and who were relieved at the different stations we passed by. We were besides accompanied by the interpreter Uebara Kumajirō, and the physician Gotō.

As we had been confined for the space of fifty days, we were glad to enjoy the recreation of walking, and we only mounted the horses when we felt ourselves fatigued. On these occasions the Japanese rolled up the ropes with which we were bound, fastened them, and suffered us to ride at liberty. This, however, they only did when our road happened to lie through open fields: whenever we had to pass through villages, they never failed to hold the ends of the ropes.

Our road from Hakodate lay along the bay close to the shore. Having arrived opposite to the tongue of land on which the city is built, we ascended a hill, on the summit of which a battery was erected. The apparent object of this battery was to prevent vessels from entering the bay: it was, however, very ill calculated for that purpose, owing to the extreme height of the hill, and the breadth of the channel which formed the entrance. The Japanese conducted us through this battery, and thereby occasioned us no small degree of uneasiness. They sought to conceal nothing from us, even in their military works. From this we inferred that they doubtless intended to detain us prisoners for life, as in that case we could not turn to their disadvantage any knowledge we might collect respecting their system of fortification. We re-considered all the circumstances that had occurred in Hakodate, from which it appeared that flight was our only means of deliverance. But we were soon convinced of the impracticability of escaping at this time; for though during the night the ropes with which we were bound were laid aside, yet the greater part of our attendants never closed their eyes, and some never quitted the apartments in which we were lodged. Our only chance was to break from them by force during the day and, considering the numbers by which we were surrounded and that our only weapon was a knife, this seemed next to impossible.

Our food was the same as that with which we had been supplied during our journey to Hakodate, and we received a meal three times every day. In this part of the island the villages are extremely numerous and populous. The inhabitants maintain themselves by fishing and collecting seaweed; besides this, they have in general large kitchen-gardens, in which they plant an extraordinary number of radishes. We not unfrequently saw entire fields thickly planted with these roots.

We spent the night of the 29th of September in a little village about half a day's journey from Matsumae. This place was rendered memorable to us by the following circumstances. The interpreter Kumajirō advised us, when we should be examined in Matsumae, to be careful that our answers corresponded with our previous declarations. He assured us that if we in the slightest degree departed from our former statements, we should be declared guilty by the Japanese laws. He besides supplied each of us with some excellent tobacco and several pieces of paper, and said that he gave us these things in order that the officers in Matsumae might not attribute our want of them to the negligence of our conductors. He desired us not to believe the physician when he told us that a fine house was being prepared for us in Matsumae, where we should all live together. This we thought was much the same as telling us that a prison was to be our doom: what this extraordinary attention respecting the paper and tobacco denoted we were however unable to divine.

On the afternoon of the 30th of September we halted in a village about three kilometers distant from Matsumae, where we were met by a party of soldiers and a vast crowd of people. We remained here about half an hour, during which time our conductors put on their best clothes, and we then entered the city with the same formalities as had been observed at Hakodate: the number of spectators was considerably greater, owing to the vast population of the city. Having proceeded through the town, to the distance of about four or five kilometers along the shore, we entered a large open space, crowded with men, who stood behind ropes, which had been extended there for the accommodation of the procession. From there we ascended a tolerably high hill, passed along the rampart encompassing the castle, and entered a courtyard, which was surrounded by a high wooden fence, entirely new. Here we met a detachment of soldiers in their military uniforms. From this courtyard a little door led through another fence, which was higher than the preceding one. We now entered a dark edifice like a barn, and we three officers were shut up together in a cage, which bore some distant resemblance to a room: the sailors and Alexei were confined in another.

On the first view of our prison, we thought we should never again enjoy the light of the sun; for, though the weather was fine, and the sky bright, when we entered, we found darkness had already commenced in this dismal abode, to which no friendly ray seemed to penetrate. The place of our confinement, the fence surrounding the yard, and the sentry boxes, were all so recently finished, that the workmen had not had time to remove their chips.

The prison was large, built of fine wood, and must have occasioned the Japanese government no inconsiderable expense. It was a quadrangular wooden building, twenty-five paces long, fifteen broad, and twelve feet high. Three sides were complete wall, without any aperture whatever. But the south side was formed of strong spars, four inches square, and placed at the distance of four inches also from each other. On the side which consisted of these spars, there was a gate, and a little door, both of which were kept fast locked. In the middle were two cages, formed of spars, similar to those on the south side of the prison. They were so placed, as to leave a passage between each, and also passages between them and the walls of the prison. One cage was six paces square, and ten feet high; the other was of an equal breadth and height, but was eight paces long. We three officers were put into the former; the sailors and Alexei were confined in the latter. The entrance to the cage was so low, that we were obliged to creep into it. The door was formed of massy spars, and was fastened by a strong iron bolt. Above the door was a small hole, through which our food was handed to us. A small water closet was constructed in the further end of each cage. The sides of the cage next each other were bounded in such a manner that we could see the sailors, but they could not perceive us. A screen was also placed between the closets, for the purpose of obstructing the view from the one to the other. A guard room was placed against the spars forming the entrance side of the prison, and which was occupied by two soldiers in the service of the imperial government, who were constantly on guard: they could see us all, and seldom turned their eyes away from us. The whole building was surrounded at the distance of from six to eight paces by a high wall or fence, with sharp pointed wooden stakes, and in which there was a door exactly opposite that of the prison. Around the first wall was a second, but less high fence, including a considerable space, within which were, on one side of the gate of the great wall, the kitchen and an apartment for the workmen, and, on the other side, a guard house.

The outer guard consisted of soldiers belonging to the *daimyō* of Tsugaru. They were not allowed to come near us, nor even to pass within the first fence, but patrolled the rounds every half hour. During the night they had fire, and struck the hours with two boards: the *bakufu* soldiers on the contrary visited us every half hour, walked round our cages, and looked through the spars. The whole structure was situated between an abrupt and deep hollow, through which a stream flowed, and the rampart of the castle, from which it was separated by a road of no great breadth. At night this prison was most horribly dismal. We had no fire: a night lamp supplied with fresh oil, and placed in a paper lantern, was kept burning in the guard room, but the feeble glimmering light it shed between the spars was scarcely capable of rendering any object visible to us. The clanking noise made every half hour by the moving of the locks and bolts, when the soldiers inspected us, rendered this gloomy place still more disagreeable, and did not allow us to enjoy a moment's repose.

We could not suppose that the Japanese would have thrown away time, labour, and expense, if they intended to set us soon at liberty. They might easily have found a suitable house for confining us two or three years. But the strength and the plan of this prison appeared to denote that it was intended to be our dwelling-place during the remainder of our existence. This idea distressed us not a little. We sat long in profound silence, looked at each other, and regarded ourselves as finally lost. A servant at length brought in our supper, which consisted of boiled rice, a piece of fish, and a handful of beans with syrup. He reached it through the spars, and, not observing me as I lay in a corner, asked in broken Russian where the third was. Mur immediately asked him where he had learned Russian, to which he replied, "in Kamchatka." Mur told him that he had also been in Kamchatka. The Japanese, however, understood him to say that he had seen him there. He was overjoyed to hear this, and repeated what he supposed Mur had said to the interpreter. We had frequently told him that we knew of no Japanese having been at Kamchatka, except the seven who had been saved from shipwreck, and who were in Nisehny Kamchatka, but whom we had not seen. On our endeavoring to make the interpreter comprehend the mistake of the servant, he exclaimed, "How artful! how artful!" and went away. This circumstance gave us much uneasiness, as it was calculated to make the Japanese suspect that there was something in the affair we wished to conceal from them.

On the 1st of October, 1811, it was notified to us, that on the following day we should be carried before the magistrate (*bugyō*) of Matsumae, Arao Shigeaki, which was accordingly done in the morning. We were conducted in the same manner as in Hakodate, except that, on this occasion, the ends of the ropes were held by *bakufu* soldiers. The road to the southern gate of the castle, or fortress, to which we were conducted, lay between the rampart and the hollow, and extended to the distance of about a quarter of a kilometer from our prison. As the road was dirty, the Japanese had laid down planks for us to walk on, and held umbrellas over us to protect us from the rain.

On entering the castle, we soon found ourselves in a sort of court or yard of considerable size, strewed with small stones or gravel, and were put into a low long-shaped building, and placed all in a row upon one bench. We waited here about an hour. At last a door was opened, and we were conveyed into a second court. Proceeding forward, we came to the door of a third court, on approaching which, the soldiers who escorted us pulled off their sandals and laid them down, with their swords and daggers, at the door: in like manner we were obliged to deposit our boots. This door being opened, we walked on very fine straw mats towards a large wooden building. Here we were placed in the front of a spacious room in which the screens, of which the walls, according to the Japanese mode of building, were formed, were thrown open on the side next the court. Mur, Khlebnikov, and myself, were placed on an elevated spot; our sailors were behind us, but somewhat lower, and Alexei sat on their left. Our servant, Heinste, who understood some Russian words, took his station on our right (this was the place of the interpreter), and Kumajirō on our left. This servant had told us that he was to be our interpreter in our conference with the magistrate, but we did not believe that he would venture to undertake a task he was so incapable of executing.

The room was very extensive. The screens which formed its sides, some of which were of paper, others of wood, were all gilded, and adorned with Japanese paintings of landscapes, quadrupeds, and birds. The curious carved work, and the various kinds of fine wood of which the doors and frames were formed, added greatly to the splendor of this extraordinary edifice. The floor was covered with finely worked tapestry. On each side of the room were five officers, with daggers in their girdles, sitting cross-legged, according to the Japanese custom. Three of them had large swords, lying beside them on the left hand: they were in their usual dress.

After we had waited about a quarter of an hour, during which the Japanese laughed and amused themselves in conversation with each other, we suddenly heard a rustling behind a screen. One of the officers called out— *Schee!* and a deep silence immediately followed. A Japanese, in ordinary dress, came forward, kneeled on his entrance, placed the palms of his hands on the floor, and bowed his head. Magistrate Arao Shigeaki Tajima no Kami now appeared. He was in a common black dress, on the sleeves of which, as is the custom with all the Japanese, his armorial bearings were embroidered. He had a dagger at his girdle, and his sword was carried by one of his suite, who were five in number, he who had previously entered included. The sword bearer held the weapon near the extremity, with the handle upward. But a cloth was wrapped round the part he grasped, to preserve his naked hand from coming in contact with it. The magistrate took his place without delay. He faced us, and looked like a president sitting at the head of his council. His suite sat down behind him at the distance of three paces, he who carried the sword laid it down on the left of the magistrate. This was no sooner done, than the Japanese all testified their respect, by laying the palms of their hands on the floor, and bending their bodies so low, that their foreheads almost touched the ground. In this position they remained for some seconds. Shigeaki returned the compliment with a pretty deep bow, in doing which he laid the palms of his hands upon his knees. We saluted him after the European manner, on which he nodded his head, repeatedly smiled, and seemed desirous of showing that he was favorably disposed towards us. He drew from his bosom a paper, into which he looked, and called each of us by our names. We answered with a bow, and he bowed in return. He then addressed himself to Heinste, who listened, with his forehead touching the ground, and when Shigeaki ceased to speak, stood up, in order to interpret what had been said. This he however did so imperfectly, that we could not comprehend him. The following was the purport of his version: "Thou art a man—I am a man—such another is a man—say what sort of a man?"

We advised him not to deceive his superior, but to confess frankly that he was incapable of performing the task he had undertaken, lest harm should befall him in consequence of his persisting. He listened with the greatest attention to what we said, and proceeded to interpret it, in doing which he resumed his former position. The Japanese wrote down what he said, and then a second question was put. The shameful assurance of this man roused our indignation so far, that we declared we would answer no more questions, in order that this impostor might not injure us by his erroneous interpretations. Heinste, however, who was not in the least ruffled by this declaration, as in fact he did not well understand what we said, made some reply to the Japanese, who took a note of his supposed interpretation; after which a new question was asked. We turned to Alexei and Kumajirō, and requested that they would explain the matter to Shigeaki. But they did not dare to speak. Meanwhile Shigeaki conversed with Heinste, and we heard him pronounce the Japanese word for father, which we knew. It is probable that he asked the names of our fathers. Heinste pulled a paper, with Russian words, out of his breast, and after stammering for a considerable time, at last acknowledged that he did not know the word, and could not find it in his list. When Shigeaki and his officers found that he was ignorant of so common a word, they laughed, dismissed him, and again appointed Kumajirō and Alexei our interpreters.

The questions commenced in the same manner as at Hakodate, with inquiries respecting our names, rank, families, and relations. In these particulars the interrogatories were even more minute than any we had answered before. And they were all put by Shigeaki himself. After examining us on the subject of Resanov's return from Japan, and the cause of our arrival among them, he asked some questions that had no relation to these subjects, and appeared to arise from mere curiosity. Of these I recollect the following—he wished to know how the Russians buried their dead; what sort of monuments they erected over their graves, and whether, in that respect, any difference was made between the rich and the poor. When, in the course of our answers, we mentioned that the funerals of the rich were attended by a number of priests, Shigeaki remarked that the same practice prevailed among the Japanese. At last he asked whether there was any request that we wished to address to him. We answered that we did not rightly know what was intended by that question, as we supposed Shigeaki himself must be aware of the only request we had to make, seeing that we had been treacherously seized, and even still unjustly detained in prison. He then observed that we might address a petition to him with regard to the place in which we wished to reside: namely, whether in Matsumae, in Edo, the capital, or in any other part of Japan; or, finally, stating whether we would rather return to Russia. We replied that we had only two things to ask: the first was, to be permitted to return to our country; the second, in case the first was not possible, to die—these were the only favors we had to request of the Japanese. Shigeaki now, with evident emotion, made a long speech, which all present listened to with the utmost attention. And an expression of commiseration was visible in the faces of all. Alexei then turned to explain to us what had been said (but he probably committed some blunders in his interpretation), and observed that he had heard so many consolatory assurances, that he despaired of being able to repeat them all; he would, however, endeavour to convey to us the substance of the speech, at which we should doubtless find some cause to rejoice. "The General," continued Alexei, "says that the Japanese are men, and have hearts as well as other people, and that we have therefore no reason either to fear or despair. They will investigate our affair. And if they find that we are not deceiving them, and that we are not implicated in the proceedings of

Khvostov, they will send us back to Russia, and will supply us with rice, *sake*, and other provisions, and presents. In the meanwhile they advise us to console ourselves, as they will look after our health, and see that we want for nothing. If we stand in need of clothes, or any particular kind of food, they desire that we will not hesitate to make our request known."

We thanked Shigeaki for this consolatory speech, and for his promise that we should have justice done to us; upon which he withdrew, having directed our attendants to conduct us back to prison. Before he retired he bowed to the officers, and they to him, as on his entrance. When he rose, his sword bearer immediately took his sword up with the cloth, holding the hilt upwards, and followed him.

Notwithstanding the singularly unfortunate combination of circumstances, which was calculated to fill the minds of the Japanese with distrust and hatred towards us, the assurance of Shigeaki tended greatly to ease our minds. We thought that no men, who were not possessed by evil spirits, could have so well assumed the mask of dissimulation, and put on such an appearance of sympathy, if they really did not feel for us. On the other hand, bitter experience had confirmed all that we had before heard or read concerning the oriental nations, and in particular the Japanese, namely: that the meanest beggars with them excel our most crafty European courtiers in the practice of falsehood and deceit. We were frequently distressed by the reflection that this subtle and cunning people were doubtless aware of the use to which they might turn us, when we should become reconciled to our fate of remaining forever in Japan. And that they, perhaps, consoled us only with empty hopes, lest we should pine our lives away in despair, and thus rob them of the advantages they might otherwise derive from our experience and knowledge of the arts of Europe.

On the following day, the 3rd of October, we were again conducted to the castle and placed in the presence of Shigeaki, with all the formalities that had been observed on the former occasion. He devoted but little attention to the main subject of investigation, but questioned us for a long time concerning the various customs and manners of the Europeans. Among other things, he inquired whether we ever witnessed such a storm in Russia as had taken place on the preceding night in Japan.

In some places, he added, the weather was much more stormy than in Matsumae. "This," he said, "was not one of our very severe storms. In mainland Japan they are both more violent and frequent than here." He endeavored to give to this examination the appearance of a friendly conversation, and in about two hour's time dismissed us, in order that we might partake of some refreshment.

We entered a spacious courtyard, and took our seats in a summer house, where the Japanese, by order of Shigeaki, served us with tea and sugar. It was not allowable to smoke tobacco in the courtyard of Shigeaki's castle. Our guards therefore went by turns into the kitchen and guardroom to smoke their pipes. In the meantime the interpreter, Kumajirō, came to us, accompanied by a civil officer and a tailor, who, he said, had been ordered by Shigeaki to make some clothes for us, either after the Japanese or the Russian form, as we ourselves might think fit. But that, if we wished to have them after the Russian fashion we must furnish the tailor with a pattern. We observed that we had clothes enough, and felt no wish to have more; upon which the Japanese replied that that was of no importance; that Shigeaki wished to make us a present, and that we must not reject it. All contradiction was therefore useless. We told him that we wished to have some warm clothes made after the pattern of a coat that had been sent from the sloop to Khlebnikov.

The tailor was then conducted to the store-house, where our things were kept. Tthe coat was shown to him, and he proceeded to take our measures—he made use of a measure that was divided into ten parts, and noted everything down in writing. When he had measured us all, we were again summoned to appear before Shigeaki, who examined us for several hours, and at length dismissed us with an exhortation not to abandon ourselves to despair, but to offer up prayers to God, and wait with patience for the issue of the investigation. "Be assured," he said, "that I will use all my influence with the emperor to obtain his consent that you may return to your native country. I will provide you with paper and ink, in order that you may draw up an account of your case in the Russian language, and with the help of the interpreters get it translated into Japanese. I will examine it, transmit it to the government, and will see that everything is terminated to your advantage. You may also draw up a petition to be presented to me."

We thanked him for his kindness, and returned to our melancholy prison, not knowing whether these consolations of the Japanese were sincere or feigned.

In the course of a few days our new clothes were brought to us. Those for Mur, Khlebnikov, and myself, were made of a cherry-colored cotton stuff, somewhat resembling frieze, which the Japanese call *monpa*, and were wadded and lined with cotton. The sailors' clothes were of common cotton stuff, wadded and lined, and of the same form as our's. They were all, however, very singularly shaped, being neither cloaks, greatcoats, nor night-gowns, though they bore some resemblance to garments of each of these denominations. Alexei had a nightdress made after the Japanese form.

We did not again appear before the magistrate until the 6th of October. Our food in Matsumae was incomparably better than it had been in Hakodate. According to the Japanese custom, stewed rice and pickled radishes served us instead of bread and seasoning. We were besides frequently furnished with good fresh and salt fish, boiled or fried; soups, in which were various wild herbs or noodle. And they sometimes prepared for us a kind of Russian soup or sauce, made with white fish and muscle broth. The fish were fried in oil of poppies, and were seasoned with grated radish and soy. When the snow began to fall, they shot for us sea dogs, bears, and frequently hares. The Japanese consider the flesh of whales and sea lions to be the most delicate of all food. Our attendants, some of whom had been in Russia, were ordered to cook our victuals in the way we liked best. We were accordingly sometimes regaled with small patties of barley-meal with fish, which were pretty savory, and they also gave us a kind of dark-colored grits boiled. These were the only imitations of Russian dishes they knew how to prepare. Our meals were usually served to us thrice every day. Our drink consisted either of luke-warm or hot tea. And when we returned from the castle, our attendants usually presented each of us with two teacups full of warm *sake*: this they never failed to do when the weather was colder than usual.

We were living almost in the open air. And, as the weather was extremely cold, the Japanese gave to each of our sailors a large nightdress, and one bear-skin: they furnished the officers and myself with two bearskins each, and placed benches for us to sleep upon, as they had heard that the Russians did nor like to lie on the ground. They besides gave the sailors a bench to sit upon. These attentions, however, corresponded very ill with our rigorous confinement, and therefore appeared to us very singular.

Besides the orderly officers, who came to us by turns during the day, a particular officer was appointed to look after our provisions. The kind manners of the Japanese emboldened us to ask one of the officers whether we could not have a window made in the back wall of the prison, as through the palisades we could discover nothing but the sky and the tops of a few trees. He did not oppose our request, but examined the wall, and asked us where we thought it would be best to make the window. We felt reason to hope that our request would be complied with. But we were deceived. On the renewal of our solicitation, a few days afterwards, the officer replied, that the Japanese were careful of our health, and feared lest the bleak north-winds might give us cold. We were consequently compelled to give up all thoughts of the window.

From the 6th of October, to the end of the month, we were conducted regularly every day, or every other day, to the magistrate, who usually detained us the greater part of the day, so that our attendants were obliged to carry our meals to the castle. About the middle of October, when the frost began, Shigeaki left off receiving us in the room, and our examinations afterwards took place in a chamber of justice, similar to that at Hakodate, and which was likewise hung round with instruments of punishment. The number of questions Shigeaki asked was incalculable. If he put one interrogatory concerning any circumstance connected with our case, he asked fifty that were unimportant, and many that were ludicrous. This so puzzled and tormented us, that we sometimes made very insolent replies. We once stated plainly, that we had rather they would put an end to our existence at once than torture us in the way they did. Who would not have lost patience on being asked such questions as the following. When I was taken, I had ten or twelve keys of my bureau and drawers, and of the astronomical instruments belonging to the ship. Shigeaki wished to be informed of the contents of every drawer, and every box. When I pointed to my shirt, and told him that my drawers contained such things as these, he asked me how many I had. I told him, with some degree of ill humor, that I did not know, and that it was my servant's business to keep that reckoning. Upon this he immediately inquired how many servants I had, and what were their names and ages. I lost all patience, and asked the Japanese why they teased us with such questions, and what use such information could be to them, since neither my servants nor property were near me. Shigeaki then, with great mildness, observed that he hoped we were not offended by his curiosity; that he did not intend to force any answers from us, but merely questioned us like a friend. This kindness immediately calmed our irritation, and we reproached ourselves for the rude answers we had given. Shigeaki then asked a few questions relative to our business, but soon resumed his old system of examination, and at length dismissed us, harnessed as usual like so many horses. In this manner we frequently quarreled, and adjusted our disputes three or four times in the course of a day.

In order to enable the reader to form some notion of the questions the Japanese put to us, and the trouble it cost us to explain the various things that excited their curiosity, I subjoin a few of their interrogatories, scarcely, however, the hundredth part of the useless inquiries which they were accustomed to make in the course of one day. It must, moreover, be considered that we had to make ourselves understood to them by means of a half-barbarous Ainu, who knew scarcely anything of the subjects on which we conversed, and who knew of no words in the Ainu language to express many of the terms we made use of. The Japanese interrogated us without any kind of regularity, and often jumped from one subject to another. The following is a specimen of one of our examinations.

What kind of dress does the Emperor of Russia wear—what does he wear on his head—what kind of birds are found in the neighborhood of St. Petersburg—what would be the price in Russia of the clothes which we were then wearing—what number of cannon was planted round the imperial palace—what wool is made use of in Europe for manufacturing cloth—what quadrupeds, birds, and fish are eaten in Russia—in what manner do the Russians eat their food—what dress do the ladies wear—what kind of horse does the emperor usually ride—who accompanies him when he goes abroad—are the Russians partial to the Dutch—how many foreigners are there in Russia—what are the chief articles of trade in Petersburg—what are the dimensions in the length, breadth, and height, of the imperial palace—how many windows does it contain—how many times do the Russians go to church in one day—how many festivals do the Russians observe in the course of the year—do the Russians wear silk clothes—at what time of life do the Russian women begin and cease to bear children. They besides inquired the names of the emperor, and all the branches of the imperial family; the names of the governors-general of Siberia and Irkutzk, and of the commandants of Okhotsk and Kamchatka, etc. etc. On our informing them that the sovereigns of Europe did not fortify their palaces, they at first seemed to doubt the truth of what we said. They, however, afterwards expressed their astonishment at what they termed so singular an instance of imprudence.

On our mentioning sheep, they requested Mur to draw them the figures of a sheep and a goat. At length they asked him for horses, asses, coaches, sledges, etc. in a word, they wished to have everything represented on paper which they could not see in Japan. They always made their requests with the utmost politeness, and therefore he could not possibly refuse them, although he found it a very tedious and troublesome task to satisfy all their demands: fortunately, he sketched with astonishing rapidity.

When we replied that we did not know, they requested that we would inform them according to supposition. This they never failed to do whenever we sought to evade their questions. They frequently put us out of humor by making inquiries respecting things of which we could not possibly possess any knowledge, such for instance as: how many harbors are there in Europe in which ships are built—and how many ships of war and merchantmen are there in all Europe. We might indeed have invented an answer of some kind or other. But we found it necessary to be upon our guard, as they frequently questioned us on the same subject at different times, and in different ways.

But the Japanese vexed us most of all by their inquiries respecting barracks. I have already observed that in Hakodate they insisted on knowing how many men were under our command, according to our rank, when we were ashore. This question was again repeated, together with a request to know where the sailors lived in Petersburg. In barracks, we replied. They then requested Mur to sketch, from the best of his recollection, a plan of Petersburg, and to point out in what part of the town the sailors' barracks were. This demand was no sooner complied with, than they made inquiries respecting the length, breadth, and height, of the barracks; the number of gates, windows, and doors, they contained. And further into how many stones they were divided; in what part of the building the sailors lived; how they employed their time; how many men were appointed to guard the barracks, etc. But this was not all: they questioned us about the military barracks; asked how many buildings of that kind there were in Petersburg, in what part of the town they were situated, and what number of men they contained. We thought it best to plead ignorance of most of these matters. But this did not induce the Japanese to discontinue their trifling. They inquired in what part of the city our dwellings were situated, how far they were from the palace, and requested us to point out the spot on the sketch which Mur had drawn. At length they wished to know how large our houses were, and how many servants we kept. I frequently thought that the Japanese took a pleasure thus to torment us; for to reply to all the questions which their insatiable curiosity induced them to put to us was a real martyrdom.

We sometimes absolutely refused to answer, and told them that they might if they pleased put us to death. Shigeaki would then endeavour to reconcile us by expressions of regard and inquiries respecting matters relative to our imprisonment, but he would soon resume his childishness. We avoided, by every possible manoeuver, giving them any opportunity for unnecessary questions: we replied in a short manner, and sometimes gave them only half an answer. But every word carried with it a train of interrogatories. They admired the fine handwriting and drawing of Mur: they looked upon him to be an exceeding learned man, and asked where he had been educated. Mur took care not to tell them that he had been brought up in the Naval Cadet College: to avoid the thousand questions that would infallibly have ensued respecting that institution, he merely said that he had received his education in his uncle's house. Then followed a string of questions concerning his uncle, who he was, whether he was rich, where he resided, and whether he had himself been Mur's instructor, etc. On his informing them that he had had tutors, they inquired their names, where they had been educated, etc. When they asked me where I was brought up, I told them in my fathers house, and naturally concluded that there would be an end of the matter. But I was under a mistake: I was obliged to inform them when and how I had acquired my education, whether my father was a man of property, and with what sciences he was acquainted.

The Japanese at last produced all the things they had taken from us, inquired their names, their uses, how they had been manufactured, and how much they cost. They took down all our answers in writing, and placed a label with a superscription on each of the articles. One day, a box full of my English and French books was brought into the presence of Shigeaki, though we had not been previously informed of their being sent from the sloop. The Japanese took up the books one by one, showed them to us, and inquired respecting their contents. With regard to some of the books, this explanation was easy enough. But with others we experienced no small difficulty. Among the latter was the *Physics* by Antoine Libes, in three volumes, in the French language. This work contains numerous plans of various instruments and machines, which powerfully excited the curiosity of the Japanese. Everything they saw filled them with amazement. They declared themselves overjoyed that such a book should have fallen into their hands, and requested an explanation of all the figures that most pleased them. In vain did we tell them that with such an interpreter as Alexei we could not possibly make them understand the meaning of the plates. They entreated that we would give them some notion of what kind of book it was. We told Alexei that the book treated of the means of raising heavy weights, and showed him one of the plates representing a crane and block. He immediately understood us, and translated what we said to the Japanese. But this did not satisfy them: they replied that such things had long since been well known to them. They pointed to one of the plates explanatory of the refraction of rays, and asked us what it meant, and whether it did not relate to the distance between the sun and the earth. I thought it would not be difficult to make Alexei comprehend this figure, and asked him whether he had not observed that when the end of an oar was in the water it had the appearance of being broken. "Oh yes!' he said, "I have observed that, though I do not know how it happens." When we tried to explain to him the refraction of rays, he asked us what a ray was. No sooner had we made him understand the meaning of the word than he burst into a loud fit of laughter. "Oh, that's impossible!" he said: "what man can break a ray?" We were likewise unable to repress our laughter, and the Japanese joined us without knowing why. They seemed at last convinced that Alexei was not a fit interpreter for such matters, though he himself was fully of the opinion that we were talking nonsense. They now took the books from us, saying "another time, another time," and began to pack them carefully up in the box. This increased our vexation. It appeared they took us all for extremely learned men, but, in particular, entertained that opinion of me, because my name was written in all the books. They questioned me concerning that circumstance, and expressed their astonishment at my having so many books in my possession. From what fell from them they seemed to expect that we would, one day or other, be able to make them understand the contents of these books, which, at present, appeared perfectly enigmatical to them.

I subjoin two observations the Japanese made concerning these books. They asked me why I had so many foreign books, and only one in the Russian language (Tatischtsehew's *French Dictionary*, in two vols.), and whether we did not know how to print books in Russia. It is, I replied, because they happen to have sent from the sloop only the chest containing the foreign books: the Russian volumes are in another box. They then asked how it happened that my foreign books were so handsomely bound, and printed on fine paper, whilst that in the Russian language was, on the contrary, printed on coarse paper. I replied that the Russians, as well as other nations, occasionally printed their books either on fine or coarse paper.

Among a number of insignificant questions, arising from mere curiosity, the Japanese wished to know the military and naval force, the number of garrisons, and the riches and strength of the Russian empire, etc. We readily replied to these questions, always bearing in mind that which we had before said. And though each interrogatory was repeated ten times over, we were constantly prepared with a corresponding answer. It seemed to them impossible that we should make use of bombs weighing nine pounds. And they laughed when we said that we preferred firing muskets with flints, as they make use of matches for that purpose.

With regard to the circumstances relative to our imprisonment, Shigeaki asked all the questions we had previously answered in Hakodate. He repeated them once, and sometimes twice during the day. But he always seemed to consider the satisfaction of his own curiosity as the most important object, and all else as mere accessary matters. He did, however, want clear and decided answers to any question relative to our own case. We learned that our two attendants were the same Japanese who had been carried off from the Island of Sachalin by Khvostov, and who were detained by him for a whole winter at Kamchatka, and then sent back to Japan. What had been his object in doing this we knew not. Those attendants constantly accompanied us to the castle, and were always present during the examinations, or rather conversations. Shigeaki once asked a question concerning Khvostov, and immediately spoke to one of the attendants. The latter answered (for we understood the purport of what he said perfectly well,) that Khvostov wore a uniform ornamented with gold lace, the same as mine and Mur's. The Japanese looked at us and smiled. Shigeaki then said that the two attendants, Heinste and Fukumasa, who had been taken before the chief commandant of Kamchatka, had heard him declare that he would overrun Japan with a numerous army. And that, instead of merely blustering there, as Khvostov had done, he would burn and destroy everything he could find. We replied that it appeared to us improbable that the commandant of Kamchatka should have made any such declaration; that the expressions had perhaps been made use of by one of the officers of the garrison. And that, even allowing it to be true, the commandant of Kamchatka was a person of no importance in Russia, and might, if he pleased, talk nonsense as well as other people. Our government, as we have already proved to them, entertained no such intentions; otherwise its hostilities would not have been confined to empty threats, and the Japanese would soon have experienced the difference between a predatory attack made by a private individual, and a regular war declared by the emperor. Shigeaki was not in the least degree offended by this answer, and continued his questions with his usual civility.

At the close of this examination, Shigeaki informed us that we should not be conveyed to the castle for some time again, in order to afford us time to draw up a written statement of our case, with the assistance of the interpreter Kumajirō, to whom he had given every necessary instruction. He accordingly dismissed us with an exhortation not to yield to despair, but to offer up prayers to heaven, and to place confidence therein. He added that in case we stood in need of anything, we should immediately inform him, since we should experience every indulgence he could give consistently with the laws of his country.

I must not omit to mention several marks of attention the Japanese showed to us during the month of October. I have already observed that they provided us with warm clothing and bearskins. But as the cold continued to increase, they stopped up the spaces between the spars with paper, and at our earnest entreaty made windows at the top, which opened and shut by means of a rope. From these windows we could indeed discover nothing but the sky and the tops of a few trees. But in our sad condition we derived some consolation even from this prospect. They besides dug large holes for hearths, at about one and a half or two paces from each cage, which they built round with thick freestone, and filled with sand.

Several officers, the interpreter, the physician, and an architect, assembled like the members of a council, to debate concerning the precise spots where these holes should be dug. The ground was examined and measured, and upwards of an hour was spent in deliberation. At first we naturally supposed that some affair of mighty importance was in agitation, but we soon learnt what it all tended to. They wished the fires to be kindled at such a distance that we could not reach the coals with our hands, though we could smoke our pipes by means of the long tubes they supplied us with. This dilatory and trifling turn of the Japanese caused us much vexation. If (thought we) they deliberate for an hour about matters of this nature, how long will it be ere they bring the investigation of our case to an issue.

In these fireplaces they burnt charcoal from morning to night, which warmed us when we seated ourselves on the ground near the spars. In the course of a few days they supplied us with tobacco for smoking, and very long pipes, to the middle of which a wooden ball was affixed, of so large a size that it would not pass between the palisades, and which was intended to hinder us from drawing the burning pipes into our prisons. We felt irritated at this singular instance of distrust, and reproached the Japanese in pretty plain terms for the barbarous opinion they entertained of the Europeans. They laughed and referred to their laws, which obliged them to remove from the reach of their prisoners anything by which they might commit violence, either on themselves or others. They told us that we were only permitted to smoke tobacco through the particular favor of the magistrate, and that without violating their laws they had granted us some indulgences, and had kindled fires for us. They therefore observed that we ought not to murmur at any trifling restriction. This explanation consoled us: we were glad to find the Japanese did not adhere strictly to the letter of their law, and that they often made evasions in our favor. In the present case the Japanese had to take care to avoid a war with Russia: it was accordingly natural enough that they should rather choose not to be over-punctual in expounding their statutes, than to draw down upon themselves the anger of a warlike and powerful neighbor. They, moreover, assured us, that our condition would be bettered in course of time, and that at length, the highest mark of favor they could show us, would be to send us back to our native country. They observed that the Japanese never did anything rashly; that with them every measure was executed slowly and deliberately, and that, consequently, our condition could only be gradually improved. This we well knew from experience, for we had never yet received two civilities or favors in the course of the same day.

Among the many marks of kindness with which the magistrate honored us, one in particular deserves to be noticed. There were one day shown to us several models of boats and ships, which appeared to us to be Chinese; a silver rouble bearing the head of Catherine II; a Japanese bag, containing about two pounds of rice, and an elegant case of flasks, partly lacquered and partly gilt, which was the property of Shigeaki. The Japanese asked us whether we had ever seen anything in Europe like the models and the case of flasks. And, further, what was the name and value of the coin, and what quantity of rice the bag would contain, according to Russian weight. Their questions were short, and unaccompanied by the usual digressions. They then poured from the flasks some excellent *sake* and cordials, which they presented to us. The interpreter, Kumajirō, gave us to understand that this was done by order of the magistrate, who, according to their laws, could not entertain us in his own house. I must likewise observe, that the Japanese did everything they thought would contribute to our comfort, and were particularly watchful of our health. Our physician visited us daily. If we felt the slightest indisposition, he repeated his visits twice or three times in course of the day, and in cases which appeared in any degree dangerous he brought another physician along with him. Their attention to us went to so great a length, that one night, when a fire broke out in the city, our guards came into our cage and explained to us the cause of the alarm and desired us not to trouble ourselves about it. However, during the first few days of our imprisonment at Matsumae, they were far from paying such particular regard to us.

I must not omit mentioning one very laughable circumstance, the real cause of which we were unable to divine. Our meals were superintended by an old officer, sixty years of age. He behaved very civilly to us, and frequently consoled us with the assurance that we should be sent back to Russia. One day he brought to us three portraits of Japanese ladies, very richly dressed. We supposed that he meant merely to show them to us, and we were about to return them to him, when he desired us to keep them. We refused, but he insisted that we should accept of them. We asked him what use they could be to us. And he replied that we might amuse ourselves by looking at them when the time hung heavily on our hands. We then asked whether we were in a situation to be amused by the sight of such beauties. Indeed, the figures were so wretchedly designed, that they were calculated only to excite aversion and ridicule. The old man, however, insisted on our accepting of his portraits: we complied with his wish, and afterwards made the interpreter Kumajirō a present of them. Mur jokingly told him that we did not wish to keep the portraits, lest we might be induced to request his countrymen to send the fair originals to amuse us, and asked whether he thought the magistrate would accede to such a demand. "No, no," replied Kumajirō, laughing, "not now; sometime hence perhaps."

During the last fortnight of the month of October we were occupied in drawing up the statement of our case. We were furnished with paper and ink, and Kumajirō directed us how to prepare our memorial. At first we entered into a serious dispute with the Japanese on this subject, and refused to write anything at all. Kumajirō required that we should write on separate sheets of paper for ourselves and the sailors a kind of affidavit, setting forth where we were born, what were the names of our fathers and mothers, how long we had been in the naval service, etc. This we immediately did. He next wished us to state on the same sheets of paper all the absurd things respecting which we had been questioned: for instance, that the Russians buried their dead in churchyards on the outside of the city, that they erected crucifixes and other monuments over their tombs, etc. But this we refused to do;

declaring that a whole life would be insufficient to note down on paper all our answers to the silly questions which had been put to us, and that the magistrate had merely required a statement of our case to be translated into Japanese. The Japanese were at first displeased at our refusal, and endeavored to persuade us to do what they declared would be to our own advantage. We obstinately persisted in our determination. And they then requested that we would write down all the circumstances that had occurred to us since our departure from St. Petersburg; adding, that they wished everything to be made as short as possible, excepting what related to our communications with the Japanese, with every particular of which they desired to be made acquainted. This we agreed to do, and told Kumajirō that we would, during his absence, write out our case. And when he should be present, with the assistance of Alexei, we would have it translated into Japanese. He requested that we would write the copy which was to be translated in such a way as to leave room between every two lines for one or two more.

We accordingly set to work, and, in order that we might reserve a copy of the statement for ourselves, we first of all wrote it out in a rough style. But in doing this we experienced considerable difficulty: we were obliged to proceed with the greatest caution, lest we should be observed by our guards, who would have taken the papers from us. Khlebnikov usually sat near the spars, wrapped in a large nightgown, turning his back towards the Japanese. He wrote with a straw, and placed his ink in a small wooden spoon before him. I walked up and down, and winked to him whenever any of the guards changed their position so as to be able to observe what he was doing. We were afraid to use for this purpose the paper with which Kumajirō had provided us, lest the sheets might have been counted; we therefore wrote on the coarse paper which had been given to us for pocket handkerchiefs. Mur, in the meanwhile, wrote out a fair copy of our statement, which we dictated under pretense of conversing with him. The trouble which our interpreters, Alexei and Kumajirō, gave us, whilst they were making the translation, is inconceivable. We endeavored by all possible means to avoid such words and phrases as Alexei could not understand. For example, instead of very or much we were obliged to make use of the word violent; instead of hostilities, blows; instead of peaceable intentions, good meaning, etc. Our style of writing would therefore have appeared singular enough to anybody but our interpreters. Notwithstanding all this, we were frequently unable to make Alexei comprehend us, and even when he did understand our meaning, he could sometimes find no corresponding words and expressions to convey what we intended to the Japanese interpreter.

Kumajirō adopted the following plan. He first asked us how the Russians sounded particular words, and then described the pronunciation in Japanese characters, above the word itself. When he had completed a sheet in this way, he would ask us the signification of each of the words, and would write it down in Japanese above the pronunciation. This gave us no little trouble. He was a man of about fifty years of age, naturally stupid: he had no notion whatever of any European language, and was totally ignorant of grammar. If we explained to him the meaning of a word, either through Alexei's interpretation, or by gesticulations and examples, he would listen attentively to everything we said, and then exclaim "*O-o-o*;" which, in the Japanese language, is equivalent to "Yes, yes, I understand." We sometimes spent half an hour in explaining a word to him. And when we thought we had made him fully understand it, he would again ask us what it meant, declaring that he could form no idea of its signification. We frequently lost all patience, and reproached him for his stupidity. But he would excuse himself by saying that he was old, and found the acquirement of the Russian language extremely difficult. He spent two whole days in endeavoring to comprehend the word imperial.

We occupied two hours at a time, trying to explain it to him by every example we could think of. Alexei, who understood the word perfectly well, did all in his power to render it intelligible to him. Kumajirō would listen attentively to all we said, laugh, and mutter out his *O-o-sso*! but scarcely had we finished speaking, when he would say, "I understand emperor quite well, but imperial, imperial, I cannot comprehend that at all." Prepositions and conjunctions could find no access to his stupid head. It was quite inconceivable to him that we should place them before the noun substantives to which they referred, whilst, in the Japanese language, they are always placed after them. This particularly excited his astonishment, and he would not believe that anything could be well expressed in so barbarous and imperfect a language as he regarded the Russian to be. When he had once comprehended the meaning of the words, he began to labour at the construction of the sentences. Here new difficulty arose. He maintained that the Russian words ought to follow each other in the same order as those in the Japanese translation, and wished us to arrange them so, without perceiving that it made absolute nonsense. We assured him that this was impossible. But he declared that our translation would be considered incorrect, if we placed at the end of a sentence a word that ought to stand at the beginning.

At length, after long debates and disputes, we desired him to think on some Japanese and Ainu phrases, and asked him whether he could arrange them word for word in both languages. "I know that is impossible," he replied, "but the Ainu are an uncultivated people, whose language has no manuscript character; while, on the contrary, books are printed in the Russian." We laughed heartily at this observation, and Kumajirō, with his accustomed good humor, joined us. We pledged our word of honor that though the different European languages contained phrases bearing a resemblance to each other, it was impossible to arrange the vocabularies in the same manner in everyone, and that this was the case with regard to the Japanese and Russian languages. This appeared to satisfy him. When he understood the meaning of any sentence in Russian, he endeavored to construe it by corresponding expressions in Japanese, and no longer troubled himself about the order of the words. He seemed highly pleased, however, when they happened accidentally to follow each other in the same order. He then hurried on, and was sure to commit blunders; for, in cases where the Japanese words followed each other as in the Russian, but conveyed a very different sense, he wrote them down with great satisfaction, and always showed himself reluctant to make any alterations when we told him he had misunderstood our meaning.

When we had finished our translation, which was not until the middle of November, we drew up a petition to be presented to the magistrate, in which we addressed him by the title of Excellency, and entreated that he would take into consideration every circumstance tending to our justification, and request the Japanese government to set us at liberty, and send us back to Russia. The translation of this petition cost us no less trouble than our memorial. At length, after numerous questions, explanations, remarks, additions, etc. which were made in conformity to the wish of the Japanese officer who examined the translations, we were informed that we should shortly be required to appear before the magistrate, who wished to question us personally concerning our statement, and to be convinced of its accurate translation.

Whilst we were occupied in this way, Alexei had obtained permission to remain alone with us in the absence of Kumajirō. As we entertained some doubts about his attachment to us, we thought it prudent, during our conversation, to make use of uncommon, and even foreign words, which he did not understand. Alexei observed this, and told us, with great sensibility, how much he regretted that we should withhold our confidence from him, as he was as good a Russian as ourselves, and served the same emperor. He now informed us that the Japanese had sent to Kunashir a number of the Ainu they had seized on the Island of Iturup, and that the tale of their having been sent by the Russians was invented by the party who remained at Iturup; the rest continued to deny it until the Japanese threatened to put them to the torture, and promised, in case they would avow all, to liberate and reward them. They did not, however, confirm the falsehoods the others had asserted. "I am now resolved," continued Alexei, "to make known the conduct of the Ainu, and to suffer torture or even death to prove that I know God, and am as good as any Russian." To shorten his life by ten or twenty years, he said, was a trifling sacrifice, if by that means he could save his soul from eternal damnation. He, therefore, entreated that we would insert in our statement all that he had related to us. He spoke with much firmness and sensibility, and with a degree of eloquence so unusual to him, that we could not doubt the truth of what he said. We praised him for his good intention, and assured him that he would not be punished in Russia for a falsehood into which his companions had ensnared him; though we feared the Japanese would not credit what he said, and would suspect that we had persuaded him to contradict his former declarations. We told him it would be better to reflect on the best mode of explaining the affair, as the Japanese might, perhaps, ask why he had not confessed the truth on board the ship, or at least as soon as we were made prisoners. "That will not cost me a thought," answered Alexei, "whether they believe me or not is a matter of indifference to me, so as I do but justify myself in the face of Heaven. I wish only to confess the truth: the Japanese may kill me if they will: I shall think it a happiness to die in such a cause." At these words the tears started from his eyes. We were so moved, that we ardently wished for some means of discovering the affair to the Japanese, by which Alexei might not be a sufferer. But this seemed impossible.

He seized the first opportunity of disclosing the whole to Kumajirō, and told him that the Ainu had not been sent by the Russians, but that they had visited Japan of their own free will, and for the purposes of carrying on trade. Kumajirō was struck with amazement at this declaration, and called Alexei a fool and a madman. Alexei, however, insisted that he had spoken nothing but the truth, for which he was at any time ready to lay down his life. We knew not whether Kumajirō immediately communicated this declaration to his superiors. When, however, we were again conveyed to the castle, so that the magistrate himself, or some of his superior officers, might examine our translation, Alexei spoke with the same firmness and presence of mind on mention being made of the affair of the Ainu. The Japanese were astonished at his accusing himself, called him a blockhead, and apparently believed that we had persuaded him to make this confession, which they regarded as a fabrication.

The firmness with which he persisted in the truth of his story induced the Japanese to examine him several times alone. We feared that he might be led to deny his last declaration, and to confirm what he had first of all stated. On his return from the castle, we therefore endeavored to read in his face what was passing in his mind. We were frequently permitted to leave our cages, and to go to warm ourselves at the fire in the lobby. We accordingly found an opportunity of desiring the sailors to question Alexei concerning his examination: if his answers were satisfactory, we directed them to cough several times, and if not, they were to remain silent. To our great consolation, we heard a loud coughing in the evening, as if the sailors had been laboring under a severe cold. When, however, we found opportunities of discoursing with them in private, they expressed the greatest suspicion of Alexei, and firmly believed that he was deceiving us, by telling the Japanese a very different story. In support of this opinion, they told us that he had been endeavoring to learn from them the object of our visit to the Kuril Islands, and had advised them to declare to the

Japanese all they knew respecting our intentions. We were, however, convinced that Alexei was sincere, and that he had resolved to bring the truth to light, which finally proved to be the case.

When the Japanese had questioned Alexei on every necessary particular, we were again conducted into the presence of the magistrate. Shigeaki's first question was, whether the Russians had really sent the Ainu to the coast of Japan, and when Alexei had first disclosed to us that the Ainu had deceived the Japanese. Here our answers did not fully correspond with each other. Alexei had not exactly understood the agreement made between us, and consequently did not answer in the way we wished. The Japanese laughed outright. We knew not what passed between them. But the Japanese seemed to suspect that Alexei had been fabricating, in concert with us, an untruth, for the purpose of invalidating the declaration first of all made by the Ainu. Alexei's presence of mind did not forsake him: he adhered to his assertion, and requested to be confronted with his countrymen. The Japanese would not inform us whether, after the departure of the *Diana*, they had suffered the Ainu to leave Iturup. When we questioned our guards on this subject, some replied they knew nothing of the matter, some declared that the Ainu had been sent home, and others that they were still at Iturup. We retired very sorrowfully to our prison; for the Japanese, we were persuaded, looked upon Alexei's declaration as a falsehood of our invention. We were convinced that they regarded us as spies and impostors: Heaven alone was witness to our innocence. The idea of enduring everlasting imprisonment, at a distance from our dear native country, overwhelmed us with despair, and death appeared a thousand times preferable to the situation we were then in. The Japanese observed our despondency, and did all they could to console us: they supplied us with better food than usual, and under the plea of taking care of our health, provided us with new wadded nightdresses.

On the 19th of September we were again conducted to the castle. Our guards, attendants, and the interpreter, were exceedingly cheerful, and informed us that the magistrate had an agreeable piece of news to communicate to us. We were unable to divine what they alluded to. We remained for a considerable time in the ante-chamber, before we were conducted to the Hall of Justice, in which all the officers of the city were assembled. Shigeaki at length entered. Having taken his seat, he asked us whether we were well, and whether we were ready to confirm all we had said respecting Khvostov, and our not having visited their coasts with any evil intention. We reasserted all that we had before stated. And he then delivered a speech of considerable length, of which Alexei, as usual, could interpret only the principal points. It was to the following effect:

The Japanese at first supposed that we intended to plunder and burn their villages, and founded their opinion on Khvostov's conduct, and other circumstances already known to us. For this reason they had enticed us into their garrison and detained us by force in order to ascertain what had induced the Russians to commence hostilities, as the Japanese had uniformly entertained friendly dispositions towards them. Shigeaki, however, gave credit to our explanation of the affair, and regarded us as innocent. He had accordingly given orders for removing the ropes with which we were bound, and would do all that lay in his power to better our condition. If it depended on him to grant us our freedom, and send us back to Russia, he would do so without hesitation. But we must be informed that Shigeaki of Matsumae was not the chief individual of the state, but that Japan was ruled by an emperor and a superior government, whose commands he was bound to obey in all cases of importance, and without whose consent he could not grant us our freedom. On his part, he would use all his influence with the government in our favor, and to facilitate our return to Russia. With this view he had sent one of the principal officers of Matsumae to Edo, the capital, to endeavour to bring our affair to the wished-for conclusion. In the meanwhile he entreated us not to give way to despair, but to offer up prayers to Heaven, and patiently await the decision of the *shōgun*. Whenever he said anything to console us, he reminded us to rely on God, a circumstance with which we were particularly pleased. It was satisfactory to reflect that the people into whose power fate had delivered us entertained a just idea of the Supreme Being, and placed faith in the Almighty Ruler of all nations, before whom all must sooner or later render an account of their actions.

When Alexei had finished his explanation, and the Japanese perceived that we understood him, our ropes were immediately taken off, and they all sincerely congratulated us. Two of them, in particular, were so moved by this scene, that they shed tears. We returned thanks to the magistrate and officers for their kind wishes, and the sympathy they had testified for our misfortunes. The magistrate then retired, and we were conducted from the Hall of Justice. Our guards and attendants now wished us joy, as well as a number of persons, both of high and low rank, whom curiosity had attracted to the spot.

<h1 style="text-align:right">Translating</h1>

On returning to our prison, we found, to our astonishment, everything changed. And we could scarcely comprehend how the Japanese had contrived to effect so complete an alteration in so short a time. The spars or railings in front of our cages were removed; the spaces which before served us for passages were thrown into the cages, the floor was laid with planks in the direction of its length, and covered with new mats, so that our prison was converted into a roomy hall, in which we could walk about and converse at our ease. Near the fire hearth wooden compartments were formed, in which a teacup for each of us was placed. On the hearth stood copper kettles with water for tea, and a pipe, with a little pouch of tobacco, was laid ready for each. Instead of lamps with fish oil, candles were burnt. We wondered not a little at this unexpected and rapid metamorphosis.

The Japanese burn a fire on the hearth from morning till evening, both in winter and summer. Men and women sit round the fire and smoke tobacco. The kettles are never off the fire, as tea is their common beverage for quenching thirst. If they have no tea, they drink warm water, but never taste cold. Even their *sake* they like better warm than cold.

We had scarcely recovered from our astonishment, when several officers, with their children, came to visit us. They offered us their congratulations, seated themselves by the fire, and smoked and chatted with us. In a word, we seemed no longer prisoners, but guests. Supper was not handed to us as usual in cups or basins, but was served up, according to the Japanese custom, on trays. The vessels used were entirely new, and a finer sort was allotted to the officers than to the sailors. The aliments were better than before, and the *sake* was no longer dealt out to us in certain portions, in cups, but was placed before us, as wine is in Europe, so that we might fill it out as we pleased.

This kind treatment revived the hope of again seeing our country, and we passed a tranquil night for the first time since our imprisonment. The two following days were spent equally agreeably, and we considered our speedy return to Russia as certain. But our joy was not of long duration. New occurrences induced us to doubt the sincerity of the Japanese. We soon had to revert to our old meals, and nothing remained except the new utensils. The oil lamp again served to give us light, and the ropes, which had been removed, were again hung up by our guards in their former situation. We, besides, learned that the Commissioner Nasa Sezaemon Masatatsu of Kunashir who had entrapped us, his deputy, and the officer who gave us the letter in the Isle of Iturup, had arrived at Matsumae, and that Magistrate Arao Shigeaki had resolved to examine Alexei in their presence. From this we plainly perceived that the magistrate did not consider the investigation respecting us as yet brought to a conclusion. On Alexei's return to the castle, he told us that the magistrate had threatened him with death for the falsehood of his former declarations. But that he had firmly stated that he feared nothing, and was ready to die for the sake of truth. Upon hearing this the magistrate ceased to threaten, assumed a tone of good humor, desired him to think no more on what had passed, and informed him that he would soon be called upon again for another examination.

Shortly after this, Kumajirō brought to us a young man of twenty-five, named Murakami Teisuke,[1] and said the magistrate wished us to teach him Russian, in order that he might examine the translation of our manuscript, as the Japanese government required that documents of this description should be certified by two interpreters. We asked what the declaration of the magistrate then meant, when he pledged himself to better our situation, and to procure us our liberty. That is what the magistrate wishes to do, replied Kumajirō, but the government requires that every paper should be translated by two interpreters. This statement vexed us not a little, and, as we believed it insincere, we answered the interpreter with some degree of

1 Murakami Teisuke (1780–1846) was a native of Bitchū Province (present day Okayama Prefecture) who had moved to what was then still called Ezo (Hokkaido) where he became active as a linguist and artist, painting the local Ainu and studying their traditions.

irritation, saying, that we saw plainly the Japanese were deceiving us, and did not intend to set us free, because they wished to make use of us as teachers. But that they had made a great mistake. We were ready to die, but not to become the instructors of the Japanese. Were they, however, in the first place, to assure us of the certainty of our return to Russia, we would labour day and night until the period of our departure, to teach them all we knew. But after the deceit they had practised, we were not disposed to undertake any such task. Kumajirō laughed, and protested that there had been no deception, and that we could only think so in consequence of our ignorance of the Japanese laws. At last, Mur, Khlebnikov, and myself, consulted what we ought to do, and resolved to give the new interpreter some instructions until the spring, by which time we should see whether or not the Japanese were inclined to grant us our liberty.

We had scarcely intimated our consent to give instructions to Teisuke, when he appeared with a chest full of manuscripts, consisting of vocabularies, drawn up by Japanese who had been in Russia, and of information concerning Russia, as each of these individuals had been required to make a report to the government on everything he had seen. The physician Gotō and the interpreter Uebara Kumajirō frequently visited us along with Teisuke. Kumajirō informed me that the magistrate wished us, in addition to teaching Teisuke the Russian tongue, to enable him to draw up a statistical account of Russia and other European states, and that the Japanese would be extremely thankful for that information. We considered, that in the present state of things, some advantage might arise, not only to ourselves, but even to Russia, by our communicating to the Japanese such facts as we thought it advisable to make them acquainted with, and we readily agreed to undertake this task. To avoid being troubled with innumerable questions respecting trifles, we remarked, that persons who, like us, had spent almost the whole of their lives at sea, could not be expected to give all the information respecting Russia the Japanese might wish to obtain. We were then very politely informed that the Japanese would be perfectly satisfied with such information as we were capable of giving them.

Among the English books sent to us, we found William Tooke's *View of the Russian Empire*, which contained almost everything of which the Japanese would have desired to be informed. We, however, concealed the real nature of that book from them, as we were afraid they would compel us to translate it. Other reasons also induced us to adopt this course.

Teisuke showed extraordinary capacity even in the very first lessons we gave him. He had an excellent memory, and pronounced the Russian words with such facility, that we conjectured he had previously learned the language, and was purposely concealing his knowledge of it, or, at least, that he was acquainted with some other European tongues. We had scarcely commenced to instruct him, when he remarked, that Kumajirō did not pronounce the words in the same manner we did, and quickly caught the correct sound. We had therefore to go over again the whole of the dictionary which Kumajirō had drawn up, and he wrote above each word its pronunciation, according to the Japanese orthography.

Our pupils visited us daily, and remained with us from morning till night, leaving us only at the time they went to dinner. When the weather was bad they had their victuals brought to them in the prison. Teisuke soon learned to read, and proceeded to enter in a vocabulary the words he had heard us speak, spelt in the Russian alphabetic character. This Kumajirō never attempted to do; indeed Teisuke learned more in a day than Kumajirō in a fortnight. While collecting information from us respecting Russia, and other European countries, and with great diligence translating the whole into the Japanese, he never failed to enter the Russian words in his lexicon, and to annex to them his own remarks. He also endeavored to ascertain whether the reports made by the Japanese who had been in Russia were correct. This gave him occasion to propose various questions to us.

We were now allowed the use of pens, ink, and paper, and to write whatever we pleased. And we accordingly proceeded to make collections of Japanese words. We were, however, afraid to put our observations on paper, as we apprehended that the Japanese might, at some future time, take our manuscripts from us.

A few days after we became acquainted with Teisuke, he brought along with him his brother, a youth of fourteen, and told us that the magistrate desired we should also teach him Russian. "Your magistrate may desire what he pleases," we sharply replied, "but we are not inclined to do whatever he may wish. We have already declared that we would rather sacrifice our lives than remain in Japan on any conditions, still less will we submit to be made pedagogues of. We plainly see the object of all the flattering assurances we have received. We were told that one interpreter was not sufficient for the translation of our memorial, the law requiring two. Having consented to teach another we are now required to instruct a boy. In this way a whole school will soon be formed, but that we will never agree to. We are few in number, and unarmed, and our lives may soon be taken, but we are resolved not to be made schoolmasters." This answer irritated Teisuke extremely. Being of a warm temperament, he was in a rage in an instant and spoke, contrary to the custom of the Japanese, very loud, threatening we had to do what we were ordered, whether we liked it or not. We, with equal warmth, defied his power, or any that might be exercised over us, telling him that to put us to death was easy, but to force us to do what we were determined not to do was impossible. In this way the dispute was kept up for some time, and at last he left us, still in a violent passion.

We expected that this affair would be followed with some disagreeable consequences, but we experienced none. Next morning Teisuke came to us with a very friendly air, and apologized for the angry manner in which he had expressed himself on the preceding day, and for having thus indiscreetly given us offense. He attributed his conduct to a passionate character he inherited from nature, and prayed that we would forget what had passed, and again become friends. We, on our part, also thought it prudent to apologize, and a reconciliation was soon accomplished. Teisuke now brought his brother with him, but merely in the quality of a visitor. Some days after, however, he again spoke of the magistrate's wish to make him a Russian interpreter, and said, as if in jest, that it would be better for us if we consented to teach him. We replied, that if the Japanese desired to live in a state of peace and friendship with Russia, we would take his brother and several other youths home with us, where they would not only have the opportunity of learning the Russian language, but a great many other useful branches of knowledge. After this he spoke no more on the subject.

Meanwhile we could not learn whether the assurances the magistrate had given us were likely to be realized, but it appeared probable that the Japanese government was not inclined to credit our state merits. It was evident that a doubt was entertained respecting the correctness of our translation of the letter from the officers of the *Diana*. And the Japanese fell at last on the following expedient to discover whether we had not deceived them. They ruled some paper in four columns, in one of which they inserted, in alphabetic order, all the words of the letter, omitting only the words they already knew: such as, my name, the word Japanese, the names of the officers who subscribed the letter, etc. At the bottom of the paper were some words which intimated that the Japanese wished us to fill up the other columns with the meaning of each word in English, French, and Dutch. This paper, we were told, had been sent from the capital, but by whom the words were collected we were not informed. It was supposed that a Japanese who understood Dutch had drawn it up. On observing the artifice, we also thought it prudent to dissemble: we pretended to have no idea from where these words had originated, and that we could extract no meaning from them, particularly as many of them were not Russian. We observed among the words some that commenced with a C (the Russian S) in which an E was written instead of that letter.

From the form of the character we concluded that some European had written the manuscript (some time after Teisuke owned to us that a Dutchman, named Laxman,[2] had written the words) who, however, did not understand Russian, as besides the above mentioned blunder, all the words were left in the same number and case as they stood in the letter, and, in some instances, N was changed into R. We, however, positively refused to comply with the request of the Japanese. We declared we had reason to believe, if we did write the words in the different languages required, that the Dutch interpreters, who were hostile to the Russians, would give them a meaning favorable to their own views. As proof that we

2 Adam Kirillovich Laxman (1766 – 1806) was a Finnish–Swedish military officer and one of the first subjects of Imperial Russia to set foot in Japan. A lieutenant in the Imperial Russian military, he was commissioned to lead an expedition to Japan in 1791, bringing with him two Japanese castaways in exchange for whom he hoped to obtain trade concessions from the Tokugawa shogunate. Landing on Hokkaido in October 1792, he was met by members of the Matsumae clan, and was treated hospitably. This changed when he demanded to deliver the castaways to Ed in person. He was eventually allowed to sail to the port of Hakodate, from he marched to Matsumae Castle. At Matsumae, he was told that all Japanese trade with foreign nations ran through Nagasaki, but since he had brought along castaways, he would be allowed to leave peacefully. On his departure, he was provided with papers stating Nagasaki would welcome one Russian ship.

had ground for this suspicion, we cited the acknowledgment of the Dutch themselves, that they had greatly contributed to the dispute between Resanov and the Japanese; at the same time we offered to give a translation of any document, but would not explain detached words. The Japanese immediately asked how the Dutch interpreters could know of any contention between them and Resanov. We then gave them an account of a letter found by an English ship on board of a Dutch prize, in which the Dutch boasted of having succeeded in imbuing the Japanese with an irreconcilable hatred towards the Russians, and stating that our embassy had been dismissed with such an answer as would put an end to all farther desire on the part of Russia for communicating with Japan. On their asking why we had not sooner informed them of this circumstance, we answered that we doubted whether what we stated would be credited. And, besides, that we had no idea of the Dutch having interfered in any way in our affair. Since it now appeared that some reference must have been made to them on the subject, it was our wish not to afford them an opportunity of injuring us a second time. We then related some anecdotes of the conduct of the Dutch East and West India Companies, which afforded instances of the disregard of every principle of rectitude that stood in the way of the advantageous prosecution of commercial interests.

For the truth of all that we stated, we appealed to an English work which was among the books that had been sent to us, and which detailed the transactions of those companies, in colors calculated to excite the strongest hatred and contempt of such rapacious traders. The Japanese now ceased to call upon us for the French, Dutch, and English words. But requested that we would explain to them clearly the meaning of each of the words in the first column, in order that they might fill up the blank columns with Japanese words of the same purport. This we could not refuse. And after the conclusion of the labour, which lasted several days, and gave both us and the Japanese interpreters much trouble, we had to set about a translation of Khvostov's paper, executed in the same manner.

Meanwhile we learned that the officer, who was to proceed to the capital with a report of our case, was ready to set out on his journey, and that the magistrate wished at the same time to send some of our books to the emperor. We were told, however, that it was intended we should be allowed the use of our books, as a consolation during the tedious hours of our confinement. We were, therefore, desired to pick out such as we wished to retain. The interpreter actually brought us the chest with the books, and we laid some aside in the hope that we should be allowed to keep them. But how were we deceived! The Japanese marked those we had selected, and packed them separately from the others, and finally carried off the chest, without leaving us a single book.

Whilst we were looking over the books, a circumstance occurred which embarrassed us not a little. Kumajirō, in turning over the leaves of one of the volumes, found a piece of red paper, upon which were some Japanese words. It was one of the tickets which in Japan are usually attached to goods. I recollected that it had been given to me by one of our officers in Kamchatka. Kumajirō read the ticket, and asked where it had come from, and how it had got into my book. I said it was perhaps Chinese. But I had got it accidentally in Kamchatka, and had put it into my book as a mark. "Yes, yes," he replied, "it is Chinese," and put it again into the place in the book from which he had taken it. I was afraid lest this would occasion new investigations, and be taken by the Japanese as a proof of our having participated in Chwostov's depredations. It was, indeed, most singular, that such a multitude of circumstances, though some of them were totally insignificant and unworthy of observation in any other case, should conspire to make this jealous, timid, and mistrustful people regard us as implicated in that unfortunate affair. I had accidentally been reading when this bit of paper was brought to me, and being in want of a mark at the moment, I used it for that purpose. And by another accident this book was put into one of the seven or eight chests our shipmates had sent on shore to us. We often remarked among ourselves that the writer of a romance could, with difficulty, surround his hero with as many unlucky events as those in which fate had actually involved us. Jesting with Mur, who was young and handsome, we used to advise him to try to win the affections of some distinguished Japanese lady, through whose aid we might be enabled to escape. Our adventures would then have been truly romantic—unfortunately we wanted a heroine to complete our story.

Before the departure of the officer for the capital we were conducted into the presence of the magistrate. Shigeaki wished that we should show him how the Europeans wore hats and swords, and for this purpose a hat and sword were brought to us. Their curiosity went so far, that they inquired what was denoted by officers wearing their hats sometimes lengthways, and sometimes crossways. They were surprised when we informed them that they might on the parade wear their hats as they pleased, and that no distinction of rank was denoted thereby. They also asked how the sailors wore their hats. The magistrate then said, that it would be interesting to the inhabitants of the capital to be enabled to form a notion of the tall stature of the Russians, and therefore wished to have us measured, to which we immediately agreed to. But the curiosity of the Japanese was not yet satisfied. They wished to have our portraits taken in full length. Teisuke, who knew how to draw, was appointed to execute them. He drew them in India ink, but in such a style, that each portrait would have passed for that of any other individual, as well as of him it was intended for: except the long beard, we could trace no resemblance in them. The Japanese, however, sent them to the capital, where they were probably hung up in some of their galleries of pictures.

Two days before his departure, the officer came to our prison, as he said, for the purpose of taking leave of us, and observing how we lived, in order that he might communicate some information to the government on this particular. He assured us that he would do all in his power to bring our affair to a happy end, and took his leave, after having wished us good health. At the end of December he departed from Matsumae, taking along with him the commander of Kunashir, his deputy, the officer who had given us the letter at Iturup, and the Ainu interpreter who had served us in our communications with the Japanese on that island.

After his departure we hoped we should be allowed some rest. But our expectations were quickly disappointed. The more progress Teisuke made in his knowledge of the Russian language, the more trouble he gave us. He was, however, a kind and generous-hearted creature. He frequently informed us of things at which Kumajirō had never hinted. And the latter frequently checked him when he thought he was too unreserved in his communications. Teisuke was evidently more attached to us than any other Japanese. He seldom visited us without bringing along with him, as a present, something he considered a dainty. And we had to thank him for many of the favors we experienced from the magistrate. We now learnt that Teisuke filled the office of secretary to the magistrate, with whom he stood in high favor, and that he exerted all his influence to our advantage, though we frequently quarrelled. Our disputes were chiefly occasioned by his unbounded curiosity, which proved extremely troublesome.

We now thought ourselves fairly rid of all our translations. But the Japanese adhered to their grand maxim that nothing should be done at once, but everything gradually. Teisuke and Kumajirō brought to us the following inscription on Japanese paper: "The Russian frigate *Juno* visited this place, and named this village the Village of Doubt." We were informed that Khvostov had left such an inscription on a copper plate in a pagoda in one of the Japanese villages. They wished that we should explain its meaning. Here we had new difficulties to encounter. How were we to translate this name, Village of Doubt. And why was the place so called? When we succeeded in explaining the word Doubt to the Japanese, they themselves doubted whether they had not misunderstood our meaning, as they supposed it impossible that in such a case the word could have been so applied. We, on our part, were equally unable to form any notion of the sense in which Khvostov had used this phrase. When we assured them that no Russian could explain the meaning of the writer of the inscription, they suspected that we wished to deceive them, and to conceal something that might tend to our own disadvantage. This business occupied us several days. They then wished us to translate an epitaph, which the pilot Lozov had cut upon the trunk of a tree at Nemuro, under which a sailor had been buried who died of the scurvy during the time that Laxman wintered in that place. This task was completed in an hour; for the Japanese had, doubtlessly, been informed of the meaning of this inscription by Laxman himself, and were satisfied on finding that our explanation corresponded with his.

The Japanese kept us constantly employed in translating, with the view of making themselves acquainted with the Russian language, but still more out of curiosity and distrust. They brought to us, for example, a copy of the communication which Resanov had delivered to the Japanese from our emperor. Of the title, in which the Emperor of Japan was mentioned, they could understand only the words "of Japan." They assured us that their emperor had never borne such a title, and were unable to divine what had induced the Russians to make use of it.[3]

When we made inquiries respecting his real title, they told us it was extremely long and difficult to remember. In the same manner they concealed from us their emperor's name. They did not, indeed, exactly refuse to make us acquainted with it. But every individual to whom we addressed ourselves for information on this point gave us a different answer, so that we could never learn his real name. We, however, understood, that, according to the Japanese laws, no subject could bear the name of the reigning emperor, and that every individual who may happen to have the same name as the hereditary prince, is obliged to adopt a new one on his ascending the throne. In the document mention was made of all the presents which had been sent from the Russian court to the emperor of Japan, We had learnt from Captain Adam Johann von Krusenstern's narrative that all these things had been exhibited to the Japanese, and yet our interpreter asked us to give him a description of them. We afterwards found that they had in their possession a minute description of these articles, which not merely pointed out the size and use of each, but likewise mentioned the time and place at which they had been manufactured. They showed us this description, from which they translated several passages. The cunning of the Japanese is truly astonishing. When they wish to discover anything, they put their questions in such a way as would induce a belief that they entertain not the slightest notion of it, and have heard it mentioned for the first time in their lives. If, on the contrary, they fancy they possess sufficient information on any subject, they never pretend ignorance, but frankly acknowledge all they know respecting it.

In addition to the Russian papers of which the Japanese wished to have translations, Teisuke and Kumajirō brought to us a number of other things, and some translations of European books, of which they requested us to state our opinion. They showed themselves most anxious for the translation, and our communication with them on those subjects afforded us many oppor-

3 The confusion over the emperor's identity was the result of the Russians (like many other early foreign visitors to Japan) conflating and confusing of the Japanese (spiritual) emperor, who held court in Kyoto with the *shōgun*, the country's ruler, whose *bakufu* government was located in Edo..

tunities of remarking their distrustful disposition. Among other things, they showed us a Chinese painting, representing the city of Canton, where flags were flying on the factories of different European nations, and they asked us how it happened that the Russian flag was not there. We told them the reason of this, and they then inquired why we had intended to enter a harbor in which there were no Russian merchants. They were not a little astonished, and would scarcely credit what we said, when we told them that in such cases the people of Europe were accustomed to assist each other, to whatever nation they might happen to belong. Teisuke, besides, showed us the drawing of a brass eighteen pounder, which had been cast in Holland. He made a great parade about it, and told us that the Japanese had taken it along with many other pieces of cannon, after a great victory, which they had gained during their last war with the Koreans, about two hundred years ago. We, however, perceived, from a Latin inscription, that it had been cast scarcely a century ago, for the Dutch East India Company. But that we might not put Teisuke to the blush, we expressed much astonishment at the exemplary valor of the Japanese. He, besides, showed us a drawing of the *Nadeschda*, in which Resanov had sailed to Nagasaki, and inquired what was meant by the flag at the stern of that vessel, and other European flags, which Captain Krusenstern had probably hoisted for the purpose of ornamenting his ship. But we were most of all astonished on seeing some charts, which had been executed by the Japanese, whom Resanov brought with him from Petersburg, and which described the course of the vessel. On these maps were marked Denmark, England, the Canary Islands, Brazil, Cape Horn, the Marquesas Islands, Kamchatka, and Japan: in a word, every sea through which they had sailed, and every coast they had visited. The distances and situations of places were, it is true, quite inaccurate. But when it is considered that these men were, probably, only common sailors, that they executed these charts from recollection, and that the situation of the sun was their only guide in determining in what quarter of the world they were sailing, this inaccuracy is no proof against the general capability of the Japanese.

Teisuke informed us that a number of Japanese translations of European books had been sent from the capital, in order that we might examine them, and pronounce our opinion of them. He added that as nothing had yet been decided in our favor: the magistrate did not wish to distress us, but merely requested that we would compare three of these translations, and that the rest might remain until he received orders for our liberation, in case we should then have time to inspect them. The following are the titles of the three books Teisuke named: Count Maurice Benyovszky's *Conspiracy and Escape from Kamchatka. An Account of the Expedition of the Russians and English to Holland in the year 1799*, and *Geography of the Russian Empire*.

Teisuke paid but little attention to the two first mentioned books, but he read the last from beginning to end. We constantly found it necessary to make observations and contradictions on this work, which was a description of Russia at a period in which the country was in a very crude state; though the remarks it contained were for the most part correct, they related to our ancestors, and not to us. The Japanese, who adhere to their old laws and customs with a most extraordinary pertinacity, were unable to conceive how a whole nation V could have undergone so great a change in such a short period.

Our religion was likewise a subject that excited the curiosity of the Japanese. Teisuke requested, in the name of the magistrate, that we would make him acquainted with the doctrine of our faith, and on what it was founded. As a reason for making this solicitation, he said that the governor of Nagasaki, the place visited by the Dutch, was very well acquainted with their religion, and it would be very discreditable to the governor of Matsumae to return to the capital without being able to state any particulars respecting our's.

We were very willing to communicate to them the moral tenets of the Christian religion, the ten commandments, and to give them some notion of the evangelists. But this was not what the Japanese wanted. They told us that these principles were not peculiar to Christians, but that they were common to all individuals who had good hearts; and that the Japanese themselves had long been familiar with them. They most particularly wished to be made acquainted with our form of worship, as their countrymen who had been in Russia had frequently visited our churches, and had written down all the observations they made respecting the liturgy. They asked us why the priests several times opened and shut a door, and what was contained in the goblets they brought out, etc. But these were circumstances which, with the limited means we possessed of making ourselves understood, we found it impossible to explain. We, therefore, observed, that in order to make them acquainted with the secrets of our faith, it was necessary either that we should speak Japanese perfectly well, or they understand Russian better. And that, since both parties were deficient in these requisites, we dared not undertake to communicate with them on matters of such importance; since they might probably imbibe false notions of our religion, and even be led to regard as ridiculous things that are sacred. But we did not thus get rid of the importunity of the Japanese. They continually repeated their questions concerning our mode of worship. And we were, at length, compelled positively to declare, that we would not converse on these matters until we were fully competent to understand each other.

Even Alexei was not left unemployed. The Japanese endeavored to extract information from him respecting the Kuril Islands, of which they made him draw maps in the best way he could. Alexei blotted abundance of paper, and furnished ample contributions for the geographical depots of the Japanese. To account for their applications, they said that their laws required that they should seek information from all foreigners who visited them, and observe and write down everything, whether true or false, which they might be told. They alleged, that by comparing the different accounts they thus received, they were enabled to separate truth from fiction, and to derive much advantage from this practice.

When we inquired whether any news concerning us had arrived from the capital, the interpreters usually replied they did not know. Sometimes, they assured us that the investigation of our case was going on well, and that we had reason to expect a favorable end. In January, 1812, Teisuke, and afterwards Kumajirō, told us as a secret, that the magistrate had received orders to remove us to a convenient house, and to render our situation altogether more comfortable, and that this change would take place on the Japanese New Year's Day. We had previously received the same information from our guards. But as they had often made statements that were never realized, we supposed that this was only a new invention with which they wished to console us. Yet we did believe the interpreters, and rejoiced not at the idea of the improved accommodation which was promised us, but at the ray of hope of being permitted to return to our country, which such a change of system afforded. We therefore looked forward to the month of February with the greatest impatience.

The magistrate wished to present us with new clothes on the approach of the new year. He, therefore, ordered that some questions should be put to us respecting the colors and materials, and also the form in which we might wish them to be made. We thanked him for his attention, but wished to decline his offer, as we had already a superfluity of clothes, and needed no addition to our wardrobe while in prison. He, however, persisted, and the interpreter took away Khlebnikov's uniform coat for a pattern. After some days had elapsed new clothes were brought to us. Those intended for the officers were made of taffetas, with linings of the same, and wadded. But the dress provided for me was of a green color, while that given to Khlebnikov and Mur was brown. The sailors received wadded cotton clothes of a grey color. The Japanese could not imitate the fashion of our uniforms. They perceived themselves the want of resemblance, and expressed astonishment at the skill of the European tailors.

It became the practice, after the alterations had been made in our prison, for the guards to be constantly beside us: they sat down with us at the fire, smoked tobacco, and chatted. They were in general extremely friendly, giving us comfits, fine tea, and other delicacies. But all this was privately, as they were prohibited from making us any presents without the permission of their officers. One of these men, who spoke the Ainu tongue, told us as a secret that the pelt hunters who ran away from Khvostov on the Island of Iturup had, after the departure of the ship, been found drunk on the shore, and killed by the Ainu. The Japanese government was very much displeased with this. For though they might have ordered them to be executed, they believed their premature death had deprived them of much important information, which might perhaps long since have brought about a reconciliation between Russia and Japan.

We learned likewise, that an Aleutian, named Jacov, had escaped from Khvostov, at Sachalin, and had died there, some time since, of the scurvy. His statements were calculated to contribute not a little to our justification; for he maintained, that the Company's ships had attacked the Japanese without any superior authority; declaring, that he was assured of this by all the Russians who were on board of those vessels. His hatred of Khvostov was carried so far, that he painted him in the blackest colors, and had requested the Japanese officers to furnish him with a musket, in order that he might lie in wait for the Russian commander, and shoot him when he came on shore, in revenge for the injuries he had received from him. The cause of this violent hatred was his having on one occasion been flogged for drunkenness, by order of Khvostov. According to Alexei's representation, the Japanese themselves, and not the Ainu, had killed the pelt hunters— the latter certainly would not have committed that atrocity of their own accord. As a proof of his statement, he related the following story, which, though certainly deciding nothing for the truth of his asseveration, deserves, on other grounds, to be mentioned here:

The Japanese had for several years carried on war against the Ainu inhabiting the mountains in the northern parts of Hokkaido. Unable to subdue them by force, they resolved to obtain their object by artifice and treachery. They accordingly made proposals of peace, which the Ainu accepted with the greatest joy. And it was agreed between the parties that the treaty should be publicly celebrated. The Japanese built for that purpose a large house, and to an entertainment given in it, forty of the Ainu chiefs, and a number of their bravest warriors, were invited. The Ainu, who are fond of ardent liquors, were easily prevailed upon by their new friends to drink deeply. The Japanese, on their part, feigned intoxication, and gradually withdrew. When they were all out of the house, the doors were closed, and the Japanese murdered their guests, by shooting them with arrows, through apertures that had been prepared for that purpose in the walls. They then cut off the heads of the Ainu, salted them, and sent them to the capital as trophies of victory.

This was a relation that could not have failed to excite horror in men at perfect liberty. What feelings, then, was it not calculated to rouse in us, who were actually in the power of a people capable of perpetrating so perfidious and atrocious a deed? Poor Alexei excused himself for not having given us this information before, by saying, that he was afraid it would render us uneasy. He added that he could describe several similar transactions of the Japanese, but that he saw this first relation had not particularly gratified us. We smiled at his simplicity and observed that as he had already told us the worst, we wished to hear the rest merely to satisfy our curiosity. Alexei, however, did not rightly comprehend us, and retained his idea that his narrative had displeased us.

Meanwhile February arrived, and the Japanese new year commenced, but we heard not a word of the promised house. We supposed that the Japanese, who were busy keeping their holidays, could not find time to think on us, and therefore did not expect the fulfilment of their promise before the middle of the month. Our expectation was not only deceived, but our situation was rendered worse than it had been. We were supplied with nothing but rice and salted fish for our meals. During the first five or six days of the festival, neither the interpreters nor any officer visited us. When we saw the former, we reproached them with having deceived us. Kumajirō assured me that the reason we had not been removed to the house was that the fish at that season approached the coast and that all the inhabitants were, from morning till night, so busily engaged in the fishery, that no men could be found to clear away the snow, which had nearly buried up to the roof the house allotted for us, as it had been all the winter unoccupied. This excuse was truly laughable, for it was difficult to believe that in a town, the population of which amounted to fifty thousand men, could not be found to do this work. It now appeared to us absolutely certain, that the Japanese practised deception for the purpose of tranquillizing us, and gradually reconciling us to our fate. We spoke our minds frankly on this subject to the interpreters. But they laughed, and assured us that we were laboring under a mistake. While this uncertainty prevailed respecting the house, the magistrate took the opportunity of conferring upon us two favors: he sent us some of our books to read, and razors that we might shave ourselves. Our beards were very long, and their growth was at first exceedingly disagreeable, but we were now accustomed to the inconvenience. Khlebnikov and I refused to avail ourselves of the permission to shave, especially as it was required we should perform the operation in the presence of an officer and other guards, lest we should commit suicide. The Japanese at first left it to us to shave or not as we pleased, but when they found that Khlebnikov and I did not use the razors, they intimated a disposition to compel us, telling us that the magistrate wished to see us without our beards. We replied that it was the magistrate's duty to do us justice and that for that purpose it must be indifferent to him whether we appeared before him with or without beards.

At last we learned from the interpreters that our case did not stand in the most favorable situation in the capital. Teisuke told us that all the officers in Matsumae, and even all the inhabitants of that town, were convinced of the truth of our declarations. But the members of the supreme government were not of the same opinion, and believed that the interpreter Kumajirō did not sufficiently understand Russian to give a correct translation of our answers and our memorial, particularly as his version of the latter was in several passages totally unintelligible. We asked Teisuke what he thought the government intended to do with us? He answered that it was not exactly known, as nothing was yet decided on. Many were of opinion that we would be set at liberty. We plainly perceived that it was his wish to save us from complete despair, but his assurances afforded us little consolation. In a consultation, we all concurred in opinion, that' there was no hope of our being set at liberty by the Japanese; flight, therefore, was the only means of deliverance. But Mur, and the two sailors, Simanov and Vassiliev, would by no means consent to adopt this desperate course, though Khlebnikov and I did all we could to persuade them. We explained to them that it was not impossible to escape from the place of our confinement to make ourselves masters of a vessel on the sea shore, and then, with the help of Heaven, to proceed either to Kamchatka or the coast of Tartary, as circumstances might render necessary. We represented that, instead of lingering and wasting away our lives in prison, it would be far more glorious to die at sea, the element to which we had consecrated our lives, and in which, every year, so many of our brother sailors were buried. We allowed the undertaking to be difficult, but not totally desperate and impracticable; since storms and waves had repeatedly driven Japanese vessels to the Russian coasts, why, we asked, might we not hope to reach the point to which we should be steering? But all our arguments and representations were in vain. Mur absolutely refused to enter into our design, and, together with the two sailors, turned a deaf ear to all our persuasions. In the hope that they might one day or other be induced to undertake the. execution of this project, we began to collect a store of provisions. Unperceived by our guards, we daily laid by a portion of our boiled rice. And, during the night, when it had become dry, deposited it in small bags.

An Escape Plan

Meanwhile the spring season commenced. The days became longer, and the cold, which gradually diminished, was superseded by the genial rays of the sun. At the commencement of March, we were, by order of the magistrate, frequently permitted to walk in the yard. On the 4th of that month Teisuke informed us that it would be much better were we permitted to go to the capital, where we might have an opportunity of convincing the members of the government of the truth of our memorial, and of interceding for our liberation, as it was very doubtful whether that object would be attained without our personal appearance there. He added that every individual in the capital entertained the conviction that Khvostov had acted by command of the Russian government, and that our sole object in visiting them was to inspect their harbors, with the view of afterwards overwhelming them with a greater force.

We, besides, learned from Teisuke another circumstance, which was of the utmost importance to us. He told us that Khvostov, during his first attack, had carried off some Japanese, whom he detained at Kamchatka during the winter. In the following year he landed them on the Island of Lissel (Rishiri Island), giving them a paper addressed to the magistrate of Matsumae, which would be shown to us in course of time. Teisuke either could not or would not inform us by whom this paper was signed. But as the Japanese had already, as we believed, shown us every bit of paper on which any Russian words were written, even the prayers distributed by the Ainu, and had anxiously required translations, and yet had made no mention of this paper, it appeared to us that it must be a declaration of war, or some other important document of Khvostov. It seemed to us highly probable that Teisuke was acquainted with the contents of this paper, and that the Japanese concealed it from us, under the supposition that they could, in the end, fully convict us of deception. What then could we urge in our justification. Teisuke had no sooner quitted us, than Mur declared that he perceived plainly all the horrors of our situation, and was ready to attempt his escape along with us. And Simanov and Vassiljev expressed the same determination.

One thing only remained doubtful, whether it would be prudent to trust Alexei with our secret and persuade him to escape along with us, or whether we should leave him behind. We feared to make him acquainted with our design, lest he might betray us. On the other hand, we were distressed at the idea of abandoning him, to endure the hard punishment the Japanese would not fail to inflict upon him. We at first resolved to leave a letter, addressed to the magistrate, assuring him of Alexei's innocence. Mur, however, advised us to make him acquainted with our plan, and to take him along with us, as we might find him extremely useful, owing to his knowledge of the various roots and herbs which were fit to eat, and his experience in navigating the waters of that part of the world. We accordingly unfolded our design to him. He at first testified the utmost amazement, changed color, and was unable to utter a syllable. But he quickly recovered himself, declared that he was as good a Russian as any one of us, that he acknowledged the same God and emperor, that whether we were right or wrong, he was ready to escape along with us, and though we might be swallowed up by the waves, or put to death by the Japanese, he would share in every misfortune we might encounter. We were not a little astonished at Alexei's resolution and firmness, and we now began to deliberate on the means of carrying our design into execution.

There were two ways by which we might succeed in escaping from our confinement. Two of the soldiers who were set to guard us usually sat sound asleep by the fire until midnight, and some of the rest were so addicted to drinking strong liquors, that they frequently came to us in a state of intoxication, when they supposed there was no danger of their being detected by their superiors. During the night, and taking advantage of a favorable wind, it would be easy suddenly to seize our guards, and bind and gag them to prevent their giving any alarm. We might then gain possession of their swords, and climbing over the fence into the hollow, we might cautiously reach the seashore, and there endeavour to make ourselves masters of a vessel in which we might sail to the coast of Tartary. This project, however, appeared impracticable, and we accordingly laid down another plan. At midnight our guards, having closed our doors, were accustomed to retire to the guard room, were they generally fell asleep, without thinking it necessary to watch us with that degree of rigor they had at first observed. At the further corner of their guard room was a small door, which was kept fast locked and sealed. But as we had in our possession a large sharp knife, we might cut through the beam to which the hinges were affixed, and having effected our escape from the guard room, we might soon cross the fence, or wooden wall, by means of a ship-ladder which we had made out of a sailcloth hammock. In order not to be totally unarmed, we intended, before the execution of our enterprise, to make some pikes out of the long poles on which our linen was hung to dry after it had been washed.

We waited with impatience for the first favorable night to attempt the execution of our plan. At length, on the 8th of March, the wind began to blow from the east, accompanied by fogs and rain, and we were persuaded that if it continued without change for a few days, we might reach the Tartar coast, in case we succeeded in gaining possession of a vessel. At the approach of twilight we began secretly to make preparations unperceived by our guards. But night had no sooner set in, than the clouds dispersed, the stars began to twinkle, and the wind changed to the west. We were thus compelled to postpone our attempt.

Two days after, the wind again blew in a favorable direction, and the weather was as fine as we could have wished it to be. Khlebnikov expressed a hope that on the following night, with the help of Heaven, we should attempt the execution of our plan, when, to our great astonishment and vexation, Mur replied, that he would neither dissuade us from our purpose, nor do anything to prevent our carrying it into effect. But that, for his own part, he was resolved to submit to the destiny that awaited him, and never to make any attempt towards effecting his own liberation. We endeavored to prevail on him to resume his former determination, and conjured him to reflect on the inconsistency of his conduct. But all our representations were of no avail. He replied, with ill humor and warmth, that he was no child, and knew very well how to act, that he would place no obstacle in the way of our escape, which we might effect without him, and desired us never more to mention the business in his hearing, since all our arguments and persuasions would be to no purpose.

From that moment a complete change took place in the behavior of Mur. He avoided entering into conversation with us, and when we spoke to him he would answer us briefly, and sometimes even with rudeness; though, to the Japanese, he adopted quite an opposite mode of conduct. He began to imitate their customs: he no longer addressed the officers in the European way, as he before used to do, but spoke to them as if they had been his superiors, and even treated them with a degree of awe and veneration that excited the amazement and laughter of the Japanese themselves.

In this critical situation I scarcely knew how to act. I determined on requiring that Mur should promise, on oath, not to make known our escape until the morning after it should have taken place, and that in return we would leave behind us a letter to the magistrate, and would pledge ourselves, in case of our being taken, to declare that Mur had no knowledge of our enterprise. The sailors, however, were of opinion that no reliance could be placed on Mur's assurances. In support of their assertion, they related so many things respecting this officer, that I was at length convinced it would be unsafe to trust him in these important circumstances. The interpreter having assured us that, when the warm weather set in, we should be permitted to walk about the city, escorted by a party of Japanese, we resolved to delay the execution of our enterprise, in the hope that we might likewise be conducted to the outskirts of the city, where we might find an opportunity of effecting our liberation by force; we should then have had no reason to fear Mur. He had not hitherto manifested any intention of discovering our design to the Japanese. We therefore pretended that we had, like him, relinquished every thought of escaping, and had come to the determination of patiently awaiting the fate destiny had allotted for us; though he did not change his suspicious conduct.

In the meanwhile we formed an acquaintance with a geometrician and astronomer, named Mamiya Rinzō, who had been sent from the Japanese capital. The first time he came to visit us, he was accompanied by our interpreter, who informed us that he had shortly before quitted Edo, from where the government, by the advice of a physician, who was skilled in the European practice, had sent us some medicines to prevent the scurvy, a disorder which is extremely frequent and dangerous in Japan. These medicines consisted of two flasks of lemon juice, a number of lemons and oranges, and a considerable quantity of dried herbs, of very fragrant smell, and which, according to the directions of the Japanese, we sprinkled in our soup. The magistrate, besides, took this opportunity of sending us three or four pounds of brown sugar, and a box full of red pepper in husks, boiled in sugar, of which the Japanese are very fond. But we quickly discovered that these presents were intended to persuade, or rather to force us to communicate to the Japanese geometrician our methods of taking nautical and astronomical observations. To this end he was continually making solicitations. He showed us his instruments, which consisted of an English sector, and astrolabe, with a compass, a case of mathematical instruments, and quicksilver for forming the artificial horizon, and requested that we would show him how the Europeans employed these things. He visited us every day, and frequently remained with us from morning until evening, during which time he gave us an account of his travels, and produced his plans and sketches of the different countries he had visited. We inspected them with the greatest curiosity. The Japanese looked upon him as a very learned man. They always listened to him with the utmost attention, and wondered how he could have travelled to so many different places: he had visited all the Kuril Islands, as far as the seventeenth, Sachalin, and even the land of Manchuria, and had sailed through the river Amur. He manifested his pride by a constant boasting of the deeds he had performed, and the labours he had endured. In recounting his adventures, he showed us his travelling pan, in which he cooked his food during his journies. He daily stewed or boiled something on our fire, and treated us with it. He had a small still, with which he made spirits from rice, and which was kept constantly going. He drank freely of the liquor himself, and shared it as readily with us, to the no little satisfaction of our sailors. He could ascertain the sun's height, from the natural or artificial horizon, with his sector, and knew how to find the latitude of a place by observing the sun's altitude at noon. In his calculations he used some tables of declination, and other helps of that kind, which he said had been translated into Japanese from a Dutch book. As we had none of our tables in our possession, we could not well decide on the accuracy of those he employed.

Mamiya Rinzō communicated to us several pieces of interesting information, the authenticity of which we verified by a comparison with the statements made by other Japanese, and an account of which cannot be indifferent to our government. I shall take another occasion of mentioning these communications.

Soon after our first acquaintance with this man, we learned that he was not only celebrated among the Japanese for his learning, but was regarded as a most distinguished warrior. He was in the island of Iturup at the time that Khvostov landed, and fled with some other soldiers to the mountains. He was hit by a Russian ball, and received a flesh wound, from the effects of which he soon recovered. It was a fortunate wound for him, since it was the means of procuring him promotion and a pension. He declared that after Khvostov's attack, the Japanese had it in contemplation to send three ships to Okhotsk, in order to raze that place to the ground. We used to laugh at this boast, observing that we were sorry the Japanese had not sent thither thirty, or even three hundred ships instead of three, as we were certain none of them would ever have got back. He, on his part, appeared offended at this observation, and asserted that the Japanese were not inferior in war to other nations. I must here remark, that this was the first Japanese who ventured, in our presence, to swagger and assume importance on account of his military skill, and his vaporing made not only us but even his own countrymen sometimes laugh at him. He had heard that besides ascertaining the latitude by the sun's altitude, the longitude could be found by lunar and astral observations, and wished us to show him how that was done. We were unable to comply with his request, as we had not the necessary tables, and could not make ourselves understood on such subjects with all the assistance of our interpreters. He showed great displeasure at our refusal, and said that Japanese men of learning would soon arrive, with Dutch interpreters, from the capital, to extract explanations from us on scientific subjects, and that we would be compelled to answer their questions.

This news was not very consoling, for it indicated that the Japanese intended to force us to give them instructions. Mur had voluntarily offered his services in that respect, but had declined teaching mathematics on the ground of inability. He instead advised the Japanese to resort to Khlebnikov for instruction in the mathematical sciences, as he was well acquainted with those branches of knowledge.

Though Mamiya Rinzō was decidedly inimical to us, we were not always engaged in disputes with him; on the contrary, we conversed together in an apparent friendly manner on various subjects, among which the political was the most important. He maintained that the Japanese had well founded reasons for believing that the Russians entertained evil designs upon them, and that the Dutch had spoken truth in their information respecting several European courts. Teisuke was not of this opinion. He believed that the Dutch had designedly infused suspicion among the Japanese government against the Russians and the English. They asserted that these two nations, then united against France and her allies, had determined to extend their power towards the east; that England acting by sea, and Russia by land, and reciprocally supporting each other, had for their ultimate object to divide China and Japan between them. As proofs of this intention, the Dutch cited the progress those nations had in a short time made in their approaches towards Japan; Russia being in possession of Siberia and the Aleutian Islands, and England of India. Captain Broughton, who twice visited the Japanese coasts, and on both occasions had intercourse with the natives, performed these voyages at the time when Russia and England were at war with France and Holland. According to Teisuke's statement, the Dutch then asserted that the English were examining the Japanese harbors with the view of afterwards attacking them. We protested that this notion was groundless, and endeavored to explain to the Japanese the real cause of Captain Broughton's visits to their coasts, which was well known to the Dutch, and also to convince them that the false representations of that people originated in selfishness and jealousy, as they were afraid that the Japanese might consent to a commercial intercourse with England and Russia, whereby they would be deprived of the immense advantages they derived from their fraudulent traffic, and the sale of trifling articles at a most exorbitant price. Teisuke agreed with me, and appeared firmly persuaded that the representations of the Dutch proceeded solely from avarice and envy. But Mamiya Rinzō still retained his favorable opinion of them. On this occasion,

Teisuke gave an account of a transaction that had rendered the Japanese government so inimical to the English, that he was of opinion, if a ship of that nation arrived on the coast, the crew would be liable to be dealt with as we had been. One or two years after Resanov's departure, a large ship, under Russian colors, appeared at the entrance of the harbor of Nagasaki. Some Dutch and Japanese were, by order of the magistrate, sent on board, where the former, one excepted, were detained; the latter, and the Dutchman, were directed to return ashore with a notification that the vessel was an English ship; that the rest of the Dutch were kept on board in consequence of the two nations being at war, and that they would be carried off as prisoners, unless the Japanese supplied the ship with a certain number of bullocks and pigs. While waiting for an answer, the English sailed up and down the harbor in boats, and made soundings. Meanwhile the Dutch persuaded the magistrate to pay the ransom demanded, and the Dutchmen were sent on shore. The magistrate had to atone with his life for his conduct in this affair. And orders were immediately issued to act hostilely against the English wherever they might be found.

On our remarking that the Dutch cheated the Japanese by selling them wretched merchandize at high prices, Teisuke replied that the Japanese government was perfectly sensible of that. But, notwithstanding, would not alter the old arrangements. In our conversation on this subject, he related the following anecdote. The war with England having prevented the Dutch from trading direct to Japan, they freighted ships in the United States of America, with valuable cargoes for Japan. These ships entered Nagasaki under the Dutch flag. The cargoes were delivered before the Japanese began to take particular notice that both these ships and their crews differed very much in appearance from the vessels and seamen they had been accustomed to see. But suspicion was in particular excited by the superior quality of the goods, which were, in fact, all English. The *bakufu*, on discovering this, immediately ordered the ships to be reloaded and dismissed from the harbor.

About the middle of the month of March, 1812, the magistrate gave us permission to walk about the town and its environs. We twice made excursions to the distance of four leagues, accompanied by five or six *bakufu* soldiers, and three or four of the principality soldiers, under the direction of one of the interpreters. Besides this escort, we were attended by several servants, who carried our tea equipage, *sake*, mats, and not unfrequently provisions for our dinner. A police officer from the town was also attached to our escort; he preceded us, and pointed out the road we were to take.

The Japanese often took us four kilometers from the town to the hills, and along the sea coast. We perceived that it would not be difficult to break loose from our guards, by using their own arms. The question was, where should we then fly. We resolved to wait for an opportunity when there should be a vessel on the coast, to which we might push off. And for that reason we always requested the Japanese to take us along the shore. We did not forget, at the same time, to carry our supply of provisions with us. Mur, who could not fail to conjecture our design, told the Japanese that he felt pain in his feet, and begged they would not go so far from the town.

At the latter end of March, the interpreter and our guards again informed us that we should soon be released from our confinement, and that we were only kept in prison until the completion of the necessary repairs in the house designed for us. Soon afterwards Kumajirō requested that Mur would describe to him, by a drawing, in what part of their houses the Russians place images of their saints, in order that some might be put into our new residence. We laughed at this, and assured him that the Japanese might fix up the images wherever they pleased. But Kumajirō repeated his solicitation, and Mur at length gave him a drawing. We soon learned that Kumajirō had really made a very serious matter of it, for everything was arranged precisely according to Mur's drawing.

On the morning of the 1st of April, the Japanese began to remove our things to the house, and at noon we were conducted before Magistrate Arao Shigeaki at the castle. In the presence of all the chief officers of the city, he informed us that we were now to be released from our imprisonment, and lodged in a fine house, which had previously been the residence of a Japanese officer, that we should live in a much better style than before, and that we ought therefore to regard the Japanese as our countrymen and brothers. With these words he withdrew.

A New Home

From the castle we were conducted to the house that had been prepared for us. It was situated opposite to the southern gate of the fortress, between the rampart and a sloping rock, at the foot of which the middle quarter of the city was built. It had a pretty extensive yard, and was surrounded by a wooden wall, or fence, with *chevaux-de-frise*. The yard was divided by a wooden fence into two separate parts, one of which was appropriated to us. In this place, three or four trees and a few shrubs were planted. And the Japanese, in drawing our attention to all the elegancies of our new dwelling, called it a garden. There was a puddle of dirty water in the further corner of the yard, which they styled a lake, and a hillock of mud in the centre was intended to represent an island.

From this yard, or garden, a small door, which was always closed, communicated with the adjoining yard. It was only opened when the commander of the Tsugaru soldiers or one of the officers came to inspect our yard, or when we were led out to walk. At sunset our guards began to walk their rounds at every half hour. The gate leading to the road next the rampart was in the other part of the yard, and was only closed during the night. Our house was divided by wooden palisades into two separate parts, each of which communicated with the corresponding half of the yard. One half of the house contained three apartments, which were assigned to our use, and separated from each other by screens.

The other part behind the palisades was occupied by a party of soldiers, and an officer of the *daimyō* of Tsugaru, by whom we were guarded. They could observe all our motions with the greatest ease. And there was besides a door, which communicated from their part of the house to our's, but which was always closed. These soldiers, in addition to their swords and daggers, were armed with guns and pikes. The officer was constantly seated near the palisades, looking into our apartment. Besides this guard room, there was another little chamber, in which two *bakufu* soldiers were stationed, who were occasionally relieved, and who could likewise see ail that passed in our apartments. The door that led from their chamber to our lodgings was closed only at night. These soldiers were frequently with us in the course of the day. They sometimes visited us during the night, when we were first removed to our new abode. Behind these guard rooms, and in the same part of the house, were chambers for the servants, kitchens, and storerooms. The part of the house we occupied was surrounded by a balcony, or gallery, from which we could see over the fence, and could descry towards the south the Straits of Tsuruga, the opposite coast of Japan, and the masts of several vessels lying close in shore. Through the openings in the fence we could discover the vessels themselves, together with a part of the city. On the northern side we had a view of the castle and the hills of Hokkaido.

Our residence was in various respects changed for the better. We could at least enjoy the sight of the sky, the stars, and many other objects. We could, when we chose, walk out into the yard and enjoy the fresh air. We had before been debarred from all these comforts. Our food was likewise considerably better. But, notwithstanding this, we were inconsolable whenever we recollected the last words of the magistrate. He desired us to regard the Japanese as our brothers and countrymen, and mentioned not a word about Russia, as he had before been accustomed to do. He had formerly used every effort to console us, by appearing to take an interest in our behalf, and promising to exert all his influence to facilitate our return to our native country. But he now told us to look upon the Japanese as our countrymen. We could construe this in no other way than that we must make up our minds to remain in Japan, and banish every thought of Russia. But we had firmly resolved that such should not be our fate. We had even bound ourselves by an oath, that, whatever might be the consequence, we would attempt either to liberate ourselves by force from the power of the Japanese, or to escape secretly during the night. We had all, with the exception of Mur, formed a determination to perish rather than remain forever in Japan.

When the Japanese officers and the interpreter came, according to custom, to congratulate us on our removal to our new abode, they immediately observed that the house had not made the impression upon us they expected, and that we were as dull and melancholy as ever. We perceive, said they, that your change of residence has not contributed to cheer your spirits, and that all your thoughts are bent on returning to Russia. Though the Japanese government has not yet come to any decision on your case, yet the magistrate, when he visits the capital in the summer season, will use all his influence with the government to obtain your freedom, and to send you home. Teisuke, who had repeatedly assured us of the interest the magistrate took in our case, on this occasion mentioned to us a circumstance that determined us on attempting our escape before the commencement of the summer.

It appeared that the magistrate had, a short time before, received a letter from the capital, which he opened in the presence of Teisuke. On reading it he let it fall from his hand, and his face evinced the deepest agitation and distress. When Teisuke inquired the cause of his emotion, he replied that the government had paid no regard to his representation. Instead of granting him permission to maintain a friendly understanding with the Russian vessels that might in future approach the Japanese coasts, he had been directed to burn them, and make their crews prisoners. The *daimyō* of Nambu had accordingly, been ordered to provide a considerable detachment of troops, under the command of a distinguished general, with artillery and ammunition, and to strengthen the fortifications, and reinforce the garrisons of Kunashir and other seaports. Then, we exclaimed, war is unavoidable. And the Japanese, and not the Russians, are the guilty promoters of bloodshed. War will doubtless ensue, replied Teisuke, but it will not last forever: whenever peace is concluded, you will be set at liberty. Set at liberty! thought we; yes, when our bones have rotted in Japan. We were well aware that the harbor of Okhotsk did not contain so considerable a force as would compel the Japanese to come to a reconciliation; for this purpose, it would have been necessary to send an expedition from the Baltic. And the practicability of that event depended on the peace with England. All these things required time, and time might banish all recollection of our case.

These considerations urged us to attempt the speedy execution of our project, and, if possible, to effect our escape before the arrival of any Russian vessels, as we reflected that, when they came within sight of the Japanese coasts, our guards would probably be doubled, or we might again be shut up in our cages.

Teisuke used every endeavour to console us. He assured us that if the new magistrate should be as kindly disposed towards us as Arao Shigeaki had been, he might, in consequence of the personal intercessions his colleague would make in our behalf, easily give another turn to our affair. The new magistrate was expected in two months. But the Russian ships might appear in the interim. As they had no reason to expect a friendly reception from the Japanese, they might probably themselves be the first to adopt measures of hostility. We, moreover, learned from Teisuke, that the new magistrate would bring along with him the secret paper Khvostov had sent to the Japanese, and which had not yet been shown to us.

In the meanwhile the Japanese were constantly questioning us on various subjects. This was chiefly by the advice of Mamiya Rinzō. We learned from Teisuke that this man had become our irreconcilable enemy; that he had declared to the magistrate that our arrival at Japan was not accidental, but that we had been sent thither for the express purpose of acting as spies. We were not informed of all the arguments he adduced in support of his assertion. But those which Teisuke mentioned to us were highly ludicrous. For instance, it appeared to him a very suspicious circumstance that we should have along with us a letter of credit for five thousand *piastres*, which were to be paid by an English merchant at Canton: he was fully persuaded that some improper motives must have induced us to make provision for so much foreign gold, which might be brought to Japan. He therefore inquired the name of the merchant, whether he had ever been in Russia, whether he spoke the Russian language, etc. Teisuke assured us that, though Mamiya Rinzō had not succeeded in altering the good opinion the magistrate entertained of our conduct, yet his representations had had a considerable effect in the capital, where not only the government, but the greater part of the people were prejudiced against us.

In the meanwhile the interpreters neglected no opportunity of making themselves acquainted with the Russian language, and they took notes of everything they learned. They frequently mentioned the men of learning who were to come in the suite of the new magistrate for the purpose of conversing with us on philosophical subjects, and making themselves acquainted with the contents of our books. In short, every ray of hope that the Japanese would of their own accord grant us our liberty had now vanished. They had, it is true, ameliorated our condition. But this we attributed merely to their wish of reconciling us to our fate, in order that our lives might be preserved, and they reap the benefit of our instruction.

On this subject we all entertained but one opinion, and our thoughts were wholly occupied with the means of carrying into effect our hazardous enterprise, to which our own companion, Mur, proved the greatest obstacle. This unfortunate circumstance rendered our situation doubly wretched. He was, as it were, transformed into another being. He no longer regarded himself as a Russian, and assured the Japanese that all his relations resided in Germany, etc. His conversations with the interpreters proved to us what we might expect from him. Alexei secretly informed us that Mur had acquainted him with his design of entering the Japanese service as European interpreter, and had advised him to do the same, for which he promised him his protection when he should become a distinguished man. It was evident that he was to us a very dangerous person, and this was an additional reason for inducing us to hasten the execution of our project.

Had we been all of one mind, an attempt to escape might easily have been carried into execution. Though the Tsugaru soldiers scarcely ever fell asleep during the night, yet they concerned themselves but little about us, and usually sat by the fire smoking tobacco. Their whole duty consisted in going every half hour round the yard, and striking the hour. The officer, it is true, always sat near the palisades, yet he seldom looked into our apartment, and was almost constantly occupied in reading. As for the *bakufu* soldiers, they strictly fulfilled their duty at first, but they afterwards slept during the whole of the night, or amused themselves with reading or playing at cards or draughts.

We might easily, at midnight, have crept one after another into the yard, previously taking the precaution to place some of our clothes on the beds, and covering them up beneath the quilts, from which it would appear that we were still lying soundly asleep. There was an aperture under the fence, through which the water ran off from the yard: this opening might easily have been increased so as to admit of our creeping through it. We must then have stolen softly through the town, until we reached the shore, from where, in a small boat, we might row to one of the vessels we had observed during our walks, and on gaining possession of it put to sea. But to insure the success of such an enterprise, it was necessary that a brisk wind should be blowing from the land. And Mur, who suspected our design, watched us closely at every motion. We therefore thought it impossible to make an attempt of this nature without his participation, as he would have immediately discovered our flight and raised an alarm among the guards. None of the inhabitants of the city being permitted to go out at night without lanterns, to elude the observation of the patrols, it would be requisite to creep cautiously along the streets, which would at least have required several hours, and before that time our escape would probably have been prevented. We therefore abandoned all thoughts of carrying this design into effect.

We had, however, formed two other plans. Instead of proceeding to the shore, we might ascend a mound covered with trees, which formed a kind of glacis, behind the ditch on the western side of the fortress; for, during our walks, we had observed that no guards were stationed either on the rampart or the glacis, but that, within the gate of the garrison, two soldiers only were seated in a large guard room, who were usually amusing themselves by smoking tobacco. From the glacis we might gain a long alley of high tree, and from thence enter the city graveyard, which was situated in an extensive plain that stretched along the side of a deep valley. After passing through the cemetery we should be in the open fields, about the distance of two kilometers from the hills. It would then require three days to be spent in crossing the hills in a northerly direction, in order to reach the coast, there to await the opportunity of making ourselves masters of a vessel. Our other plan was to break from our guards by force, in case, during our walks, we should meet with a ship near the shore.

We gave the preference to the latter scheme, as we reflected that whilst we were crossing the hills, the Japanese might gain time to issue orders for keeping a strict watch over their ships. But this project was likewise extremely uncertain, since it required the combination of two circumstances; namely, a brisk favorable wind, and the meeting with a vessel suited to our purpose. Though we had no time for delay, yet we resolved to wait for a day or two, in the hope that an opportunity might arise to enable us to carry the latter plan into execution.

In the meanwhile we made every possible preparation for our departure. In one of our walks in the outskirts of the city we found a piece of steel, which one of the sailors picked up, under pretense of drawing up his boot, and slipped it into his pocket. We likewise found means to provide ourselves with some flints, unperceived by our attendants. The fragments of an old shirt, which we threw upon the fire as if by accident, served us for tinder: we besides daily increased our store of provisions by secreting a portion of our allowance. These were merely economical arrangements. But we did not, on the other hand, neglect to make warlike preparations. We found amongst the grass in our yard a large sharp chisel, which had probably been left behind by the carpenters who repaired our house: we immediately hid it, and resolved, on the first favorable opportunity, to fasten it to a long pole, in order that it might serve as a pike. To a similar purpose we destined a spade, which had been left by accident in our yard, and which we carefully concealed. But this was not all: the proverb that necessity is the mother of invention, was fully realized, for Khlebnikov even managed to make a compass. We requested our attendants to let us have two large needles for mending our clothes, and afterwards pretended that we had lost them. The Japanese sometimes fasten together the beams of their houses with copper; this had been done in our house, although the copper was very rusty. Khlebnikov cleaned a piece of this copper, in the middle of which he bored a hole, so that a needle might be placed upon it: by frequently rubbing this needle on a stone which he selected for the purpose, he succeeded in magnetizing it, and finally gave it such a degree of polarity, that it pointed with tolerable accuracy towards the north. The case was composed of a few sheets of paper pasted together with rice. This compass cost Khlebnikov much labour, and he was, besides, obliged to proceed with the greatest caution. Had the Japanese observed him rubbing the needle against the flint, they would never have guessed his real design, but would probably supposed that he was sharpening the point. But it would have been impossible to deceive Mur. It was therefore so arranged, that whilst

Khlebnikov was at work in a corner of the yard, one of our party always walked up and down, and gave him a signal when any suspicious person approached. The Japanese now took us out to walk more frequently than before, and the interpreters, or some of the inhabitants of the city, often invited us to call on them, and gave us refreshments. According to the Japanese laws a native cannot receive strangers into the body of his house, and we always entered under the pretense of being so fatigued by our walk, that it was necessary we should rest awhile. We generally found everything prepared for our reception, and we took our seats in the galleries, which were previously spread with clean mats. According to the Japanese custom, they presented to us tea, tobacco for smoking, *sake*, sweet cakes, fruits, etc.

One day, as we were walking along the beach, we came up with two fishing boats. As it were, in fulfilment of our wishes, a sloop chanced to be lying at a short distance from the shore. I deliberated with Khlebnikov, but the execution of our enterprise seemed so doubtful, that we deemed it imprudent to make the attempt. Whilst we were contending with the soldiers, the fishermen might have rowed off from the shore. And even had we succeeded in getting on board their boats, it would have been extremely uncertain whether or not we could have gained possession of the vessel. Mur, who watched every motion we made, immediately understood what was passing in our minds. On our return home, Alexei secretly informed us that we were in the greatest danger, as Mur had ordered him to reveal our design to the Japanese, and had threatened to do so himself in case of his refusal. Alexei asked us whether we were determined on attempting our escape, and if so, entreated that we would not leave him behind us. I must here observe, that we had not made Alexei acquainted with our last plan, fearing lest he might be terrified at the thought of so desperate an undertaking, and consequently be induced to betray us. We, besides, observed, that he was engaged for several hours every day in private conversation with Mur, and this circumstance roused our suspicion. Mur was probably uncertain whether or not we had entirely relinquished our project, and thrown away our store of provisions. Had he made so important a communication to the Japanese without being able to prove what he asserted, he would have been overwhelmed with shame by such an act of treachery towards his unfortunate companions, who had neither the will nor the power to do him harm. If by any miracle we had all safely returned to Russia, what would have been his feelings, after such conduct! These reflections, doubtless passed within his mind, and convinced him that he must have incontestable proofs of our design, before he could venture to disclose his suspicions to the Japanese. It appeared, therefore, probable that he wished to make Alexei the instrument for obtaining those proofs. Khlebnikov, indeed, was of opinion, that this Ainu was sincerely attached to us, and that we might safely trust him with the secret. But I did not think this altogether prudent.

The sailors were all averse to making him a participator in the business, and assured us that Mur, by his representations, had alienated him from us, and drawn him over to his side. In such a situation as our's it was necessary to consult the feelings of all. We therefore followed the advice of the sailors, and told Alexei that we had for that time abandoned all thought of escaping, but that we might perhaps think of it again on the return of summer, and asked him how he supposed we could best execute our purpose.

In order to remove suspicion from the mind of Mur, we told him we still wished to escape, but that we had resolved not to go without him, and would not make any attempt until after the arrival of the new magistrate. We added that we wished to know the contents of Khvostov's paper, and to see how the new magistrate should be disposed towards us, and that he might by that time probably change his mind, and like us resolve to venture everything. Mur replied, that his determination was totally independent of any information the magistrate might bring, and that he had resolved to remain in Japan. We were happy to find that our dissimulation had the desired effect: Mur seemed perfectly satisfied, and no longer kept a watchful eye upon us. The reader will no doubt pardon this conduct, when he considers what a web of wickedness, cunning, and calumny, had been woven around us, can we be condemned for dealing thus with our faithless companion, who would for his own selfish purposes have hindered us from escaping eternal imprisonment, and returning to our native country?

At length the 20th of April arrived. The time was near at hand when we might expect our ships to reach Japan, supposing that the *Diana* had sailed from Okhotsk to winter in Kamchatka. To all appearance it was vain to look forward to an opportunity of forcibly breaking from our guards, and getting on board a vessel. In the meanwhile some little imprudence on the part of our sailors had probably occasioned Mur to renew his suspicions, for he now began to watch us with as much circumspection as before. We again deliberated on what we should do. The coasts of Hokkaido are thickly covered with villages of various sizes. We knew that vessels and boats were lying on every part of the shore. We reflected that these vessels might be strongly armed and guarded. But then Heaven assists the bold, and force must be opposed to force.—We determined to make our escape into the mountains.

On the 23d of April, we were conducted to the outskirts of the city to walk. Under pretense of mere curiosity, we requested the Japanese to lead us to a pagoda, which stood near the cemetery, and which had recently been built after a fire. We had thus an opportunity of observing the footpaths we might pursue in the course of our flight.

It may be here observed, that the island of Hokkaido is entirely covered with hills. The ground is nowhere level, except on the coast, and at short distances from the base of the mountains, which raise their summits in every direction, and are separated from each other by deep ravines. This extraordinary chain of mountains, which is high and low by turns, extends over the whole island, the midland parts of which are uninhabited. All the Ainu and Japanese villages lie along the coast.

As we passed through the fields we gathered wild leeks and garlic, in such great quantities, that Mur, who thought we wanted it for present use, could have no idea that we were on the eve of making our escape.

On our return home, we felt extremely fatigued, and threw ourselves on our beds. During the twilight the sailors entered the kitchen, and carried off two knives without being perceived. About half an hour before midnight, Simanov and Skajev stole into the yard, and concealed themselves under the steps. When twelve o'clock struck, and the Tsugaru soldiers had gone their rounds, they began to make a hole under the fence, through which we all (Mur and Alexei excepted) crept one after another. I stumbled in going out, slipped down, and struck my knee against a stake which was sunk in the ground close to the opening. The blow was extremely violent, but the pain soon diminished.

We found ourselves on a very narrow path between the fence and the hollow, so that it was with the utmost difficulty we succeeded in gaining the high road. With hasty steps we then passed between the tree, crossed the mound and the cemetery. In about half an hour we reached the foot of the first hill we had to ascend.

Proceeding in our hazardous enterprise, we began, at the distance of about two miles from the shore, to climb the hills, and endeavored, wherever it was possible, to direct our course towards the north. The stars served to guide us. Whilst we were ascending the first hill I felt a violent pain in my knee, which in a short time swelled prodigiously. When we proceeded along places which were level, I could, with the assistance of a stick, walk without much difficulty. But I experienced severe pain either in ascending or descending, as I was then obliged to tread heavily with the leg which had been hurt. Being thus unable to make an equal use of both feet,

I was quickly overcome with fatigue. My companions were, therefore, under the necessity of stopping every half hour, in order that I might recover myself, and ease my knee by resting. Our object was to reach, before daybreak, some hills, along which a thick forest extended, in order to conceal ourselves from the observation of the enemy; for we had now reason to regard the Japanese as implacably hostile to us. During our walks in the vicinity of the town, this forest appeared to us to be at no considerable distance, but we soon found how greatly we had mistaken its situation. We could trace no footpath leading directly to the forest, and we therefore advanced straight forward. Owing to the darkness of the night, we could see no farther than a few paces around us, and we sometimes unexpectedly found ourselves at the foot of a steep precipice, which it was impossible to climb. We had then to search for a more practicable road, which, when found, we continued to ascend until new obstacles presented themselves.

In this way we spent three anxious hours, and having at last gained the summit, we proceeded northward along the level height. But fate had everywhere thrown interruptions and difficulties in our way. At the height we had now reached, the snow lay in some parts extremely thick, and the Japanese might easily have traced our footsteps across it. We were therefore obliged to search for such places as were not covered with snow. In doing this we crossed from one side to the other, and frequently turned back, by which we were greatly fatigued, and advanced but slowly. About an hour before daybreak we unexpectedly found ourselves proceeding, in a direct line, for the forest, along a good road, which the Japanese had made for the purpose of conveying wood to the city on packhorses. This road was thickly imprinted with the tracks of horses and men: there was no snow upon it, and therefore the Japanese could not trace our footsteps. It led in a straight northerly direction, and passed over the level summits of the hills. We were not a little delighted at the discovery, and advanced with increased rapidity. I still felt much pain in my knee, and through the whole of my leg. But as we were walking on level ground, it was nothing to equal that which I experienced when ascending the side of the hill.

We hoped shortly to reach the forest, in the heart of which we intended to pass the day. But the sailor, Vassiliev, who accidently looked behind him, suddenly exclaimed, "they are pursuing us on horseback with lanterns."

With these words he quickly descended into a hollow on one side of the road. On looking round, we perceived some lights, which appeared to be at no great distance from us. We immediately followed the example of Vassiliev, and precipitated ourselves into a deep hollow. We descended to a considerable distance, without finding either a tree or thicket under which we could conceal ourselves, and day was already beginning to dawn. Had it been broad daylight we might easily have been observed from any of the surrounding hills. We at length reached the bottom of the hollow, which was on every side overhung with naked precipices. The hollow itself was covered with thick snow, but no place of concealment presented itself, and the sun had now completely risen.

We stood still for a few moments, not knowing how to proceed. At last we perceived a small aperture in a rock, and on approaching it, found that it was a cavity that might, perhaps, though with difficulty, contain us all. A waterfall, which descended from the hill, and passed by the side of this cavity, had hollowed out a pit about ten feet deep almost directly under it. We were enabled to get near the cavity by advancing along the snow, which was very high on the one side. This hole, in which we hoped to find shelter, was situated in the side of a rock, about nine feet from the bottom of the hollow, but the cataract had driven away so much of the snow, that it was with the greatest difficulty we could reach the aperture, our only assistance in climbing being a small tree growing beside it. Had any of us missed a step, or had the tree failed to support our weight, we might have been precipitated into the pit, from which we could not easily have extricated ourselves. With my lame leg, it would have been next to impossible for me to have got out. Yet we succeeded in reaching the hole in safety. When in it, we found that we had not sufficient room to sit down. And our grotto was, besides, half rilled with a kind of sand stones, of which the whole hill was composed. Many of the stones lay with their sharp points and edges upwards, and we dared not to stir without the greatest caution, as there was a considerable slope towards the mouth of the hole. Had any of the stones given way we might have rolled out along with them. We could neither lie down nor stretch out our feet, but were obliged to rest ourselves first on one elbow and then on the other. In other respects our hiding place was well adapted to our purpose. The Japanese could not have traced us to it from any distance, for fortunately a keen frosty morning had so hardened the snow that our footsteps were no longer visible. But there was one circumstance that excited our apprehension: our companion Skajev, as he was descending the hollow, lost his cap, which he had himself made out of a worsted stocking. Had it been picked up by the Japanese, they would have immediately recognized it as a part of our wardrobe, and it might perhaps have assisted them in discovering our asylum. We were, besides, afraid that the rays of the sun might melt the snow at the entrance of the cavity. And in that case we should have found it impossible to get out, as even in the morning we could not reach it without considerable difficulty.

In this situation we remained until sunset, reflecting on our fate, and deliberating how we should proceed. The day was extremely clear, but the rays of the sun did not penetrate to our retreat, and the neighboring waterfall increased the coolness of the atmosphere, so that we frequently shivered till our teeth knocked against each other. During the whole day we distinctly heard the sound of hatchets in the forest, which was at no great distance from us. At sunset we peeped out of our hole, and saw a number of people on the hills. No other remarkable circumstance occurred, except that we heard a rustling noise, as if somebody had been slipping down the hill towards us. The noise became louder and louder. We even fancied that we beheld soldiers in search of us, and prepared for our defense, when we suddenly perceived a wild deer. But the animal no sooner smelt us than it darted off at full speed.

When the stars began to appear we left our hole, and proceeded northwards to a high hill, which was here and there overgrown with underwood. My situation was dreadful. Whilst we were in the cave I had constantly kept my lame leg in one position, and therefore experienced but little uneasiness. But when I attempted to walk, and particularly to ascend the hill, the pain, which was not confined to my knee, but extended from the heel to the hip, was unbearable. I endured the utmost agony in climbing this hill, and we had yet many more to ascend. The circumstances of our case required that we should advance without loss of time. Finding that I retarded my companions, and that I might perhaps occasion them to be overtaken by their pursuers, I entreated that they would abandon me to my fate, and proceed without me, but to this suggestion they would not listen. I represented that, from the commencement of our enterprise, fate had destined me to suffer, by rendering me incapable of following them. I begged that they would not sacrifice themselves for my sake, as I only occasioned them to linger. And from the excruciating pain I endured, they must, sooner or later, leave me behind. But they were not to be prevailed on by my entreaties. They all protested that so long as I lived they would not abandon me, and that they would stop to let me rest at every quarter of a mile. And that, when they reached a safe place of concealment, they would stop for two or three days, during which time I might recover the use of my leg. Makarov besides offered to assist me in climbing the hills, if I would go behind him, and hold by the skirts of his jacket or his girdle. In this manner I resolved to follow my companions. I was unable to walk, and was dragged along by the sailors. Having ascended another hill, we reached a level covered with bamboo reeds and grass of the preceding year. Here we rested for a short time, and then advanced in a northerly direction, taking the stars for our guides.

The night was calm and clear, and the snow-topped hills, which we had yet to ascend, shone in the distance. The level eminence which we were now crossing was separated from the adjoining hill by a ravine of extraordinary depth, which we thought it imprudent to descend during the night, as we might have experienced considerable difficulty in extricating ourselves from the abyss. Instead, therefore, of advancing straight northwards, we turned a little towards the west, and proceeded along the edge of the ravine, in the hope of finding some convenient place for crossing it. Our embarrassment was not of long duration. We soon discovered a kind of mound, which appeared to be indebted to art for its existence, and which connected together the summits of the hills, which were otherwise separated by the precipitous ravine. It was on account of its magnitude only that it could be regarded as a production of nature. As we were proceeding onward, we discovered, as we supposed, two huts, and at intervals heard the sound of a pipe, resembling that which is used in Russia for alluring quails. We stooped down among the grass, and for a long while listened attentively, without knowing whether the sound proceeded from a bird, or from some hunters, whom we suspected might be in the huts. We at length resolved to advance, being well aware that their number could not be so considerable as to prevent our resisting them with success in case they attacked us. On approaching, we discovered that what we had in the dark taken for huts were merely two heaps of poles. We armed ourselves with some of these poles, and then pursued our course.

On reaching the next hill we discovered a wide road leading to the north, along which coals and wood are conveyed on packhorses to the city. We observed plainly that this road had not been trodden during the present spring, though we perceived in all directions fires, which were doubtless kindled for making charcoal. The sides of this road were overgrown with thickets and high grass, among which we lay down to rest at midnight, for owing to the sharp stones with which the cave was filled, we had not enjoyed a moment's repose during the day. We slept for two or three hours, and then resumed our course. From the summit of the hill we descended, by various turnings and windings, into a small valley, which was watered by a little stream, on the surface of which the ice and deep snow were in many places sufficiently strong to bear our weight. We now lost sight of the road, and proceeded over the snow in an oblique direction across the valley, in the hope of finding the road again. But our attempt was unsuccessful. Instead, we discovered a footpath leading to the summit of a hill, which was higher than any we had hitherto crossed. As the precipice was extremely difficult to ascend, and we frequently found it necessary to stop to rest ourselves, we did not reach the summit until day was about to dawn. We then found a convenient resting place, where we resolved to halt for the day. We crept in among the thickest of the bushes, and for the sake of a little warmth lay close to each other, as the morning was extremely cold, and our clothing was not calculated to protect us from its influence. We did not lie in this place above two hours. And we suffered so severely from the cold, that to sleep was quite impossible.

When daylight was completely set in, we arose to take a view of the objects around us. We found ourselves on a lofty eminence, which was on every side surrounded by mountains. Those towards the south were somewhat lower than the one on which we stood, but those to the north were, on the contrary, considerably higher. Hills, forests, and snow, were the only objects which met our eyes; yet the prospect was sublime. We observed that the tops of all the hills were enveloped in mist, and we consequently concluded, that if we kindled a fire among the bushes it would not be perceptible from any of the surrounding eminences. We therefore resolved to try the experiment, for the double purpose of warming ourselves and boiling our kettle (we had not forgotten to bring along with us a copper kettle, which our attendants had, by a lucky chance, on the night of our escape, left on the hearth in the room where the sailors slept). Not indeed to make tea, for we had none with us, but to warm and render more palatable our rice, which was by this time dry and moldy. We likewise searched for wild herbs, but in vain, for among these hills winter still raged with the utmost severity. We collected some dry twigs, kindled a fire, and warmed some snow water, which we sucked up with small bamboo reeds, and ate the rice along with it.

In the meantime some heavy clouds arose behind the hills from the east, and the wind began to howl among the rocks. The clouds spread in every direction, and the wind blew with more and more violence. A storm appeared to be gathering. Persuaded that we should now meet nobody among the hills, and that our pursuers therefore could not discover us, we resolved to proceed without waiting for night. We were, moreover, induced to adopt this resolution on account of the extreme cold, from which, notwithstanding the fire, we suffered most severely.

We proceeded straight northwards, along the footpath that had been traced on the ridges of the mountains. This path soon inclined to one side, and at length turned completely round; we therefore abandoned it, and pursued our course among the thickets. The declivity of the hill, which was covered with snow, soon conducted us into a hollow. The pain in my foot had not in the least abated, and I was dragged along, holding by the girdle of Makarov. When we were descending the precipice, the violence of the pain forced me to sit down on the snow, and slide along. In doing this I guided my course with the pole to which the chisel was fixed, which also served to diminish the velocity of my motion where the declivity was very abrupt. Contrary to our expectations the storm did not arise, the clouds dispersed, and all the surrounding hills became perceptible.

This did not induce us to alter our determination, and we still continued to advance. On reaching the hollow, we discovered on the banks of a little rivulet two or three earthen huts, but there was nobody within them. We waded through the water, and again ascended a hill, which had the advantage of being covered with trees, against which we frequently rested, and by which we were at the same time concealed from observation.

Having ascended to a considerable height, we suddenly found ourselves at the foot of a steep rock, which we could not climb without the greatest difficulty and danger. I had nearly reached the top of the rock, when I found myself under the necessity of loosening my hold of the girdle of Makarov, who otherwise, overburthened as he was, would not have been able to have gained the summit. I therefore placed the toes of my sound foot firmly against a stone, and throwing my right arm round a young tree, which was so much bent down that it inclined almost to a horizontal direction, I resolved to wait until Makarov should reach the top, and be able to release me from my perilous situation. But, powerful and vigorous as Makarov was, his great exertions had so overcome him, that he no sooner reached the summit, than he fell to the ground almost in a lifeless state. At this moment, the stone against which I had rested my foot detached itself, and rolled to the bottom of a deep hollow which the rock overhung. I was thus left hanging by one hand, without the possibility of obtaining any other support, owing to the excessive smoothness of the rock.

The rest of the sailors were at no great distance, but fatigue rendered them unable to afford me any assistance. Makarov still lay stretched upon the ground, and Khlebnikov was laboring to climb the rock at another point. Having remained in this dreadful situation for several minutes, my hand began to smart severely, and I was on the point of ending my sufferings by precipitating myself into the gulf, more than a hundred fathoms beneath me, when Makarov, suddenly recovering, beheld my situation, and hastened to my assistance. He rested his foot upon a stone that projected from the rock under my breast, and with one hand grasped a branch of the tree. With my hand that was free I then seized his girdle, and, by a great effort on his part, I was drawn to the top of the rock. We were no sooner both safe, than Makarov again fell down in a state of insensibility. Had either the stone or the branch of the tree given way, we must both have been precipitated to the bottom and have perished.

In the meanwhile, Khlebnikov had climbed to the middle of the rock, when such obstacles presented themselves that he could neither move backwards nor forwards. The sailors immediately tied together the sashes they wore as girdles, and, having lowered one end until he was enabled to take hold of it, drew him from his perilous situation.

We rested for a short time on the top of this rock, and then proceeded to ascend the next hill, on the submit of which we perceived, in the distance, an earthen hut, or something resembling one, which we supposed would afford a convenient shelter for the night. Before sunset we reached the summit of this hill, one of the highest in Hokkaido: it was overgrown with reeds, between which the snow lay very deep, and only a few scattered trees were to be seen. Contrary to our expectations, we found no earthen hut. But we were convinced we were now secure, as the Japanese would not look for us in that terrific spot. We immediately kindled a fire, and prepared a supper, consisting of wild garlic and sorrel, which we had gathered on the banks of the river through which we had that day (April 25th) waded. We likewise dried our clothes, which were completely soaked, as the water had in many places been more than knee deep. Towards night we collected some reeds and built a hut.

Having eaten heartily of boiled herbs and a portion of our store of provisions, we laid ourselves down to rest, as night had already set in. In consequence of the extreme fatigue we had undergone, we quickly fell asleep. My repose was not, however, of long duration: being oppressed by the excessive heat of our hut, I awoke and walked out into the open air. I leant myself against a tree near the hut, and the majestic image of nature which I then beheld excited all my admiration. The sky was clear, and numerous black clouds were floating around the nearest hills. It probably rained in the plains. The snow glistened on the tops of the mountains in the distance. I never saw the stars shine with such brilliancy as on that night: a deadly stillness prevailed around me.

But this sublime spectacle vanished when I suddenly recollected our situation, which now presented itself to my mind in all its horrors—six men on the summit of one of the highest mountains in Hokkaido, without clothing, provisions, or even arms, by the help of which we might have obtained something to save us from starvation, and surrounded by enemies and wild beasts, wandering over a strange island, uncertain whether or not we should succeed in gaining possession of a vessel. And I in a state of lameness which occasioned the severest agony at every step. To reflect on so helpless a condition, was indeed to be verging on despair. In the meanwhile some of my companions also awoke, and their sighs and prayers served only to increase my distress. I forgot my own misfortunes, and shed bitter tears for their unhappy fate. In this situation I remained for upwards of an hour, when the cold forced me again to take refuge in the hut. I stretched myself upon the ground but to sleep was impossible.

We arose at daybreak, (on the 26th of April) kindled a fire, cooked some wild garlic and sorrel, ate our breakfast, and then continued our journey. We now resolved no longer to climb the hills, but to pursue our course along the banks of a little stream, which flowed in a westerly direction, and then to turn towards the north, to await on the seashore an opportunity of getting on board a vessel. We descended into a deep valley below the hill, and directed our course towards the west, along the side of the stream. But the road we had chosen was by no means an easy one. The stream frequently flowed with violence between narrow cliffs of rocks, which we could not pass without the greatest difficulty and danger. The least slip of the foot would have plunged us into the water, and we should have been carried down by the current, and dashed to pieces against some of the projecting masses of rock. In addition to this, we were compelled at every quarter of a mile, and even at shorter distances, to wade across the rivulet, as the banks on one side were frequently so steep that it was impossible to walk along them. Whenever we found it necessary to cross from one side to the other, we, of course, chose those parts in which the water was shallow, and flowed with little violence. But we frequently found it, even with the assistance of poles, difficult to resist the force of the current. The depth of the stream was various, sometimes reaching to our knees, and at other times above our waists.

Having travelled in this way to some distance, we discovered on the banks of the rivulet several empty huts, which during the summer season had been inhabited by woodcutters and coalburners. We entered them and searched for provisions, but we found only an old hatchet and a chisel, both completely covered with rust, and two lackered cups, which we carried away. The day was clear and excessively warm. We therefore resolved, though the sun had not yet set behind the hills, to pass the night in one of the huts, in which we found a stove for making charcoal. We were afraid to kindle a blazing fire, lest it should be perceived by the Japanese: we, however, made one sufficiently large to roast some wild garlic, lysimachia, and sorrel, and to dry our clothes. We then lay down to rest in the hut, of which one half of the roof had fallen in, so that we slept, as it were, in the open air. The night was extremely cold. But from this we did not suffer much inconvenience, as we lay among straw, with which we completely covered ourselves.

On the following morning, the 27th of April, we took our usual breakfast, and pursued our course along the banks of the river. Having proceeded about two miles we discovered a hut, from the roof of which smoke was issuing. To attack the poor inhabitants would have been an unprovoked act of cruelty. And we, besides, thought it imprudent to show ourselves, lest they should give our pursuers information respecting us. We, therefore, ascended a hill, which was covered with thickets, and proceeded westward. We then descended by a footpath into a valley, where at noon we seated ourselves by the side of a little brook, and ate some beans and rice.

On reaching the summit of another hill, we observed various roads leading to the seaside. The hills in this part of the island were entirely barren, without either bushes or high grass, and crossed by paths in various directions. The weather was so extremely clear, that we observed a dog running along a footpath on a distant hill. It seemed imprudent to advance, as owing to our number and size the Japanese might easily have recognized us, and yet we were unwilling to lose time. Our object was to reach the coast by the evening, and, after having taken a little rest, to proceed along the shore during the night. We therefore resolved to advance separately, stooping down, and keeping a strict watch on every side. We accordingly turned back about the distance of a mile, and reached a hill somewhat lower than the rest. But here we were still in danger, for it would have been easy to see us from the highway which lay along the shore. We therefore sat down among the grass, and deliberated on the most prudent mode of pro-ceeding. At that moment we discovered a party of soldiers on horseback, who were galloping along a footpath, in a direction towards us. We crept immediately into a hollow, and hid ourselves among the bushes, with which it was on both sides covered, and the soldiers rode past without perceiving us. We were now convinced of the danger of proceeding across the hills; for had we not been sitting down at the moment the soldiers were riding up the hill, we should doubtless have been discovered and taken.

The valley in which we had concealed ourselves was watered by a small brook, the bed of which was dirty, and filled with decayed roots and leaves. We stirred up the mud, and found some small crabs, about half an inch in length, which were indeed calculated rather to excite disgust than to provoke appetite. But we ate them with as much pleasure as if they had been the most exquisite dainties. Having sat about an hour in the valley, we resolved to advance in it as long as we should find bushes capable of concealing us, and to endeavour to regain the hills by some other road. The valley led straight towards the sea. We walked on for upwards of a mile, and came to a spot that could be seen from various roads. We therefore seated ourselves amidst shrubs and reeds. There we found several fine young trees, some of which we cut down to make pikes, fastening our knife to one, the chisel to another, and merely cutting the ends of others into sharp points with the hatchet we had found in the hut, and with which one of the sailors was armed. Whilst we were busy at this work, we suddenly heard the sound of voices approaching. They appeared to proceed from some persons on the other side of the valley. Khlebnikov, who at this time was seated the highest up of any of us, saw a number of working people pass by, among whom were several women.

When it began to grow dark we resumed our journey, and at night reached the shore, along which we proceeded in a northerly direction. I cannot state with any precision at what distance from the city we reached the shore. Whilst we were ascending and descending the hills, we frequently found it necessary to take a lateral direction, and even to turn back, by which means we made but little progress, though we had passed over considerable spaces of ground. From the situation of two small uninhabited islands, which we observed on looking towards the shore, and which we had before seen at Matsumae, we concluded that we were about twenty miles from the city.

We had scarcely advanced to the distance of a kilometer, when we unexpectedly found ourselves in front of a village, which was built beside a steep rock, a circumstance that accounted for our not having sooner perceived it. We immediately halted, fearing to proceed, lest guards might be stationed in the village. But finding that the rock was extremely high, and difficult to climb, we resolved at all hazards to venture onwards. We succeeded in passing unperceived: even the dogs never once barked at us. We found here two boats, which were good in their kind, but too small for our purpose, and we proceeded, in the hope of falling in with some larger vessels.

This occurrence afforded us much satisfaction. We were convinced that the villages were not all so strictly guarded as we had supposed. In the course of the night we passed with equal boldness through one or two other villages, near which we saw several boats, but they were all too small. Besides, the road along the shore was not so passable and good as we had at first supposed. There was a large plain between the hills and the beach, which was frequently intersected by hollows through which streams and brooks flowed from the hills into the sea. When the direct course towards the sea was obstructed by perpendicular rocks, the road passed along the plain through the hollows, in which the ascent and descent were very steep, and exceedingly difficult. We frequently lost the footpaths, particularly in the valleys, where the soil was usually composed of gravel and sand, and we sometimes knew not how to get out of them. We often spent whole hours in searching for the road, and when we did not succeed in finding it, we were compelled to climb the heights in the dark with the greatest difficulty and danger. There was in general no trace of footsteps left among the sand in the hollows, and we were obliged to go forward, trusting to chance for finding an outlet. But we frequently found our progress stopped by rocks, which it was necessary to avoid by making a circuit, or to attempt to surmount at the risk of breaking our necks.

At daybreak, on the 28th of April, 1812, we again turned back to the mountains, where we proposed to remain during the day. When the sun had fully risen we found ourselves upon a high hill, which was totally barren, and consequently afforded us no means of concealment. We at length discovered some bushes in a hollow, and tearing up others from different places, we fixed them into the ground, and crept in beneath them. Unfortunately there was neither water nor snow upon this hill, and we suffered excessively from thirst. On the other side of the hollow, and opposite to us, was a path leading to a wood, along which we frequently observed men and packhorses going backwards and forwards, and saw them so plainly, that had the former been our acquaintances, we should have found no difficulty in recognizing them. They did not observe us, though a glance directed towards that part of the hollow in which we had taken refuge would inevitably have betrayed us.

We were busily employed during the whole of this day. We stitched our shirts together for the purpose of forming two sails, and made all the necessary appurtenances out of the ropes and pieces of woollen cloth we had carried off with us. There was a village at no great distance from our hiding place. And as evening approached, we observed that one of the vessels sailing along the coast anchored near it. We resolved, in case the wind should prove favorable, to board the vessel that very night.

At sunset we descended the hill, and proceeded towards the shore. But as we approached the vessel, we heard a noise and the sound of voices on board. We withdrew, intending to wait until the dead of the night before we attempted the execution of our enterprise. But we soon discovered that the vessel was weighing anchor, and that the noise was occasioned by that labour. Our design was therefore frustrated, and we pursued our course along the shore.

We had this night many more obstacles to contend with than on the preceding. The hollows were more numerous and deeper, and we frequently found it necessary to wade through streams. Towards midnight we arrived at a village of considerable size. We at first wished to pass along the principal street. But we found it extremely long, and we besides heard the guards striking the hour with their boards. We then proposed going round the outside of the village. But the kitchen gardens were so large, that we must have made a very considerable circuit. We therefore proceeded across the gardens, and left traces of our footsteps behind us, which must have been remarkable on account of their size.

We found it inconvenient to wear the Japanese shoes, and requested that we might be furnished with leather, as one of the sailors, who understood the shoe-making business, could make boots for us. The Japanese gave us seadog's skin for the legs, and the hide of bear's heads for the soles. Out of these materials Simanov made a kind of peasant's boots, called Siberian *torbasses*. They were extremely large, and the traces of our sailors' footsteps were twice the size of those of the Japanese. It might, therefore, easily be guessed who imprinted the marks we left behind us.

On the shore we observed several large fires, and at first were at a loss to conjecture what was meant by them. We imagined they were intended as watchfires for the soldiers. But we soon discovered that they were signals for the vessels sailing past the coast, for they were lighted up immediately upon lanterns being hoisted on board the ships.

On the 29th of April, the morning dawn drove us to the adjoining heights. At sunrise we found ourselves on the summit of a high and barren hill, which afforded us no place of refuge. We perceived on every side footpaths, along which the inhabitants passed from the villages to the forests. We turned to the opposite side, and entered a deep woody valley, in which there was a brook. We seated ourselves in a concealed place, and kindled a fire to dry our clothes and warm us, for the weather was extremely cold and windy. And having gathered some wild garlic and water angelica, we cooked and ate it. These herbs were none of the most palatable, and without the addition of other food, such as a handful of beans or rice, we could not possibly have eaten them. I lost all appetite, though I drank considerable quantities of water wherever it was to be found. We now began to consider how we should furnish ourselves with provisions. And our situation rendered it necessary that we should search for a convenient place in the forest, where we might repose and recover our strength, which, owing to want of sustenance, and excessive fatigue, was nearly exhausted. Unfortunately for us, the hills at a certain distance from the shore were completely barren.

On the eastern side of Matsumae the coast is covered, to the very margin of the sea, with wood, and we concluded it would be the same on the western side. But we found, on the contrary, that from the shore to the centre of the island, the woods were almost all cut down for the sake of procuring firewood and coal. The Japanese consume great quantities of wood and charcoal, as they have no stoves, and keep fires constantly burning on the hearths. As the winter is both severe and of long duration, the extensive population renders a great supply of coal and wood necessary.

The scarcity of wood on the hills on the western side of Matsumae proves that the Japanese must have first established themselves on that part of the island, and have afterwards extended themselves to the east. The city of Matsumae is supposed to be four hundred years old.

At every three kilometers there were villages, whose inhabitants were, during the day, continually going backward and forward to the forest. In the daytime it was impossible to conceal ourselves close to the shore, and we were obliged, before sunrise, to hasten across the hills into the forest, and when night approached again to direct our weary steps towards the sea. When we reached the beach, we were usually so overcome with fatigue, that we were scarcely able to move along. We wished to procure a supply of provisions. But we determined that nothing but the most urgent necessity should induce us to resort to measures of violence, which might irritate the Japanese, and give them reason to guard their coasts more strictly. Our great object was to obtain, as speedily as possible, possession of a vessel, confident that it would, according to the Japanese custom, be plentifully supplied with provisions and fresh water. We likewise resolved, when we should be passing through the villages, to search for the spot where the Japanese lay out their fish to dry, or, if possible, to catch two or three horses in the fields carry them into the forest, and kill them, and live upon their flesh.

At sunset we quitted our hiding place and proceeded, as usual, to grope our way to the coast. The obstacles which we before had to contend with were now increased; the valleys were deeper than any we had hitherto met with, the rivulets flowed with violence, and in wading through them the water frequently rose above our waists. In addition to this the rain poured in torrents, so that we found it impossible to lie down on the grass to rest.

We this night encountered two adventures. Close to the shore, at some distance from us, we beheld a flame, which suddenly vanished at our approach. On reaching the spot where we had seen it, we discovered an extremely high rock, but neither hole nor hut from which flame could have issued. It was perhaps merely the effect of illusion.

We now descended into a deep valley, from where we had to ascend to the level summit of a hill by a steep, winding, and well-beaten footpath, when we met with an accident which not a little distressed us. Khlebnikov slipped his foot and fell into a hole. We once heard him stop, but he again rolled further down, and at length we knew not what had become of him. He returned no answer to our questions, and we dared not call loudly, as there were villages within hearing of us. The night was so extremely dark that no object could be recognized at the distance of ten paces. We tied our girdles together and, fastening the one end about Vassiliev, let him down into the hole into which Khlebnikov had fallen. We lowered him gradually as far as the length of our united sashes would admit, and then drew him up again. Vassiliev informed us, that, notwithstanding the depth to which he had descended, he could not discover the extent of the hole. And that he called Khlebnikov, but received no answer. We resolved to remain on the spot until daylight, and then to lower another of our party into the hole, to ascertain whether Khlebnikov was yet living.

We remained for two hours, in a state of the most painful uncertainty respecting the fate of our worthy companion. We at length heard a rustling among the grass, and, on looking round, to our astonishment, beheld Khlebnikov. He had first rolled down about two fathoms from the surface, when something stopped him, and he endeavored to climb up again, but slipped a second time and fell perpendicularly into a pit, to the depth of four fathoms. Fortunately, there were no stones at the bottom of the pit, but he was, notwithstanding, severely bruised. He at length succeeded in climbing up the side of the hole, and reached the spot where he surprised us by his unexpected appearance. After having rested for a short time, he again accompanied us on our journey, although he felt severe pain in every part of his body.

Even now, I never look back without horror upon the frightful gulfs and huge rocks of Hokkaido. Millions of money would not tempt me to travel over them again, even in the open day. Whilst we were ascending steep eminences and beheld beneath us on every side nothing but masses of rock and torrents, we were frequently obliged to hold by small bushes, without being certain whether they might not be too weak or decayed. Had any of them given way, those who were trusting to their feeble support must have been precipitated into the abyss below, and dashed to pieces. A loose stone projecting from a rock was frequently our only reliance. But Heaven watched over us, and, excepting Khlebnikov's fall, no serious accident occurred. Our desperate situation made us disregard every danger. We climbed up the steepest rocks without ever thinking on death and with as much indifference as if we had been proceeding along a level road. My only wish was, in case an accident should occur to me, that it might be a decisive one, that my fall might be from such an immense height as would put a speedy end to my suffering.

Before sunrise on the 30th of April, we proceeded towards the hills, and entered a wood, where we stationed ourselves not far from the road. We dared not kindle a fire, though we should have found it extremely acceptable, for the rain, which still continued with violence, had soaked our clothes completely through. We lay down close to each other and covered ourselves over with our sails. In the course of the day, my companions ate some portion of their store of provisions, but I had lost all appetite for food, though I still suffered severely from thirst.

When night set in we again directed our course towards the shore. In all the villages through which we passed we neither found a good boat nor saw any fish laid out to dry. Either the fishing season had not commenced, or the fish had been removed into houses during the night. We saw several horses in the fields, and endeavored to catch one, but they were all so extremely wild that we found it impossible. This night we descended down the side of a steep hill for the purpose of proceeding to the shore. We had scarcely got half way, when we found we were advancing straight upon a village. In the dark we missed the footpath, and mistook a heap of straw for a part of the declivity. We had no sooner set our feet upon it than we rolled down and unexpectedly found ourselves in front of a house and barn. A dog rushed out upon us, but we calmly proceeded on our way, though we were doubtless observed by two men who came out with lanterns.

We all suffered severely from thirst, and never passed a brook without taking hearty draughts of water. But immediately after I drank water I felt myself affected with nausea, and the saliva flowed from my mouth. In the course of half an hour I was usually so overcome with thirst, that on hearing the murmuring of a rivulet at a distance I promised myself a speedy relief, and redoubled my pace in order to reach it quickly. But as soon as I had taken a draught of water the nausea returned, and I was thus alternately a martyr to thirst and sickness, and could eat nothing.

On the first of May we rested on a declivity by the side of a rivulet in a thick wood, near which there was a village built on a sandy point of land. We saw several horsemen and foot passengers cross the stream, on the outside of the wood, and people passing along a road near us.

We were therefore obliged to remain the whole day without fire. At night we again departed, but as we met several men with lanterns, we were obliged to hide ourselves behind the trees until they passed by. On approaching close to a village we heard the hours striking, and, of course, were pretty certain that the place had a guard of soldiers, who, as it was not perfectly dark, might discover us. We therefore determined to halt. In the meantime we observed a mare tied to a tree, in a meadow near the village. We determined to carry her off, and had already cut the rope, when a foal suddenly sprang up, ran about, and neighed loudly. We found it impossible to catch it, and were obliged to run off and leave the mare behind, lest the noise should alarm the Japanese. We returned a short time afterwards, recollecting that the milk of the mare would be extremely acceptable to us. But the sailor who set about milking her received so severe a kick, that we thought it prudent to have nothing more to do with her.

When it grew darker we proceeded along the strand, and came close to a village, from which the dogs rushed out upon us. We were afraid lest the barking of these animals should attract the attention of the Japanese, who would immediately have perceived us, and we sat down behind a heap of sand. The dogs then stood still and growled, but no sooner did we attempt to rise than they flew at us, and by their barking compelled us to resume our station. We were thus obliged to remain in the same spot for the space of half an hour, the dogs having by that time left us; we started up, and passed through the village without any further interruption.

Soon after, as we were passing through another village, we observed a boat in the water, close to the shore, and a tent near it. We advanced to inspect the boat, but Skajev, hoping to find something eatable in the tent, thrust in his hand, and grasped the head of a man who was sleeping there. The man roared out loudly, and fearing that the noise might alarm the inhabitants of the village, and being, besides, uncertain whether the boat would contain us all, we ran off, and concealed ourselves behind some stones. After a short time we dispatched two of our party to take a survey of the boat, but there was a man seated in it, who was looking round him on every side, so we thought it best to depart.

Before we reached the other extremity of this village, we observed a large boat that had been dragged ashore as far as the houses. On examination we found that it was well adapted to our purpose, but it was so far from the water that we despaired of getting it afloat, and we therefore proceeded onwards. We soon after discovered, under a shed on the shore, a very large boat. It was without sails, but was furnished with every other necessary appurtenance, and had even small buckets, in which we might have laid in a supply of fresh water. The wind and weather were moreover favorable. Unfortunately, the boat lay with one side towards the water, and we must consequently have turned it in order to get it afloat, but to accomplish this object we found our strength insufficient. Had either the head or the stern been towards the water we would soon have launched it. And after carrying off a supply of provisions from one of the houses, would have put to sea. But this was impossible; we therefore contented ourselves with merely taking a watering pot we found in the boat, and which we thought would serve us to drink out of.

The approach of the morning drove us once more among the hills. Daylight surprised us on the side of a barren mountain, covered only here and there with a few bushes. We beheld footpaths on every side, and villages along the shore, as far as our eyes could see. A thick forest, in which we might have concealed ourselves, lay at such a distance, that it would have taken us a long time to reach it, so we were obliged to lie down under the bushes around us. The day being fine, we dried our clothes and deliberated on new plans of escape. We were well aware that we could obtain provisions only by forcible means, and that, after having committed violence, we should no longer be in safety, as the Japanese would doubtless redouble their vigilance, and station guards along the coast. All chance, therefore, of getting on board a vessel would have been entirely at an end. We thought it a more advisable scheme to gain possession of a couple of fishing boats, which were to be met with at every point along the shore, and to row to a small island covered with wood, which lay between twenty-five and thirty kilometers from the coast, and which, when we were at Matsumae, we had heard was uninhabited. We might there build a convenient hut, kindle fire when we pleased, and during the day gather, without danger of detection, shellfish and seaweeds for our support. It would thus be very easy for us to wait until an opportunity presented itself, in calm weather, of boarding a loaded vessel sailing past the island. This was a part of our plan, which we were of opinion could be executed without difficulty, as during the three days we had been on this part of the coast we had observed that all vessels and boats passed between the island and the coast of Hokkaido, and it appeared always stood near the island. We were also aware, that in the summer calms very frequently occur in those seas. If this project should fail we still might, during the summer, when the wind is never violent, and almost always blowing from the east, trust to the fishing boats for carrying us to the coast of Tartary, which is about four hundred and six kilometers distant from Hokkaido.

While we were forming plans for our deliverance, an adverse fate was preparing for us. We saw people walking backwards and forwards on the footpaths by which we were surrounded, but it did not appear that we were observed by them. At length, on a hill at some distance, Khlebnikov perceived a woman, who frequently pointed to the place in which we were, and turned round on every side, beckoning with her hand, as if calling on persons to approach her. We soon understood that these signs concerned us, and we descended into a hollow in the hope of escaping through it into the heart of the forest. Before we reached the bottom of the hollow, we found it suddenly surrounded by men, who hastened to the spot from every side, on foot and on horseback. The moment they discovered us they raised a frightful cry. Makarov and I fled to a part covered with bushes, and soon succeeded in getting out of sight. But we could not venture to move farther off, and lay down to wait for our companions, and observe the number of our enemies, and how they were armed. Our first supposition was that they were country people. But to our astonishment we found that they were soldiers, headed by an officer on horseback. They were armed with muskets, and bows and arrows, in addition to their swords and daggers. Our companions were immediately surrounded, and compelled to surrender. From between the bushes we saw the Japanese bind their hands behind their backs, and, after inquiring respecting Makarov and me, lead them towards the shore.

Meanwhile more Japanese had assembled, and a search for us was commenced. Makarov now asked how we should proceed. Perhaps, said I, the Japanese may not discover us today. And, when it is dark, we may find our way to the shore, get into a boat, row to the uninhabited island, and from thence to the coast of Tartary. But where were our sails, our tea kettle, our tinder box, and the knife. Those things were with our companions, and all had now fallen into the hands of the Japanese. We had only two pikes j mine mounted with the chisel, and Makarov's with a small knife. Nevertheless, I proposed to my companion, that in case we succeeded in eluding the search of the Japanese, we should look out for a fishing boat on the coast, and supply ourselves, by force, with whatever was necessary for our expedition. This was resolved upon.

From the thicket in which we sat, we saw soldiers and peasants searching about for us on both sides of the hollow. At length four soldiers advanced into the centre, two armed with swords, and two with pikes. The rest ranged themselves in rows on each side of the hollow and held their muskets and bows and arrows in readiness. Those who approached us thrust their pikes into every bush capable of hiding a dog. And, at last, came direct upon the one in which we were concealed. When they had advanced pretty near us, Makarov, who observed me seizing my pike, entreated, with tears, that I would not attempt to defend myself, or kill any of the Japanese, as such a proceeding might prove highly injurious to the rest of our companions. He further observed, that I might, perhaps, be the means of saving all their lives if I delivered myself up to the Japanese, and declared that as I, who was their commander, had ordered them to attempt their escape, they were bound to do so, lest they should ever chance to return to Russia, where they would be severely punished for disobedience. These words made so deep an impression on me, that I immediately struck my pike in the ground, rose, and stepped out of the bush. Makarov followed me. The Japanese were filled with amazement at our unexpected appearance. They started back when they first beheld us, but finding that we were unarmed, they advanced boldly, seized us, bound our hands slightly behind our backs, and conducted us to a village on the shore. Our guards never permitted themselves to offer us the slightest insult, or illtreatment of any kind; on the contrary, when they observed that I limped, and walked with pain, two of the soldiers took me by the arms, and assisted me in ascending the hill and passing over slippery places. When we arrived at the village, they led us into a house, where we found our companions.

Here they gave us *sake*, boiled rice, salted herrings, radishes, and finally tea. Our hands were then tied behind us. But there was no repetition of the severity we had experienced at Kunashir. Having spent about an hour in the village, we proceeded along the shore, under a strong escort, on our return to Matsumae. We observed that the Japanese had fixed small stakes in the ground, in every place marked by our footsteps, during our nightly wanderings. Where we had turned to ascend the hills they lost all traces of us, but recognized our course again among the sand. It was evident that they had continually followed us, but had avoided seizing us lest we might have made a desperate resistance, and killed some of their party: perhaps other reasons also induced them to forbear attacking us.

When we passed through villages, the inhabitants flocked from all sides to look at us, but to the honor of the Japanese it ought to be observed that not one of them treated us with anything like derision or mockery; they all seemed to commiserate us, and some of the women even shed tears whilst they presented us with something to eat or drink. Such was the expression of feeling among a people whom enlightened Europe has regarded as barbarians. However, the chief of our escort showed us none of that benevolent kindness we had before experienced from other Japanese officers. For instance, we were obliged to walk, though we might as well have rode on horseback; we were not carried across the brooks and rivulets as before, but were desired to wade through them. And instead of being provided with umbrellas, mats were thrown over us to protect us from the rain. In several of the villages through which we passed, we expressed a wish to remain for the whole day. But we were hurried away, after having rested only a short time. We were provided with boiled rice, muscles or herrings, and tea without sugar. We were all excessively fatigued, but I particularly suffered. Owing to the pain in my foot, I could proceed only at a very slow pace. The chief of the escort, therefore, directed that two soldiers should support me by the arms, and that they should be regularly relieved in performing that duty. This order was executed with the strictest punctuality. If, during our journey, we complained of thirst, we were permitted to stop and drink water at the first brook we came to. During the night, which was extremely dark, we were led, one behind the other, with the greatest caution, and a lantern was carried before each of us, as well as before the Japanese chief. In addition to this, men bearing lanterns preceded and followed the escort. When we had to ascend or descend steep hills, a number of country people who accompanied us from the neighboring villages proceeded before us. Each carried a large bundle of straw. Those bundles were laid down at dangerous parts of the road, and when we approached set on fire, so that we enjoyed, for a moment, a light as bright as day. Had a European viewed, from a distance, our nocturnal procession, he would doubtless have supposed he beheld the obsequies of a person of high rank.

On the following day, the 3d of May, as we entered a little village, about ten kilometers from Matsumae, we met one of the chief officers of the city, and our interpreter Teisuke, accompanied by a detachment of *bakufu* soldiers. We immediately halted. The officer said not a word, and manifested neither anger nor displeasure. Teisuke, however, reproached us for having attempted to escape, and began to search us. One of the sailors told him that he might spare himself the trouble since he would find nothing; upon which he replied, "I know very well that I shall find nothing upon you, but the Japanese laws require that you should be searched." In this village, the officer and soldiers who had taken us put on their state uniforms, over which they threw mantles, because it rained. On coming near the town they took off their mantles, and the order of the procession being arranged, we advanced at a slow pace. The concourse of people was very great. Owing to the rain, all the spectators carried umbrellas over their heads, so that they presented a most singular spectacle. Our escort proceeded in the following order: two guides on each side, bearing wooden staves. Behind them nine soldiers strutting along, with their muskets on their shoulders; we followed one after the other, guarded on each side by soldiers. Behind us were nine soldiers with muskets, one after the other. And last of all the officer who arrested us, on horseback. He wore a rich silken dress, and looked down on the multitude that lined both sides of the road, like a proud conqueror who had earned laurels, and laid claim to the admiration and gratitude of his countrymen.

We were conducted directly to the castle. Formerly we had been permitted to enter the courtyard with our hats on, but we were now directed to uncover as soon as we reached the gate. We sat down on benches in the ante-room leading to the Hall of Justice, where boiled rice, pickled radishes, and tea without sugar, were handed to us. At length we were conducted into the Hall of Justice, where, in a few moments, Mur and Alexei entered, and were directed to station themselves at some distance from us.

All the officers having taken their places, the magistrate entered. No change was perceptible in his face: he maintained his accustomed cheerfulness, and expressed not the slightest displeasure at our conduct. Having taken his seat, he inquired, in his usual benevolent manner, what had induced us to try to escape. I requested the interpreter to state to the magistrate, that, before I answered his question, I wished to inform him that I alone was guilty, and had forced the rest to fly with me, which they were obliged to do, for a refusal to obey my orders would render them liable to severe punishment, should they ever return to Russia. I further declared, that they might put me to death, but that it would be unjust to injure a hair of the head of any of my companions. The magistrate replied, that if the Japanese thought fit to put me to death, they would do so without any suggestion on my part. But that if, on the contrary, they did not see the necessity of such a proceeding, all my entreaties would be of no avail.

The magistrate repeated his question. I declared that we had fled because we saw no probability of our being set at liberty, but that everything tended to convince us that the Japanese meant to keep us in perpetual imprisonment. "Who told you that?" said the magistrate, "I never gave you reason to suppose that your confinement would be eternal." "The orders," I replied, "which were received from the capital, directing that all Russian vessels should be seized, and the preparations that were made in consequence of that order, augured nothing favorable to us." "Who informed you of that? "We learned it from Teisuke." The magistrate then addressed himself to Teisuke, but what he said we could not comprehend, though we observed that Teisuke, during his replies, frequently changed color.

The magistrate had hitherto addressed his questions to me alone. But he now asked Khlebnikov and the sailors what motives had induced them to escape. They replied, that they had merely followed the directions which I, who was their commander, had given them. On hearing this, Mur laughed, and said they were no more bound to obey my orders than he, and might have remained behind if they had chosen. He called the sailors blockheads, and assured the Japanese that for prisoners to make their escape was a thing unknown in Europe. The Japanese, however, seemed to pay but little attention to what Mur said, and proceeded to inquire by what means we had effected our escape. They desired to be informed of every particular: at what hour and in what manner we had left the house; what course we had pursued how far we proceeded each day; what articles and provisions we had carried off with us. And, finally, whether any of our guards or attendants had assisted us in our escape, or whether we had made our intention known to any Japanese whatever. We answered all these questions by a faithful relation of the whole affair.

The magistrate then wished to know how long we had entertained this resolution, and how long we had imagined it possible to carry it into effect. Mur now turned towards the sailors, and exhorted them to tell the truth as they would before God, since he had already disclosed everything to the Japanese. Independently of this admonition, we entertained no design to conceal any circumstance. We however observed, that, notwithstanding Mur's exhortations to the sailors, he had not adhered very strictly to the truth in giving an account of our deliberations and plans, nor even in relating the projects he had himself formed. He had represented that his consent to escape with us was merely a pretense, in order that he might detect our plans, and, by disclosing them to the Japanese, perform a service to the magistrate. He stated, that, as far as regarded himself, he would submit to the will of the emperor of Japan. If he obtained permission to return to his native country, he would immediately depart; if not, he was ready to remain in Japan. When the magistrate afterwards inquired who had written a letter, that had been addressed to him concerning Alexei, Mur replied he had written it. But, immediately recollecting himself, he added, that he had merely done so in conformity to my orders. At this answer the Japanese themselves smiled.

The magistrate then asked what had been our object in escaping. We replied, that we wished to return to our native country. "But by what means did you expect to execute this design?" "We intended to get on board a large boat, and to sail from Hokkaido to the Russian Kuril Islands, or to the coast of Tartary." "Did you not think it probable, that, after your escape, orders would be issued for keeping a strict watch on all vessels near the coast?" "Yes, that we expected would be the case. But, after a certain time should have elapsed, we hoped to execute our enterprise at some point from where our escape would be least suspected."

"You must have observed," continued the magistrate, "during your first conveyance hither, as well as during the walks you were permitted to take, that Hokkaido is covered with high hills; you must have been aware of the difficulty of crossing these hills, and that the populous villages, which lie almost close to each other along the shore, must have precluded the possibility of your escaping: the whole plan was indeed ill-contrived and childish." "Notwithstanding this," I replied, "we spent six nights on the coast, and passed through several villages without being perceived. Our enterprise was, indeed, extremely desperate, and to the Japanese may appear childish. We, however, thought otherwise. Our situation was an excuse for any hazardous attempt; we saw no other means of returning to our homes: to waste our lives in eternal imprisonment was the only prospect to which we could look forward. We therefore resolved to perish, either at sea or in the forests of Hokkaido." "It was unnecessary to go to the forests or to the sea to end your lives; you might, if you pleased, have terminated them here." "That would have been self-murder. But when we risked our lives for the sake of recovering our liberty, we threw ourselves on the protection of Heaven, and might hope to gain our object."

"Suppose you had succeeded," he asked, "what would you have said of the Japanese when you returned to Russia?" I repled, "All that we have seen and heard among them; without either adding or concealing any circumstances whatever."

"Had you returned to Russia without Mur, your emperor surely would not have approved of your conduct in leaving one of your companions behind you."

"Had Mur been in a state of ill-health, which rendered him unable to accompany us, notwithstanding his inclination to do so, our conduct would indeed have been most unmanly, but he wished to remain in Japan of his own freewill."

"Did you know that, if you had succeeded in your project, the magistrate and several other officers must have answered for your escape with their lives?"

"We supposed that the guards might, as is the custom in Europe, have suffered some punishment. But we never could have imagined that the Japanese laws were so severe as to condemn innocent men to death." Here Mur assured the magistrate that we were very well aware of the existence of such a law, since he had himself explained it to us. We replied, that Mur had indeed mentioned something of the kind. But that our European ideas of justice prevented us from giving credit to what he said, and we looked upon it merely as a fabrication he had invented for the purpose of dissuading us from our design.

"Is there," inquired the magistrate, "any European law by which prisoners are justified in making their escape?"

"There is no written law to that effect. But when a prisoner has not pledged his parole of honor, he is never considered culpable in making his escape." Upon this Mur made some observations, calculated to render our answer ridiculous, and he even assured the Japanese that we had made a false assertion. We called to his recollection the cases of General Beresford, Colonel Pack, Sir Sydney Smith, and other individuals, who, within our own recollection, had escaped from imprisonment without any disgrace being attached to them. But Mur continued his forced laughter, and even said that no such examples had ever existed.

The magistrate then delivered a long speech, the substance of which, according to the translation of our interpreter, was as follows: "Had you been natives of Japan, and secretly escaped from your prison, the consequence might have been fatal to you. But as you are foreigners, and ignorant of the Japanese laws, and more particularly as you did not escape with a view to injure the Japanese, but for the sake of returning to your native country, which it is natural you should prefer to every other, our good opinion of you remains unaltered. The magistrate cannot be answerable for the way in which the government may view your conduct. But he will still continue to exert all his endeavours to gain permission for you to return to Russia. Until your case be decided, according to the Japanese laws, the sailors must be confined in prison. But you officers will be lodged in *unaya*."

When the magistrate had concluded his speech he withdrew, and we were conducted into the antechamber. We had hitherto been guarded by *bakufu* soldiers, whom we did not know, and who were under the command of the officer who arrested us. That officer entered the ante-chamber, accompanied by an officer named Nagakawa Matatarō, who was the fourth in rank next to the magistrate, and whose office was that of a judge in criminal matters. The officer having delivered us over to his custody, he immediately ordered the soldiers who had accompanied us to retire, and our old acquaintances, the Matsumae soldiers, entered in their stead. Matatarō then directed them to bind Khlebnikov and me as Japanese officers are bound, and the sailors like common people. The Japanese bind their officers by fastening a rope round their waists, and tying their hands down by their sides, so that they cannot move them. They tie the hands of common people behind them, as we were bound when in Kunashir.

This being done, we were conducted, between five and six o'clock, to a place of imprisonment, situated about a half or three-quarters of a kilometer from the castle. It rained, but the multitude of persons, all carrying umbrellas, who assembled to see us was immense.

The city prison was situated at the foot of a steep rock, and was surrounded by two wooden fences, and an earthen wall surmounted by spikes. Within the inner fence we beheld a large gloomy building, similar to that in which we had been confined when we first arrived at Matsumae, excepting that there were here four cages, one of which was tolerably large, and the other three small. On reaching this prison, the head gaoler, who was named Keisuke, unbound us one after the other, and searched us from head to foot, making us strip to our shirts. Having searched me first, he directed me to enter the smallest of the four cages. Khlebnikov was put into the next cage, which was somewhat larger and lighter than mine; the third cage was occupied by a Japanese prisoner. And the sailors were all shut up together in the fourth, which was the largest of all, and from its situation by far the best.

We were still unable to guess what the magistrate meant, when he told us that the sailors would be confined in a real prison, but that we should live in *unaya*; for we now found that our accommodation was considerably worse than their's. We afterwards learned that the difference consisted in Khlebnikov and myself having separate cells, whilst the sailors were confined in one. But this was a favor on which we were not inclined to set much value. Our cages, however, stood close to each other, so that Khlebnikov and I could converse without difficulty. The Japanese prisoner began to discourse with Khlebnikov: he told him his name, and said that he should be set at liberty in six days. He handed him a piece of saltfish, in return for which Khlebnikov gave him a white cravat.

Late in the evening, our old attendant Fukumasa, accompanied by two other servants, brought us our supper, which consisted of thin boiled rice, two small pieces of pickled radish for each of us, and warm water to drink. Fukumasa appeared out of humor; he answered our questions roughly, but never offered to reproach us on the subject of our escape.

We at first supposed that Fukumasa was to attend on us as before, but we soon found that this was not the case, and that he had merely brought two lads with him in order to show them the proper mode of attending on us, and teaching them the Russian names of the most necessary things. There was no occasion for this, as we could express our wants distinctly enough in Japanese.

After I had finished my meal, the Japanese handed an old nightgown through the railings of my cage. They likewise gave some things to my companions. The door of our prison was now closed, and we were enveloped in total darkness, for the spars that formed the front railing, and divided the whole from the guard room, were closed up with boards, so that there was no aperture through which the light could penetrate to our cages. After sunset the guards came every half hour with lanterns to inspect our cages, and they even awoke us from our sleep to make us answer their calls. During the summer the night hours are extremely short in Hokkaido, so that they were everlastingly disturbing us, and we were not allowed to enjoy a moment's repose.

On the 4th of May, 1812, at daybreak, an officer opened the doors of our cages, and called us all by our names. At noon we were conducted before the magistrate, with our hands bound in the same way as before. On arriving at the castle, we were ordered to sit down in the ante-chamber of the Hall of Justice, and in a few moments Mur and Alexei passed by us, and were conducted into the hall.

After a short time, Khlebnikov and I were unbound, though the ropes were left round our waists. The sailors had merely their hands and not their elbows loosened. Mur and Alexei were not bound in any way. We were then led into the Hall of Justice. When the magistrate had taken his seat, he repeated many of his old questions, respecting which he now merely required explanations. He then asked me what I thought of my conduct, and whether I supposed I had acted justly or unjustly towards the Japanese. The Japanese, I replied, have driven us to the course we adopted: they first of all treacherously seized us, and then refused to credit the statement we made, or to hold any communication with our ships, in case they should come on the part of our government to confirm our declarations. What were we then to do? The circumstances of our case fully justify our conduct. The magistrate expressed astonishment at what I said. "Your seizure," he said, "is an old affair, which ought not to be spoken of now. I merely ask whether you consider yourselves guilty or innocent. If you declare yourselves not guilty, I can, by no means, represent your case favorably to the emperor." I immediately perceived that he wished us all to acknowledge that we were guilty. And I replied that were we in a situation to be fairly tried, I could urge many circumstances in our justification. But we were in the power of the Japanese. They might judge of our conduct as they pleased. But I alone should be considered guilty, since my companions had acted in conformity to my orders.

The magistrate appeared satisfied with this declaration: he observed, that it was praiseworthy to take the blame upon myself, for the sake of justifying my countrymen, but that obedience to my commands could only be urged in exculpation of the sailors; that Khlebnikov was an officer himself, and ought to have known that he was bound to obey my orders only whilst on board our ship, and not during his imprisonment. Then, turning to Khlebnikov, he inquired whether he was ready to acknowledge himself guilty. Far from making any such acknowledgment, Khlebnikov began to justify our conduct, and to prove that we could not be condemned by any rule either of equity or humanity. At this the Japanese appeared irritated, and repeated that they could not make their emperor acquainted with declarations of that kind. Finally, partly by persuasion, and partly by menaces, they induced us to admit that we had done wrong, and that our conduct would in no way operate to our advantage. With this confession they seemed perfectly satisfied.

The magistrate then dismissed us, ordering Mur and Alexei to remain behind. I must here observe, that on my complaining that the severe pain in my foot scarcely permitted me to stand upright, the magistrate desired a seat to be placed for me, and permitted me to sit during the whole of the examination. When we quitted the Hall of Justice, our hands were again bound, and we were conducted back to prison in the usual way. On entering the cell, I found my old worn-out nightgown taken away, and the wadded one, which had been formerly given me, together with my coverlet, substituted in its stead. My companions had likewise been provided for in the same manner during their absence.

We were now treated in all respects like criminals: no distinction was observed between us and the Japanese prisoner who was in the adjacent cage. We, indeed, thought this treatment extremely severe; yet, it must nevertheless be acknowledged, that the Japanese laws respecting criminals are far more humane than those of most, I might perhaps say of all, European nations. We were now confined in a real prison, in the same place with a criminal! I shall describe our treatment, leaving to the reader to institute what comparisons he may think fit.

I have already mentioned the cages in which we were confined. They were kept extremely clean, and even the lobby was swept every day by our attendants. When we were conducted to the castle, our cages were cleaned out, and our coverlets and nightdresses aired in the sun during our absence. Food was brought to us every morning, noon, and evening. At each meal we received thick boiled rice instead of bread. It was dealt out to us in portions more than sufficient for Khlebnikov and me. But the sailors found the allowance scanty enough at the commencement of their imprisonment, when their appetites were keen, owing to the great fatigue and privations they had endured. Khlebnikov and I being unable to eat all that was given us, we sent the remainder of our allowance to the sailors, and the attendants very willingly conveyed it to them. But Keisuke at length observed what we did, and was cruel enough to forbid it.

In addition to the rice, we were served with soup made of seaweed, and other wild plants, such as, sweet cabbage, wild garlick, and water angelica; to which, for the sake of rendering it savory, pickled beans (Japanese *miso*) and some pieces of whale fat were added. In the evening we occasionally received, instead of soup, two pieces of salt fish, with pickled wild cabbage. Our drink consisted of warm water, which was brought to us as often as we wished. If we happened to ask for drink during the night, our guards, without a murmur, called up the servants, and ordered them to bring us water. At first we were not allowed to have combs. And in order that we might have water to wash ourselves with, we were obliged to reserve a part of that which was given us to drink. We were, after some time, provided with a comb, which seemed to have been intended for a prison, as the teeth were extremely small, probably to prevent the prisoners from doing themselves any injury with it.

On many occasions the Japanese showed particular attention to us in other respects. One night a violent earthquake took place: our prison shook, and we heard a great tumult in the yard, and in the streets. Our guards immediately came to us with lanterns, and desired us not to be alarmed, informing us that it was only an earthquake, which was a very common occurrence in Japan, but was seldom attended with danger. They probably did this of their own accord; for, to the honor of the Japanese, I must declare that many of them treated us with great kindness, and did all they could to afford us consolation. One in particular, named Yamada Gooiso, frequently brought us refreshments unperceived by his comrades. He sometimes desired us to ask for water, and to keep the vessel beside us. Then, having watched for a favorable opportunity, he would throw away the water, and fill the vessel with tea in its stead. We experienced similar kindness from two other guards. But a soldier, who had been one of the inner guard on the night of our escape, presented the most striking example of humanity. He had accompanied the detachment sent in pursuit of us, but not in the rank of a soldier, as on account of his neglect he was degraded to that of a common servant. From the moment of our arrest, until our arrival in Matsumae, he never quitted us. His loose hair, unshaven beard, and pale face, sufficiently indicated the grief of which we were the cause; yet he saluted us kindly the first moment he beheld us. And, far from testifying the least hatred or ill-will, made every exertion to serve us during the journey, though these attentions were in no way connected with his duty. The generosity and nobleness of his conduct often moved us to tears.

A day or two after our last conference with the magistrate, I was conducted alone to the castle, where the two officers next in rank questioned me in the presence of several others. Before I entered the hall, Teisuke came to me, and said that Mur was much exasperated against us, and had said many things to our disadvantage. He added that I need give myself no uneasiness about it, since the Japanese were not inclined to believe what Mur said. He informed me that Mur had offered to enter the Japanese service. I, therefore, before the officers began their interrogatories, requested that they would permit me to state my sentiments freely, and that they would direct the interpreter to translate what I should say as faithfully as possible. The officers replied that they were very ready to hear whatever I might wish to communicate to them. I then asked them, whether, supposing three Japanese officers should be made prisoners in any part of the world, they would be well pleased to find that one of the three had conducted himself as Mur had done? They laughed, and said certainly not. The eldest of the officers at last remarked, that I had nothing to fear on that ground, for all Russians were alike to the Japanese, and they only wanted to be made acquainted with the real circumstances of the case. "According to the Japanese laws, added he, nothing can be done with precipitation. Though you are now in a prison, when the new magistrate comes, a better place of abode, and even a house will be allotted to you, and I have reason to believe that the government will send you back to Russia."

They then asked very earnestly whether, as the Ainu had assured them, it was true that Resanov had participated in the attacks of the company's ships, by first giving to Khvostov orders for that aggression, which, though afterwards withdrawn, were ultimately followed by Khvostov. It was easy to conjecture who the Ainu was who had given this information: it was no other than Mur. I replied, that I did not know precisely whether or not Resanov had taken any part in the affair, but that a report prevailed of his having intended to attack the Japanese.

The officers then referred to a manuscript spread out before them, and asked a great number of questions concerning our navigation, the object of the expedition, the situation of Russia, and its political relations with other European states, particularly with France. I perceived that they derived all their information from the same source, and found it frequently necessary to correct the erroneous notions they had imbibed.

This unpleasant business being over, the elder of the officers again assured me that I had nothing to fear, that the Japanese were as just as other nations, and would not act basely with regard to us. With this consolatory assurance I was dismissed. On returning to the prison, I related to Khlebnikov all that had passed.

We were shortly afterwards visited by the officer Nagakawa Matatarō, accompanied by the two interpreters. They brought along with them copies of our declarations, in order to read them over and verify them. We perceived that our statements concerning the way in which we had procured the knife, and obtained information of the orders given for attacking the Russian vessels, and for dispatching troops and cannon to Kunashir, were all struck out. The officers informed us that we must say nothing more on those subjects in the presence of the magistrate. They doubtless wished to screen the Japanese who were implicated in the affair. We had been much distressed at the idea of any evil befalling either Teisuke or the innocent soldiers and attendants, through whose negligence we had obtained the knife, and were consequently very well pleased with this proposal. But we could not so readily agree to what they next required. And a warm dispute arose, in the course of which Matatarō, according to custom, flew into a rage, reproached, and even threatened us. They proposed that we should justify Mur, by declaring that his consent to escape was a mere pretense, and that he had never mentioned to Simanov and Vassiliev that he was ready to join us in the attempt. To this we would not assent, and even positively refused to contradict any of the statements we had before made on the subject of Mur. We observed that whatever that officer's real intentions might be, his declarations certainly bore the appearance of sincerity, and that we were convinced he would have escaped along with us, had not cowardice prevented him. We had very good reasons for not assisting him in extricating himself from the affair. And I think it necessary to state them, lest the reader should accuse us of revenge, and a wish to injure him.

I have already mentioned that Mur endeavored to convince the Japanese that he was a German, and not a Russian. Had we asserted that he had no participation in our plans, the Japanese would probably have sent him in a Dutch ship to Germany, his pretended native country, from where he might easily have proceeded to Russia. He might then, without fear of contradiction, have related a tale of his own contrivance, declared his conduct to be the effect of ill-treatment he had received from us, and thus forever have branded the recollection of our names. This idea was constantly present to our minds, and we resolved not to depart in the slightest degree from the truth, for the sake of justifying Mur. If our testimony could have been the means of procuring for him the situation of chief officer in Japan, instead of bringing about his return to Europe, we would readily have agreed to anything, though he had endeavored to injure us by all possible means. Matatarō visited us for three or four successive days, and urged us to contradict what we had before said of Mur. But finding our resolution unalterable, he at length desisted from his useless persuasion. We are ignorant whether or not any alteration was made in our testimony in this respect.

I will merely mention the following circumstance: When we were searched at Kunashir, the Japanese took from me a pocket book. I shortly afterwards recollected that among many other things, the names of Davydov and Khvostov were written down in this book. And I consulted with Mur and Khlebnikovon what I should say, if the Japanese demanded an explanation of that memorandum. We then regarded each other as brothers: we were animated by one spirit and one heart! Mur had, however, since told the Japanese that the names of Davydov and Khvostov were inserted in my pocket book, and that they were, moreover, my friends. Teisuke informed us of this circumstance, and observed, that we need be apprehensive of no ill consequences, since, as he expressed himself, Mur had unnecessarily communicated the affair to the Japanese. In fact, no questions were ever asked on this subject.

I was now afraid that Mur would, by his artifice, at last succeed in so far conciliating the Japanese, as to gain permission to return to Russia, where his misrepresentations might brand out names with eternal disgrace. This horrible reflection filled me with despair, and brought on a serious indisposition. For the space of a week or ten days no physician appeared, though the sailors had long before applied for medical attendance. But the Japanese at length took compassion on us, and sent a physician daily. So little did I value life, that I concealed the real cause of my illness, and took medicine, which instead of operating beneficially, had quite a contrary effect. Notwithstanding the weak state to which I was reduced, I insisted that the physician should bleed me. With a trembling hand he proceeded to open a vein, but his courage failed him, and he was unable to perform the operation. Much as I had suffered, my constitution, which was naturally vigorous, and improved by the habits of my life from youth upwards, successfully resisted the pernicious operation of the medicine. To the honor of the worthy Magistrate Arao Shigeaki, I must observe that when he suspected the real cause of my illness, he sent Nagakawa Matatarō to assure me that the Japanese would not act with severity towards us; that on the arrival of the new magistrate, we should be removed to a better place of residence, and that both magistrates would then exert all their influence to obtain our liberation. In interpreting this message, Kumajirō was so deeply moved, that he melted into tears. And though I doubted the sincerity of the Japanese, yet this assurance afforded me some consolation.

We were now supplied with better food: we were frequently treated with a kind of pudding, which the Japanese call *tōfu*: fine beans were boiled with our rice, forming a dish considered a great delicacy in Japan; even chicken soup was given us on one or two occasions. And for our drink we had always tea instead of water. This change was a consequence of an order of the magistrate, and obtained through Teisuke's intercession.

During our confinement in the city prison, a circumstance occurred I cannot pass over in silence. Our neighbor, the Japanese, who remained with us much longer than the six days he told us would terminate his imprisonment underwent the punishment to which he had been adjudged, in the courtyard. We heard his cries.

The crime which this man had committed was as follows: Having visited a public bathing house, he changed his old clothes, as if by mistake, for a better suit belonging to some other individual. He was several times conveyed before a judge, with his hands tied behind his back. At length he received twenty-five stripes, and the same punishment was repeated after the lapse of three days. What instrument was used in the infliction of this chastisement we know not, but we distinctly heard the stripes, and the cries of the offender. He returned with his back naked and bloody to prison. The attendants spat on his shoulders, and rubbed the saliva over the lacerated parts, and thus cured him. His hands were afterwards marked, to show that he had been punished, and he was then sent to the northern Kuril Islands, in the possession of the Japanese.

On the same day an officer, with the criminal Judge, Matatarō, and the interpreter Kumajirō, came, by order of the magistrate, to say that we must not suppose, in consequence of the execution of the sentence on this criminal, that a similar fate awaited us; for, according to the Japanese laws, no foreigner could be condemned to suffer corporal punishment. We looked upon this assurance as merely intended to console us. But we afterwards learnt, that a law to this effect really exists. And that the only foreigners to whom its protection does not extend are those who attempt to induce Japanese subjects to embrace Christianity. The laws are extremely rigorous against teachers of the Christian religion.

In the middle of June we were carried twice every day before the magistrate, in whose presence, and that of several officers, our depositions were read, and our opinion asked with respect to their correctness. Every circumstance that might have tended to criminate the Japanese was carefully omitted, and, in conformity with our promise, we made no allusion to them. When Mur's declaration was read, we made no hesitation to contradict several of his assertions. He protested that he was entirely blameless, and declared that he had never persuaded the sailors to attempt their escape. On hearing this, Skajev exclaimed, "Think on Heaven and your conscience, Feodor Feodorowytsch! Can you ever hope to return to Russia?" Khlebnikov and I desired him to be silent. But these few words made a deep impression on Mur, and we paid dearly for them, as will appear in the sequel. The Japanese, who observed our disagreement, took upon themselves the task of correcting our depositions, and dismissed us.

The new magistrate, Ogasawara Osayuki,[1] arrived at Matsumae on 29 June, and on 2 July we were conducted to the castle. We found assembled in the Hall of Justice all the officers who were usually present at our examinations, together with Mur and Alexei. On my entering the hall, Mur addressed me and said that we had no reason to fear, as all was going on well. When we had waited about half an hour, the two magistrates appeared, with their suites. They were each preceded by an officer.

The new magistrate was the oldest man of the two, and in his suite there were two officers more than in that of the late magistrate. He looked like a giant among the Japanese; he was as tall as our sailors. His countrymen looked upon him as a wonder. Before his arrival, they often told us that a giant was coming, and that we should see there were people in Japan as tall as the Russians. He entered first, and having taken his seat, the former magistrate seated himself on his right. The Japanese testified their respect to him in their usual way, and we bowed after the European fashion. The former magistrate then pointing to his colleague, observed that he, Ogasawara Osayuki, was the new magistrate, appointed to relieve him, and desired us to tell him our names and ranks. We did so with a bow, which he returned by smiling and nodding his head. The former magistrate then directed an officer to bring in a roll of paper, which he said had been written by Mur, who called it a memoir. He desired us to read it, and then to say whether we approved of its contents. The two magistrate then retired, and left us to deliver our opinion to the officers. Mur himself read his paper, in which, after many compliments to both magistrates, he described all the plans we had formed for our escape, such as they really were. He asserted that his agreeing to escape with us was a mere pretense; construed all we had said in a way calculated to injure us in the opinion of the Japanese; explained the object of our voyage, and minutely described the situation of eastern Russia, and the political relations between France and Russia after the peace of Tilsit. In conclusion, he entreated that the Japanese would pardon us.

Having heard the paper to an end, we began to contradict all that was not conformable to truth. But of this the Japanese expressed their disapprobation, and declared that we had no right to dispute with Mur. I replied, that if they were resolved to give full credit to Mur's declarations, it would be of no use for us to say anything on the subject, as there were no witnesses to decide between us. Khlebnikov still wished to contradict some statements in the paper, but the Japanese became irritated, and he desisted. We resolved not to sign Mur's declaration in case the Japanese should require us so to do. But no such proposal was made.

The two magistrates now entered, and one of the officers informed them that the paper had been read to us. But what he stated, as our opinion of it, we could not understand. The new magistrate then drew from his bosom a letter, folded in the European manner, which he handed to his predecessor. The latter delivered it to one of the officers, who gave it to the interpreter, and it was at last handed to me. The Russian superscription was as follows:

---

1 Ogasawara Osayuki (1746–1812) was a native of Iwami Province (today's Shimane Prefecture) with a long career as a *bakufu* administrator. He had begun as a *kanjō* (financial officer) and gradually climbed the bureaucratic ladder until, in 1800, he was appointed *kanjō bugyō* (financial magistrate). Twelve years later, in 1812, he was appointed to his final post as the magistrate of Matsumae (Matsumae *bugyō*), where he passed away that same year.

"To the Governor of Matsumae." Within the cover was a paper containing the following words, with a French translation:

The proximity of Russia and Japan renders it desirable that friendly and commercial relations should be established between them, which could not fail to operate to the advantage of the inhabitants of the latter empire. With this view an embassy was dispatched to Nagasaki. But the offensive and repulsive answer given by the Japanese to the proposals made to them, and the extension of their trade to the Kuril Islands and Sachalin, which are Russian possessions, render it at last necessary for the emperor of Russia to adopt measures that may prove his power to injure the trade of the Japanese, until the Russians be informed, by the inhabitants of Urup or Sachalin, that the Japanese are ready to enter into commercial relations with them. The Russians intend, by resorting to these mild measures against Japan, merely to demonstrate that the northern parts of that empire are entirely at their mercy, and that the obstinacy of the Japanese government in opposing all intercourse, must, if persisted, terminate in the loss of these countries.

This paper had neither date nor signature, and contained no indication of the authority under which it had been sent to Japan. We therefore endeavored to prove, and in this instance Mur supported us, that Khvostov had been the author of it; adding that we were ready to declare upon oath, that our government had no knowledge of the affair, though the writer pretended to speak of measures the emperor of Russia was to adopt. Even the anonymous nature of the document proved it had never issued from our government. Mention was, besides, made of the inhabitants of Urup, one of the Kuril Islands, which had long been uninhabited. This circumstance was well known to our government, and so glaring an error could never have crept into an official document. The Japanese having paid attention to our explanations, the new magistrate observed, that he did not mean to inquire whether the paper had been forged, or whether it had been sent to Japan by order of the Russian government; he merely wished to be made acquainted with its contents, in order that he might communicate them to his emperor. We immediately gave him a verbal translation, and Mur drew up a written one. They then showed us two documents Khvostov had presented to the inhabitants of Sachalin along with the medals. The contents of these two papers perfectly corresponded with the preceding, so that we were not required to translate them.

In conclusion, the new magistrate informed us that in a short time we should be removed to a new place of abode; that our condition would be, in all respects, ameliorated. The two magistrates then withdrew, and we were conveyed back to prison.

From this day a visible change took place in the Japanese who attended us. They became much more friendly and civil than before. Teisuke informed us that after our escape Mur and Alexei had been removed to our first place of confinement in Matsumae, which was now again preparing for us. A separate apartment was fitting up for Mur and Alexei, and we could not be removed until that was completed. Teisuke, besides, assured us that, at the farewell audience of the new magistrate, the emperor had ordered him to take the greatest care of our healths, and after his arrival at Matsumae to do everything to render our situation comfortable.

In the meanwhile, a circumstance occurred that displayed in the strongest light the kind-heartedness and generosity of our interpreter Teisuke. When I landed at Kunashir, I had accidentally in my pocket the rough copy of a letter, which I had been preparing with the view of sending it to the Japanese, in case of their still declining any intercourse with us. In this letter I upbraided them with their cowardly conduct in firing upon unarmed men, and even held out several threats to them. I added, that without the consent of our government, no officer could adopt measures of hostility even in self-defense, and that this circumstance, and not fear, made me refrain from resenting their baseness. The latter observations might be considered as explaining our sentiments, but the first part could not fail to wound the pride of the haughty Japanese. Mur knew that I had the letter, and informed the Japanese of is contents. It had been preserved along with the rest of our things, and being produced, Teisuke was ordered to translate it. Mur explained every syllable to Teisuke. But the latter, observing that many words, and even whole sentences were struck out, turned this circumstance to our advantage, by omitting all expressions that might give offense to the

Japanese government, and translating only such as tended to justify us; the rest he declared could not be deciphered. It would not have been in his power to have done this, had I written out a clean copy of the letter.

On the 9th of July we were again carried before the two magistrates. The new magistrate told us that since we had escaped merely in the hope of returning to our native country, and not with the view of injuring the Japanese, he had resolved, with the consent of his predecessor, to better our situation; trusting that we would not make any such attempt again, but patiently await the decision of the Japanese emperor. He added, that they would both employ all the interest they possessed to obtain our freedom. He had no sooner uttered these words, than the ropes with which we were bound were taken off; the soldiers who were stationed behind us had, without our knowledge, loosened them, and disposed them in such a way that they could remove them in an instant.

The former magistrate assured us, that his friendship for us continued unabated, and that he would take the same interest in our fate as he had hitherto done. He then wished us good health, and took his leave, exhorting us to pray to God, and to trust to his mercy.

The magistrates having withdrawn, we left the castle.

Instead of being conveyed back to the city prison, we were carried to our old residence, which was assigned to us on our first arrival at Matsumae. Khlebnikov, myself, and the sailors, were confined together. But for Mur and Alexei an additional apartment had been built, to which there was a separate entrance from the courtyard. Our change of residence was accompanied with an improvement in our diet. The articles of food brought to us were better than those formerly given to us at the same place. We were supplied with a cup of *sake* every day, and furnished with pipes, and tobacco pouches filled with very good tobacco.

The oldest of our servants, who acted as our butler, was called Iisuke. This man, who was extremely fond of strong liquors, laid it down as a maxim, that to drink seldom, but heartily when at it, was better than to tipple frequently and in small quantities. Accordingly, instead of giving us one cup of *sake* regularly each day, he supplied us with two cups at once. But he never neglected to help himself abundantly at all times, and was, consequently, intoxicated almost every evening. At length the guards discovered from what source he derived constant supplies for his inebriety, and considered it an occasion for interposing their authority. After this Iisuke no longer made free with our *sake*, but waited till we thought fit to share it with him.

A kettle with tea was constantly standing on our hearth. We were allowed to have combs, hand towels, and even curtains to keep off the flies, which are here very numerous. In addition to all these favors, the Japanese sent us our books, and provided us with ink and paper. We now collected

Japanese words, and wrote them down in the Russian character. At length it occurred to us that we might learn to write Japanese. We requested that the interpreter Kumajirō would make out an alphabet for us. But this he declined doing until he obtained the permission of his superiors. He afterwards told us that the Japanese laws prohibited teaching Christians to read and write their language. And that his superiors would not permit him to write the alphabet for us. We were, therefore, obliged to content ourselves with making lists of Japanese words written in the Russian character. We were separated from Mur only by a thin wooden partition. I asked Teisuke whether we might speak to him. "Certainly," he replied, "converse as much as you please, nobody will hinder you." When I first spoke to Mur, I received no answer. But he soon agreed to our proposal of addressing a letter of thanks to the former magistrate, Arao Shigeaki, before his departure. This letter was written, and in it many compliments were likewise paid to the new magistrate.

We observed, "that fate, in ordaining we should become the prisoners of the Japanese, had, to our good fortune, singled out the period when Shigeaki was invested with the government of Hokkaido." The magistrate, on reading Teisuke's translation of the letter, laughed at this passage, and inquired whether we supposed that any other Japanese nobleman, in the like situation, would not have treated us with equal kindness.

On the 14th of July, 1812, Shigeaki departed from Matsumae, taking along with him our friend Teisuke, in the capacity of secretary. Teisuke promised to write from the capital, to inform us in what state our case stood, requested that we would not fail to reply to him, and desired us to give our letters to Kumajirō to be forwarded. We did not expect for some time to hear anything decisive from the capital, knowing that Shigeaki would not arrive there in less than twenty-three or twenty-five days, but we daily hoped to hear of the arrival of Russian ships, though we sometimes doubted whether the Japanese would tell us either when they arrived, or what was the object of their visit.

The Japanese cross the Straits of Tsuruga from Hokkaido to a well-sheltered bay near the city of Minmaya. The length of the passage is about thirteen Japanese *ri* (about 2.5 miles), and as they never undertake it except with a favorable wind, they are in general only a few hours at sea. Minmaya is about two hundred *ri*, or eight hundred kilometers from Edo. Persons of distinction travel in litters or sedan chairs, and the common people on horseback. A great number of men are, therefore, always kept at the post stations. The Japanese assured us that the litter bearers, from long experience, proceed with so much steadiness, that if a glass of water was placed in the litter not a drop would be spilt. In dry weather, when the roads are good, the journey from Minmaya to Edo may be completed in twenty-three days. The couriers from Matsumae, who perform the journey on horseback, arrive in the capital in seven, and sometimes in six days. But this is the extreme of their expedition in travelling. The general post with letters departs only once every month, and is usually fourteen days in completing the journey.

Meanwhile we passed our time in smoking tobacco, reading over again our old books, and collecting and recording Japanese words. I began to note down, on small slips of paper, all our adventures, interspersed with my own observations. In doing this, I wrote only half sentences and arbitrary signs, and mingled Russian, French, and English words together, in such a way that none but myself could decipher the manuscript. Fearing lest the Japanese might some time or other search us, and seize on these papers, I concealed them beneath my sash, in a little bag which Simanov had made me out of part of an old waistcoat. But the previous conduct of the Japanese gave us little reason to fear they would deprive us of our papers; for when we made our escape, Skajev had along with him the rough copy of our first memorial to the former magistrate, and though the Japanese took it from him, they never afterwards alluded to it in any way. Khlebnikov's compass likewise fell into their hands, but they never made it the subject of inquiry. They probably did not understand its nature. Had they been aware that it was a compass, they would doubtless have inquired how we had contrived to make it.

The conduct of the new magistrate proved that he was no less kindly disposed towards us than his predecessor. According to the Japanese laws Ogasawara Osayuki could not grant us permission to walk out. But he gave orders that the doors of our prison should be kept open all day, in order that we might enjoy the fresh air. We likewise received, by his orders, fresh fruit.

He once, on a festival day, sent us a supper that had been prepared in his own kitchen. Our guards likewise treated us with much civility. They sometimes gave us *sake*, fruit, etc. and these acts of kindness were no longer performed by stealth. An old man, seventy years of age, brought some fans and lackered spoons for Khlebnikov and me, and an inkstand, ink, and pencil, for Skajev, who, notwithstanding that he was afflicted with a painful disorder, entertained an extraordinary desire to practise reading and writing. In return for these civilities, we gave the Japanese some European articles, on which, particularly fine cloth, they set the highest value. They regard as curiosities any rags of European manufacture, and make them into purses, bags for their letters and tobacco, and cases for their pipes. We therefore distributed among them the trowsers, stockings, and handkerchiefs, which were at our own disposal, for which they overwhelmed us with thanks. It was necessary to give to each his portion privately, for had it been offered in the presence of others, it would not have been accepted.

Nothing remarkable occurred until September. But I cannot omit mentioning a circumstance characteristic of the customs of the Japanese. One day a dinner was sent to us of far better quality than that to which we had been accustomed, and served in elegant dishes. We remarked that every person who visited us congratulated us on receiving this treat, and we concluded that it came from the magistrate. But we afterwards learnt that the dinner was sent to us by a rich man, who was suffering under a dangerous fit of illness, and that in such cases it was customary for the Japanese to send presents of that sort to the poor and unfortunate.

On the afternoon of the 6th of September, Mur and I were conducted to the castle, where we found assembled all the most distinguished officers, with the exception of Ogasawara Osayuki, who was confined through illness. They showed us two papers which had been sent ashore from the *Diana*, and which were dated the 28th of August, The first was a letter from Ricord, the commander of the *Diana*, to the commander of Kunashir, in which he stated that he had, by command of the emperor of Russia, conveyed to their native country certain Japanese who had been saved on the coasts of Kamchatka after shipwreck, and among whom was a Matsumae merchant, named Nakagawa Yoshisaemon. He further informed the commander, that the *Diana* was the same vessel which, about a year before, had, in consequence of the want of wood and water, entered that harbor. And the captain of which, together with two officers, four sailors, and An Ainu, had been enticed into the garrison, treacherously detained, and of whose fate their countrymen were ignorant. He, likewise, assured the commander of Kunashir of the friendly disposition entertained by the Emperor of Russia towards the Japanese; requested to know whether the commander could himself grant us our liberty, and if not, to be informed how soon he might expect from the Japanese government an answer to his demand for our liberation. He, moreover, wished to know where we were, and intimated that he would not quit the harbor until all his inquiries were answered. In conclusion, he begged permission to take on board the vessel a supply of fresh water.

Ricord's letter was couched in highly respectful and well-chosen terms: at the same time he manifested that decision, which, in such cases, is necessary, when he intimated his determination not to quit the harbor until he should receive satisfactory answers to all his demands.

The second paper was a letter from Ricord to me. He informed me of his arrival at Kunashir, and stated that he had sent to the commander of the island an explanation of the object of his voyage, both in the Russian and Japanese languages. As he knew not whether I was dead or living, he requested, in case the Japanese would not permit me to write an answer, that I would tear out the line of his letter which contained the word "living," and return it to him by the Japanese whom he had sent on shore, to satisfy him respecting our fate. I experienced a powerful emotion on reading this letter from my worthy shipmate and intimate friend; it even made an impression on Mur, who began from that moment to manifest his former friendship to us.

In conformity with the wish of the Japanese, we gave them a verbal translation of the letters, and they desired us to take copies' of both, that, with the help of Kumajirō, we might make written translations. They kept the originals in their own possession.

My companions were overjoyed on hearing of the arrival of the *Diana*, It was evident from Ricord"s letter, that the Russian government was not disposed to adopt violent measures. But wished, by gentle means, to convince the Japanese of their error. In the meanwhile, we experienced all the agitation of alternate fear and hope. We begged permission to write to Ricord, if it were only a single line, to inform him that we were still living. Our attendants undertook to make this request known to the magistrate.

But we were informed that this permission could not be granted without an order from the capital. We asked the interpreter and the guards whether our countrymen had been well treated by the Japanese at Kunashir, and whether their inquiries had been answered. They replied that they could not give us any precise information, but that they believed all we could wish for had been done.

Meanwhile the papers were translated, and immediately sent off to Edo. But we knew nothing of the orders that were transmitted to the commander of Kunashir. Kumajirō informed us that Captain Ricord had come with two vessels, the one with two and the other with three masts, and that he had sent four Japanese ashore one after the other. The latter circumstance, as it augured nothing favorable, gave us some uneasiness. From the Japanese being sent ashore one after the other, we apprehended that Captain Ricord had received no answer to his inquiries.

Mur now endeavored to renew his friendship with us. He sent me a book, in which was concealed a slip of paper, informing me that there were eighty men on board one of our ships, and forty men and four women on board the other. This he had learnt from one of the guards.

Two commissioners (*shirabeyaku*) appeared on the 20th of September, and by order of the magistrate informed us that the Russian ships had, a few days before, sailed from Kunashir, without leaving any letters either for us or the Japanese. After a short pause the officers added, that our ships had detained a Japanese vessel bound from Iturup to Kunashir, and had carried off five of the crew. They inquired what could have been the object of our countrymen in doing this. We replied that we knew not, but that they had probably carried off the men in the hope of obtaining some positive information respecting our fate. And that in that case they would, doubtless, send them back in the following year. This is our opinion likewise, observed the officers, and immediately took their leave.

We were much concerned at hearing this news, particularly as we knew not under what circumstances the capture of the Japanese had taken place. We were at a loss to conjecture whether these five men composed the whole crew of the Japanese ship, or whether Captain Ricord had selected them from among the rest. We were moreover ignorant in what way our countrymen had treated the Japanese, and also what had become of the vessel. But we were most of all distressed by the answers of our interpreters and guards, who constantly declared that they knew nothing of the matter whenever we questioned them concerning this event. Two of the guards, at the same time, regarded us with feelings of hatred, which they could not conceal, and, in an angry tone, told the sailors that since the Russians had captured a Japanese ship, we might give up all hopes of being set at liberty.

Mur at length communicated, by writing on slips of paper, and sending them to me in books, information he had obtained from one of the guards, who was more talkative than the rest; but he begged that I would not distress my companions by discovering it completely to them. As our ships approached Kunashir, the Japanese began to fire upon them from the garrison. The shot did not reach them, and, without regarding the attack of the castle, they proceeded quietly to take on board a supply of fresh water. In the meanwhile a Japanese vessel approached the harbor, and a boat was dispatched from one of our ships to board it. On seeing this, several of the crew of the Japanese vessel, through fear, plunged into the water, and six were drowned. When the Russians took the vessel, they put all the Japanese who were on board in fetters. But on being informed that we were alive, they immediately relieved them from that situation, gave them presents, and detaining only five, set all the rest free, and restored the vessel to them.

I moreover learnt from Mur that the Japanese government had condemned Alexei's companions, the Ainu, to forfeit their heads, on discovering that they had been sent by the Russians as spies to inspect the villages and fortresses of Japan. But the generous Arao Shigeaki represented that the Japanese would disgrace themselves by putting to death these unfortunate Ainu, who, instead of acting from any will of their own, had been compelled blindly to obey the orders of the Russians. He therefore proposed that, after giving them presents, they should be set at liberty. And the government adopted his humane advice. This circumstance did not correspond with the assurance we had formerly received, namely, that no foreigner could suffer corporeal punishment in Japan. But we reflected that the Japanese might have regarded the Ainu as their subjects, though they did not publicly declare them to be such, through dread of involving themselves in a war with Russia. Besides, the information Mur received from the guard might have been false, and we dared not question the interpreters on the subject, lest an investigation should have immediately followed, to ascertain how these circumstances came to our knowledge.

When we inquired what had been said by the Japanese who returned from Russia, our interpreter Kumajirō replied that they confirmed all our declarations. He besides informed us that one of them, named Nakagawa Gorōji, had been carried off by Khvostov from the Island of Iturup. In Captain Ricord's papers this man was stated to be a Matsumae merchant named Nakagawa Yoshisaemon, because he had thought it necessary to deceive the Russians, and had, under an assumed name, represented himself to be a merchant. In fact, he had been employed by a merchant as overseer of a fishery at Iturup. One of his companions, who was carried off along with him, died, after they had made their escape from Okhotsk, in consequence of eating too great a quantity of whale flesh. Yoshisaemon had, however, been taken by the Tongusians, who delivered him up to the Russians. Kumajirō's assurance that the declarations of the Japanese who had been sent home perfectly coincided with ours, was confirmed by the magistrate sending us new silk dresses, although we by no means stood in need of a fresh supply of clothes. We were convinced, from this circumstance, that the Japanese must have spoken well of the Russians.

Some time after this Mur informed us that the magistrate had died, but that the Japanese laws required that his death should be kept secret for a certain time. Two days afterwards one of our guards, a man of seventy, likewise informed us of this event, begging we would not mention it to any of the Japanese. We were concerned to hear of the Osayuki's death, for the Japanese all assured us that he was an excellent man, and was disposed to show us every kindness.

About the middle of October, Mur and I were conducted to the castle, where the two senior officers of state, together with several others, had assembled.

One of these officers, named Takahashi Shigekata, had been but a short time in Matsumae. He was the eldest of the two, and his rank was that of deputy magistrate. We found him to be an extremely humane man. The kindness with which he treated us may, perhaps, be accounted for, from his having, in his youth, been visited by a misfortune similar to our own. He had been in the service of the reigning *daimyō* of Matsumae. As he was sailing through the Straits of Tsuruga a storm arose. The ship lost her mast and rudder, and was driven on the coast of China, where the crew were all made prisoners by the Chinese, and kept in confinement for six years. Their explanations having at last proved satisfactory, they were set at liberty, and permitted to return to Japan. The law excluding from the public service every Japanese who has lived in a foreign country, did not then exist in the principality of Matsumae, and Shigekata was accordingly restored to the service of the *daimyō*. After Khvostov's attacks the principality was converted into a *bakufu* province, but he did not, on that account, lose his post. We were assured by some that this law is not enforced against Japanese who may visit China, but merely against those who have lived among Christians.

They showed us a letter that had been given to one of the Japanese on leaving the Russian ship, and which, they observed, the man had mislaid in consequence of having occasion to dry his clothes. They had, therefore, been unable to produce it before, and now requested that we would translate it. We immediately perceived the cunning of the Japanese. The fact was, that they could not show us the letter until they received an order to that effect from the capital. I laughed, and observed that I knew the real cause that had prevented the letter from being sooner produced. Upon this the Japanese laughed likewise, and seemed not unwilling to acknowledge their readiness at inventing excuses.

The letter was from Rudakov, one of the Lieutenants of the *Diana*, to Mur. It stated that the Japanese commandant at Kunashir had sent back Ricord's messenger with the answer that we had all been put to death. Captain Ricord, therefore, resolved to commence hostilities, and accordingly captured a Japanese vessel, on board of which was the commander of ten ships. He was not only the commander, but the owner of these ships. Besides being a rich merchant, he was a man of uncommon abilities and upright principles, and his countrymen treated him with the highest consideration. Even the superior officers of state showed him particular marks of respect. He was beloved by all who knew him. Captain Ricord and his officers must have immediately recognized him to be a person of distinction, as individuals of his rank have, when abroad, the privilege of wearing a sword and dagger.

Our countrymen learned, from the crew of this vessel, that we were all living and in Matsumae. They looked upon the account of our death as a fabrication imposed on the Japanese whom they had sent ashore, and resolved to discontinue hostilities. They had, however, thought proper to detain the commander, four Japanese, and an Ainu, allowing the rest to depart with the vessel. They then determined to sail back to Kamchatka, and to obtain from the Japanese more circumstantial evidence respecting us. Rudakov concluded his letter by intimating that he would return to Matsumae in the following year, wishing us health, etc.

We were requested to explain this letter to the Japanese, and then to take a copy of it, in order to make out a written translation. Its perusal afforded us at least this satisfaction, that the ill conduct of the Japanese towards Russia was now self-evident. And that if our emperor entertained any intention of punishing their want of faith, the justifiable grounds of any attack he might make upon them could not be disputed.

Whilst Mur was copying the letter, I asked the Japanese officers, with some marks of indignation, whether the governor of Kunashir had really returned such an answer to Ricord as that stated. And if so, what could have induced him to resort to a mean falsehood, which might have been attended with very disagreeable, if not dangerous consequences to Japan. "We know nothing of the matter," was their reply. On my inquiry whether such conduct was customary among them, they expressed some displeasure.

The translation of the letter was forwarded to Edo without delay. Rudakov's letter having made us better acquainted with the circumstances of the affair between our countrymen and the Japanese at Kunashir, Kumajirō thought fit to inform us that the Japanese, who had returned from Okhotsk—in particular Nakagawa Yoshisaemon—positively asserted that Russia intended to declare war against Japan, and that she had, in the meanwhile, assumed a pacific tone merely with a view to obtain our liberation. This man, it was true, stated that Khvostov and Davydov were arrested on their arrival at Okhotsk. But he asserted that they soon made their escape from prison, and insinuated that they had been confined merely because they brought back too few Japanese prisoners, and an insufficient booty. He observed that they must have acted by order of the government, because nobody in Okhotsk had told him that they were imprisoned on account of their conduct towards the Japanese. He moreover asserted that all the Japanese property, though at first placed under sequestration, was ultimately sold in the warehouses of the Russian-American Company.

Unfortunately, we were but too certain that the Japanese spoke truth. But how could we convince them that all this was attributable to the weakness of the commandant of Okhotsk, and the misconduct of the officers of the company? How could we contradict Yoshisaemon's statement, and prove that our government intended no hostilities towards the Japanese? We had, also, the mortification to learn, that the Japanese, who had saved themselves from shipwreck on the coast of Kamchatka, and had wintered there, gave a very bad account of the Russians. They had lived for some time with a priest in Nischny Kamchatka, and were then very well satisfied with their treatment. But when they were removed to Malka, a Kamchatka village, they were supplied with nothing but dried fish for their food, and were allowed hardly a rag of clothing to cover them.

On the 1st of November, 1812, Mur and I were again conveyed to the castle, where we were shown a certificate that had been delivered to Yoshisaemon by Captain Minitzky, the governor of Okhotsk. According to custom, the Japanese officers apologized for not having produced this paper sooner, and blamed the stupidity of Yoshisaemon for having kept it so long in his possession without saying a word about it. But we were not so simple as to put faith in this tale, as we knew that it would have been impossible for the Japanese who returned in the *Diana* to have concealed anything they brought ashore with them, far less an official paper under an imperial seal, which had evidently been brought from Okhotsk. This certificate stated that Khvostov had acted without authority, and that his conduct had accordingly exposed him to the displeasure of the government. And, moreover, that Yoshisaemon with his companion had twice fled from Okhotsk, without waiting for permission to return to their native country, which was, however, granted after their second escape. Finally, Captain Minitzky expressed his approbation of the good conduct of Yoshisaemon during the time he had lived in Okhotsk. Having verbally explained this document, we carried away a copy to make a translation, which was immediately forwarded to the capital along with the original.

On the 8th of November, the Japanese, whom Captain Ricord had put ashore at Kunashir, arrived at Matsumae, and were quartered in the house from which we had made our escape. They all underwent an examination, and Kumajirō, who was present, repeated what he had before told us, namely, that his countrymen spoke unfavorably of the Russians, and that Yoshisaemon praised Irkutzk; but represented Okhotsk, and the whole eastern part of Siberia, as being a poor miserable country, where he saw scarcely any human beings, except beggars and government officers. These Japanese remained about a week in Matsumae, and were then sent to Edo.

About this time, in one of my meetings with Mur, he informed me that our friend Arao Shigeaki, the former magistrate, had fallen into disgrace, and that his property had been seized. We were much concerned at hearing this, and had, besides, the mortification to reflect that Teisuke, in his letters, though he did not state anything positively, rather hinted that our business did not stand in the most favorable state. In December, however, Kumajirō informed us, as a great secret, that he had dreamt we were all liberated. He added, that he was sure his dream would be realized, for he had learned from an officer of distinction, just returned from the capital, that our case was expected to have a favorable result. Ricord's generous treatment of the Japanese, whom he had seized on board the vessel off Kunashir, had not only gained him the esteem of the government, but likewise of all the inhabitants of the capital. A note from Mur confirmed this intelligence, with the addition, that he had learned from one of the guards, that our things, which had been conveyed to Edo, were sent back to Matsumae, and that thoughts were entertained of restoring us to our native country.

A ray of hope now began to dawn upon us, and seemed to rescue us from despair. Thus perplexed between the expectation of liberty and distrust of the Japanese, we entered upon the new year 1813.

During the month of January, 1813, we received several letters from Teisuke, in answer to those we had addressed to him. In one of these letters, he plainly told us that the decision of our affair was still very doubtful, as various circumstances tended to prepossess the government against us. And that all that had been alleged in our justification had hitherto been insufficient to remove prejudices that were of long standing and firmly rooted. Teisuke appropriately reminded us of the Japanese proverb "A fog cannot he dispelled with a fan." This communication from our best friend was very discouraging. And besides, our guards openly informed us that Arao Shigeaki had been removed from his office, and that another nobleman was already appointed to fill his place.

To this unlucky circumstance was added another, which occasioned us no less uneasiness. In the beginning of February all the letters Teisuke had addressed to Mur were seized. One of our attendants, whom Teisuke's brother had intrusted to carry a letter to Mur, was so imprudent as to deliver it in the presence of the sentinel on duty. The latter observed it, and instantly raised an alarm. The servant was discharged, a serjeant or corporal was sent to superintend our military guard, and we were treated with some degree of incivility. But on our complaining of the conduct of our attendants, they were ordered to behave as respectfully towards us as before. But what we most of all feared was that the correspondence of our friend Teisuke might be attended with serious consequences to himself, as his letters contained many expressions calculated to give offense to the Japanese government. Kumajirō and our guards assured us that no notice would be taken of the contents of these letters, but we could not place much faith in what they said.

In the middle of February Kumajirō informed us that our business was settled, but that nobody, without incurring the risk of a severe punishment, could venture to make known the decision before the arrival of the new magistrate. He assured us that the Japanese government had decided on nothing to our disadvantage. This piece of news plunged us into the most perplexing uncertainty. What resolution had been adopted we could not possibly guess, since all that could be collected from Kumajirō's information was that it was neither good nor bad. We anxiously waited for the appearance of the new magistrate, on whose arrival the riddle was to receive its solution.

Khlebnikov had been extremely melancholy ever since the 11th of March. He sometimes tasted no food for whole days together, and was unable to sleep. In the course of time, however, his spirits began to revive. But his health was never completely restored, until he re-embarked on board the *Diana*.

Mur's Conduct

On the 18th of March, 1813, the new magistrate, Hattori Sadakatsu,[1] arrived and entered on his office. His suite included several officers, our friend Teisuke, a member of the Japanese academy named Adachi Nobuakira,[2] and an interpreter of the Dutch language named Baba Sadayoshi.[3] Teisuke was eager to prove that his attachment to us was undiminished. He had no sooner landed than he hastened to visit us, even before he had seen his father or any of his relations, and brought us sweetmeats. He consoled us with the information that the new magistrate had been directed to correspond with the Russians, and that orders were to be immediately transmitted to all forts and harbors, to prohibit the firing on the Russian ships.

From the account Teisuke gave us, our benefactor Arao Shigeaki appeared more noble and generous than ever. He informed us that the Japanese government had determined not to listen to any conciliatory proposals on the part of Russia, as from all that had transpired, and in particular the declaration of Nakagawa Yoshisaemon, they could expect nothing but falsehood, fraud, and hostility.

3 Hattori Sadakatsu (1761–1824) was the scion of a long string of *bakufu* officials and first entered service in 1794 as a page to Tokogawa Ieharu. By 1806, he had climbed to the position of *metsuke* (inspector), and in 1812 he was appointed *ongoku bugyō* (magistrate to remote shogunal cities.

2 Adachi Nobuakira (1769–1845) was a native of Osaka who made his careeer as an astronomer and bakufu administrator.

3 Baba Sadayoshi (1787–1822) was a native of Nagasaki who studied Dutch and French under the commissioner of the Dutch trading post in Nagasaki, Hendrik Doeff, and went on to become a prominent rangakusha, asholar of Dutch, i.e., Western learning.

Arao Shigeaki, however, questioned Yoshisaemon in the presence of the new magistrate, convicted him of prevarication in his answers, and brought him to acknowledge that all he had asserted respecting the hostile intentions of Russia towards Japan, and Khvostov's having acted by order of the government, had been merely uttered at random. He moreover sought to overthrow the grounds on which the members of the government rested their opinions. He represented to them that they ought not to judge of the laws and customs of other nations by their own, and at length prevailed on them to resolve to enter into explanations with the nearest Russian commander. He likewise made strong representations against the Japanese government prohibiting Russian ships, even coming with explanations, from entering any other port than that of Nagasaki, and observed that the Russians would thereby be led to believe that another trap was prepared for them. For how could they be convinced that the Japanese were inclined to act candidly and honorably when they required the Russian vessels to undertake so long a voyage, to settle an affair that might be decided equally well, and infinitely more promptly, in any harbor of the Kuril Islands.

The member of the government having, in answer to his representations, urged that they could not, without violating their laws, permit Russian vessels to enter any other port than that of Nagasaki, he made the following remarkable reply: "Since the sun, the moon, and the stars, which are the creation of the Almighty, are variable in their course, the Japanese laws, the work of weak mortals, cannot be eternal and unchangeable." By these arguments he prevailed on the government to order the magistrate of Matsumae to correspond with our ships, without requiring them to sail to Nagasaki.

Teisuke, moreover, informed us, that though Arao Shigeaki was no longer the magistrate of Matsumae, he had obtained a more important post, though the emoluments attached to his present office were somewhat less considerable, because everything was much dearer in Matsumae than in the capital, where he was, in future, to reside. He was now appointed magistrate of all the *bakufu* palaces in the empire of Japan. Teisuke staid so long conversing with us that his father sent for him twice. He did not, however, take leave of us until be had completely removed all our apprehensions.

A day or two after the arrival of the new magistrate, Kumajirō informed us that the chief officer wished us to teach the academician Adachi Nobuakira and the Dutch interpreter Baba Sadayoshi, who had arrived from the capital, the Russian language, and to give them, as far as we were able, any other instruction they might desire. I expressed my surprise that before the new magistrate had given us an audience, or communicated the decision of the Japanese government, we should be required to instruct persons who had been sent from the capital.

I asked Mur, through the partition separating our apartments, what he thought of this proposal, and he made the following reply: "Until the magistrate makes us acquainted with the decision on our case, nothing shall induce me to comply with his request. But whenever he shall make that communication, I am ready to work, day and night, in giving the Japanese instructions." I proposed that we should devote an hour or two every day to instructing these men until the Russian ships arrived. We should then perceive what were the real views of the Japanese government respecting us, and be able to adopt measures accordingly. But Mur would listen to nothing of the kind. I was unable to guess the cause of this obstinacy, but supposed that he wished, by his present zeal, to make his former conduct be forgotten. But the mystery was soon unravelled in a different way.

Kumajirō went away without having received any decisive answer to his message. A few days afterwards, Mur and I were conducted to the castle, where the two principal officers, in the presence of several others, informed us that they had been directed to write to the Russians, who would probably soon approach the coasts of Japan with their ships, and to request an explanation of Khvostov's conduct from the commander of the nearest Russian government or district. They accordingly intended to send oft letters to this effect to the different harbors of the northern Japanese possessions. The translations, they observed, must be executed by Teisuke, Kumajirō, and us. The interpreter then explained the contents of the Japanese letter, in order that we might be able to state our opinion respecting the proposition it contained.

The letter appeared to me extremely well written. I thanked the Japanese for having adopted measures that would probably spare much useless bloodshed, both to Russia and Japan, and stated my conviction that our government would not fail to return a satisfactory answer. They then informed me, that in case our ships entered the ports of Matsumae or Hakodate, they proposed sending the letter on board by one or two of our sailors. I expressed my approval of this plan, as our countrymen would thereby be convinced that we were still in existence. I at the same time begged that they would permit me to write a few small notes, which might be sent along with the copies of their letter to the other fortified harbors, to intimate to our friends that we were all well in health. To this the Japanese gave their assent, but observed that these notes must be as brief as possible. And, as it would be necessary to send them to Edo, to receive the sanction of the government, they advised us to write them speedily. This advice I followed without delay, on my return to the place of our confinement, and then set about the translation of the Japanese letter, in which Mur and Alexei assisted.

About this time the two learned Japanese, namely, Adachi Nobuakira and Baba Sadayoshi, paid us their first visit. We merely exchanged compliments, and they made no allusion to the object of their journey. They brought us some sweetmeats, and urgently solicited that we would give them a French dictionary, and one or two other French books.

Soon after Mur addressed me in the following remarkable way: "You, who are the cause of our misfortune," he said, "should not be the first to go on board our ship. Andrey Ilyitsch, meaning Khlebnikov, is almost at death's door, and the sailors are too stupid to arrange anything with propriety. It will, therefore, be best to send me on board the ship, accompanied by Alexei, who has been three years in imprisonment, whilst our sailors have lived only two years in Japan. But I cannot make this request to the Japanese. You must therefore do so, for your fate depends upon it. If you neglect to follow this advice, you are lost."

"How so?" I inquired.

"For reasons that are well known to me," replied Mur, in an emphatic tone. I observed that the Japanese government must be consulted before any new arrangement could be determined on, and as this would necessarily occasion loss of time, I could not think of making the application he wished for.

"Then," he said, "you will repent of your error when it will be too late."

I was at a loss to divine the meaning of these threats. On the following day Mur again addressed me through the partition. One of the soldiers, he said, had informed him, that the Japanese intended to entrap the commander of a Russian ship, and a party of officers and sailors, equal in number to ourselves, and then to let us free, as it were, in exchange for them. This circumstance, he observed, might occasion bloodshed. He therefore advised me to reflect, and to permit him to go on board first, as he could, of course, render the matter more intelligible than the sailors. He would induce Captain Ricord to take care that we should all be safely given up to him. No child could have been imposed on by such a story as this. What soldier would have ventured to divulge so important a secret. And yet Mur stated a prudent old man of seventy to be the author of his information. I coolly replied, that no credit could be given to the statement. But Mur would not suffer the affair to rest here. He shortly afterwards told me that the Japanese intended to capture our ships, together with the whole of their crews, and then to send an embassy to Okhotsk, on board of a Japanese vessel. He said he had received this intelligence from the old man, and likewise from a young soldier, and insisted on being sent to Captain Ricord instead of the sailors. This invention was even more laughable than the former.

I merely replied, "Heaven's will be done!" and said no more on the subject.

We had now finished translating the letter that was to be sent on board our ships. It was addressed thus: "From the two chief commanders next to the magistrate of Matsumae, to the commander of the Russian ships."

The contents were briefly as follows: The Japanese, in as far as was consistent with their laws, maintained intercourse with the Ambassador Resanov, in Nagasaki. But though they offered him not the least provocation, the Russian ships had, without the slightest reason, commenced hostilities on the coasts of Japan. Accordingly, when the *Diana* appeared, the commander of Kunashir, who, of course, regarded the Russians as the enemies of his country, took seven of the crew prisoners. These men have indeed declared, that the conduct of the commander of those ships was unauthorized by the government, but as prisoners, the Japanese cannot give credit to what they say. They therefore wish to have their account confirmed by higher authority, and this confirmation must be sent to Hakodate.

The Japanese wished us to translate this document with the utmost precision, and to adhere as closely as possible to the literal meaning. They required that the words in the translation should follow each other in the same order as in the original, wherever the idiom of both languages would permit of their doing so, and they directed us to pay no regard to elegance of style. This translation accordingly occupied us for several days together, from morning to night. Even when we had finished it, the magistrate sent it back several times, requesting us to make corrections, which he pointed out. At length, the task being completed, we made several copies of the letter, which we put up under covers, in the European style, with Russian superscriptions. They were then sent off to the different harbors.

On the 27th of March we were introduced to the new magistrate. He was a young man, about thirty-five years of age, handsome, and had a very pleasing expression of face. His suite consisted of eight individuals, as he was superior in rank to the two former magistrates. After asking our names and ranks, he addressed us as the other magistrates had formerly done, and gave us reason to hope that the business between the Japanese government and us would terminate in the way we wished. He questioned us respecting our health, and whether we were satisfied with the food with which we were supplied, and then withdrew. We returned home, accompanied by the interpreters.

We this day overheard a conversation between Mur and the interpreters, that filled us with horror. He asked Teisuke to obtain for him a private interview with the magistrate, as he had something of great importance to communicate to him. Teisuke replied that the magistrate would not grant an interview, unless he were first informed, through the interpreters, what was the nature of the business which rendered a private conference necessary. Mur then declared that the object of our voyage had been to make observations on the southern Kuril Islands, which are under the dominion of the Japanese. But for what reason the Russian government had ordered me to make these observations I alone could inform them, as I never communicated my instructions to the officers. He further stated, that we had concealed various circumstances from the Japanese, and in our translations had construed many passages in a way different from their real meaning, etc. On hearing this, Teisuke asked him whether he had lost his senses, as such declarations would, of course, prove as injurious to himself as they could be to us. Mur replied that he was perfectly aware of what he was doing, and that he was resolved to confess the truth. Teisuke now lost all patience, and told him that, even allowing he did speak truth, it was now too late, as a decision had taken place, and if satisfactory explanations were received from Russia, we would be immediately set at liberty. Mur, however, insisted on being taken before the magistrate, upon which Teisuke became irritated, and left him. He then entered our apartment, and told us, that if Mur were not mad, he must have a very black heart. On the following day Mur, indeed, discoursed like one who was bereft of reason. But whether his derangement was real or counterfeit, Heaven only knows.

Two days afterwards, Mur having expressed a wish to be again confined along with us, the Japanese conducted him and Alexei to our apartment.

We were now daily visited by the Dutch interpreter, Baba Sadayoshi, and the man of learning, Adachi Nobuakira, whom we have styled the academician, because he was a member of a learned society, somewhat resembling our academies. The interpreter began to fill up and improve the Russian vocabularies. He used to refer to a French and Dutch Lexicon, in order to inquire through the French for such Russian words as he did not know. He then searched for these words in a Russian lexicon, which he had in his possession. He was a man about twenty-seven years of age. And as he possessed an excellent memory and considerable knowledge of grammar, he made a rapid progress in acquiring the Russian language. This induced me to attempt to compile a Russian grammar for him, as well as I could from mere recollection. Having no books by the help of which I could compose a complete grammar, I was forced to content myself with what I could put together from memory. I devoted more than four months to the completion of this task. In the preface I stated that, should it ever chance to fall into the hands of a Russian or any individual who understood our language, the circumstances under which it was written must be taken into account. All the examples I introduced bore a reference to the relations between Russia and Japan, and were so contrived as to recommend the approximation and friendship of both nations. With this the Japanese were highly pleased. They eagerly set about translating my manuscript and, though it formed a tolerably large volume, they soon accomplished the task. Teisuke and Baba Sadayoshi, particularly the latter, were extremely quick in comprehending the rules of grammar, but they could not find time to learn them by heart. I besides translated into Russian some French and Dutch dialogues, which were in a French grammar, and they proved very useful to the Dutch interpreter in learning our language.

Adachi Nobuakira employed himself in translating from the Russian a work on arithmetic, published at Petersburg for the use of the public schools, and which had been brought to Japan by A Japanese whom Laxman conveyed back to his native country in 1792. In explaining the arithmetical rules, we soon observed that he possessed considerable knowledge of the subject, and that he only wished to be made acquainted with the Russian demonstrations. I was curious to know how far his knowledge of mathematics extended, and frequently conversed with him on matters connected with that science. But as our interpreters entertained not the slightest notion of the subject, I found it impossible to make all the inquiries I wished. I will, however, state a few circumstances, which may enable the reader to form some idea of the mathematical knowledge of the Japanese.

Nobuakira once asked me, whether the Russians, like the Dutch, reckoned according to the new style. When I replied that the Russians reckoned by the old style, he requested me to explain to him the distinction between the old and new styles, and what occasioned the difference between them, which I accordingly did. He then observed, that the new mode of reckoning was by no means exact, because after a certain number of centuries a difference of twenty-four hours would again arise. I readily perceived that he questioned me merely to discover how far I was informed on a subject with which he was perfectly familiar. The Japanese consider the Copernican the true system of the universe. The orbit and satellites of Uranus are known to them, but they know nothing of the planets that have been more recently discovered.

Khlebnikov employed himself in the calculation of logarithms, of natural sines and tangents, and other tables connected with navigation, which he completed, after incredible labour and application. When Nobuakira was shown these tables, he immediately recognized the logarithms, and drew a figure to convince us that he was also acquainted with the nature of the sines and tangents. In order to ascertain whether the Japanese knew how to demonstrate geometrical truths, I asked whether they were perfectly convinced that in a right-angled triangle the square of the hypothenuse is equal to the squares of the other two sides? He answered in the affirmative. I then asked how they were certain of this fact, and in reply he demonstrated it very clearly. Haying drawn a figure with a pair of compasses on paper, he cut out the three squares, folded the squares of the two short sides into a number of triangles, and also cut out these triangles; then laying the several triangles on the surface of the large square, he made them exactly cover and fit it.

Nobuakira assured us that the Japanese calculate with great precision the eclipses of the sun and moon. This is not improbable, for they have a translation of Joseph Jérôme Lefrançois de Lalande's *Astronomy*, and, as I have already observed, a European astronomer resides in their capital.

Teisuke and Kumajirō generally came to visit us along with Nobuakira and Sadayoshi. They usually staid with us the whole forenoon, and sometimes all day. This time was not wholly devoted to scientific investigations; our visitors frequently entertained us by relating singular occurrences and interesting anecdotes. Among other things, Teisuke gave us an account of the examination of Yoshisaemon, the Japanese who had returned from Russia, which took place in the presence of the new magistrate and Arao Shigeaki. On being asked how he had been treated by the Russians, he spoke with the highest praise and gratitude of the magistrate of Irkutzk, the Commandant of Jakutzk.

On being asked what he knew respecting our government, he replied, "The emperor of Russia is extremely kind and condescending; his subjects regard him as their father, but his officers seek to deceive him. And in order to enrich themselves, carry on trade and provoke warfare with neighboring states." All this, he said, he had learnt from the Japanese who lived at Irkutzk.

To prove that these observations Yoshisaemon made respecting Russia were singularly erroneous, it is only necessary to reflect on our relations with China. The rash and offensive conduct of the Chinese would a thousand times have justified Russia in punishing them. Yet our government benevolently forebore to do so, reflecting that these people, like other Asiatic nations, were ignorant of the laws of Europe.

He characterized the Russian nation as being warlike and rapacious. His countrymen in Irkutzk had shown him, on the map, the boundaries of Russia in former times, and assured him that the government had not purchased a foot of ground, but had acquired their present extent of territory by conquest. He had himself made the following observations: In Russia, should a boy find a stick in the streets, he immediately takes it up and goes through the military exercise. He had, besides, frequently seen numbers of boys assemble together for the purpose of practising military exercises. And the soldiers, wherever he saw them, were constantly under arms. From all the circumstances, he concluded that Russia was meditating a war with the Japanese, for she had no neighbors in that quarter of the world, except China and Japan. With China she maintained commercial relations, consequently all her preparations must be directed against Japan. At this latter observation both the magistrates laughed, and called him a blockhead; adding, that in Japan it was customary for boys to fence with swords, and soldiers to go through their exercise, though no war was in contemplation. Yoshisaemon then excused himself by apologizing for his want of consideration in drawing such a conclusion.

The magistrates reproached him for having changed his name without any motive; observing, that had he been a person of distinction, he might have adopted this mode of insuring his safety. But whether a man in his humble condition of life were called Nakagawa Yoshisaemon or Nakagawa Gorōji, must be a matter of indifference to the Russians. He could urge nothing in his justification, but acknowledged his error, and begged pardon.

On being asked what had struck him as being most remarkable in Irkutzk, he replied that the market and churches had most engaged his attention. He made a drawing of the marketplace, and described it with tolerable precision. But with respect to the churches, he could only say that they contained many beautiful images, and that every object seemed glittering in gold. Arao Shigeaki wished that he should draw a plan of Irkutzk, its streets, and public buildings, but he plainly acknowledged that he had made no observations on the town. "Did not the Russians suffer you to go out?" inquired the magistrates. "Oh yes," he replied, "they even advised us to walk about for the sake of our health; the magistrate himself frequently desired us to do so." "Why then,"continued the magistrates, "did you not avail yourself of this indulgence, and inspect the city with attention, so that on your return home you might have been able to give an account of what you saw?' Yoshisaemon again confessed his negligence, and begged that they would pardon him.

He was then asked whether he had ever witnessed a Russian festival. "Yes," he replied, "and one of the greatest that is held. On that day all the soldiers in Irkutzk assembled on the parade, and a great firing took place (the festival of Epiphany). The magistrate desired me to go out early in the morning to see the ceremonies, and informed me that in the afternoon all the people in the streets would wear their festival dresses. I therefore went out in the morning and saw the soldiers. But I suddenly heard the firing of musketry and cannon, which so terrified me that I hastened back, and did not go out again all day." In return for this confession the magistrates again called him a blockhead, and reproached him for having let slip the opportunity of observing the ceremonies and dresses of the Russians on such an occasion.

On being asked what he did on his return home, he very coolly replied, "I employed myself in writing down my observations." The magistrate and all present burst into a fit of laughter. They inquired what observations he could possibly make since he had seen nothing. "I wrote down," he replied, "all that I had heard from my countrymen." He had, indeed, brought home with him a whole packet of papers filled with observations.

Teisuke assured us that Yoshisaemon's papers contained a great deal concerning Siberia and the trade with China by the way of Kyakhta, but what he had written on these subjects Teisuke either could not or would not inform us. The magistrates were not inclined to give much credit to the remarks made by Yoshisaemon. They told him that had he related what he had either seen himself, or heard from the Russians, his account would have merited attention. But that he had, on the contrary, received all his information from Japanese who had forsworn their native country and religion, and on whose assertions the government could place no reliance.

The magistrates questioned him at considerable length concerning that part of Siberia through which he had travelled. Yoshisaemon represented it as being extremely poor and wretched; he declared that the inhabitants of Okhotsk were mere beggars, and that the population of the whole track of country from Irkutzk to Okhotsk was not more numerous than that of a small Japanese town. In short, he constantly overstepped the truth, and represented everything worse than it really was.

In speaking of the trade with China, he accused our countrymen of fraud in their dealings, and acquitted the Chinese of all blame, alleging that the Court of Peking had frequently threatened to put a stop to the trade, but that the Russians had promised to punish the offenders, though this promise was never fulfilled. Such, he said, was the account given by the Japanese who resided in Irkutzk.

There were farther questions and answers, but Teisuke he said could recollect only a few of them: perhaps he did not wish to let us know all that had passed. He made, however, the following addition to what he had already related of the account which Yoshisaemon gave of his adventures: Whilst in Okhotsk he observed, in a warehouse belonging to the Russian-American Company, a number of Japanese books and charts, which were deposited in a corner. They had been brought from Japan by Khvostov. The attention of the officers of the Company seemed much more occupied with the rice than with these books and charts. Yoshisaemon looked over the books, and found one containing a description of Japan, which he conceived it would be improper to suffer the Russians to possess. He therefore requested permission to read it, and conveyed it to his lodging, where he burned it. He likewise found means secretly to remove the charts, one by one, from the warehouse, and on taking them home consigned them all to the flames. When he arrived at Irkutzk he related this circumstance to a Japanese with whom he lived, and who had previously become a convert to the Russian church. The latter observed that he had taken a great deal of useless trouble, as he had himself brought several books and charts from Japan, which he had explained to the Russians. On Yoshisaemon's reproaching him for his imprudence, he excused himself by saying that he had become a Russian, and was no longer a Japanese.

When Yoshisaemon attempted to escape along with his companions, in the expectation of meeting Tongusians, he carried along with him a copper image of a saint, to enable him to pass for a Russian. On entering the territory of the Giliaks, however, he passed himself for a Chinese ambassador, and showed the people the image, which he said was a likeness of the Chinese emperor. The Giliaks received him with so much cordiality, that he formed the design of passing the winter among them, and resuming his journey in the spring. However, on arriving at Udskoy Ostrog his plans were frustrated—he was seized, and conveyed to Okhotsk.

Teisuke, besides, frankly told us, that the Japanese, who was sent ashore with the letters from Captain Ricord, actually received orders from the governor of Kunashir to state that we were dead. The motive for this falsehood was as follows: the Japanese assured his countrymen that Russia would no doubt declare war against Japan, and that all her friendly representations were mere artifice. Captain Ricord had, however, stated in his letter, that he would not quit the harbor until he received a satisfactory answer. And at the approach of our ships, all the fishermen and laboring people on the southern coast of Kunashir had fled into the garrison, so that all business was suspended. It was, therefore, with a view to put an end to this state of things, and to induce the Russians to land and attempt to storm the garrison, that the assertion of our having been put to death was fabricated. The commissioner (*shirabeyaku*), Odachi Kōeki, at this time commander of Kunashir, was the same officer who had so frequently treated us with so much derision at Hakodate, and his personal hatred of the Russians had probably dictated the answer he sent to Captain Ricord. This answer, Teisuke told us, excited no displeasure on the part of the government; on the contrary, several of the ministers expressed their approbation of the conduct of Odachi Kōeki, which, in their opinion, proved him to be an extremely judicious and able man.

Teisuke, besides, informed us that his correspondence with us had involved him in considerable difficulty during his stay in the capital. The letters taken from Mur had been sent to Edo. The government required Teisuke to translate all the letters he had received from us, and those which he had written to us: but he was prudent enough to give a different interpretation to the passages in which he spoke disrespectfully of his countrymen. The officers of the government, to whose perusal these translations were submitted, asked him how he dared to correspond with foreigners, when he knew that a law existed by which that kind of intercourse was prohibited. Teisuke excused himself by saying that he was not aware that such foreigners as had been made prisoners by the Japanese were included in this law; adding that he had not corresponded with us for any improper purpose, but merely through motives of compassion. He had never imagined that this correspondence could be attended by any evil consequences, but he was ready to suffer death, should the government regard his crime as sufficiently enormous to call for such a punishment. He was, however, merely reprimanded, and admonished to be more prudent in future. The letters remained in the hands of the government, and the affair had luckily no injurious result for Teisuke. Both he and Kumajirō were afterwards promoted for their labours in translating, and the zeal they had manifested in acquiring the Russian language. Teisuke was appointed to fill the office of assistant, and Kumajirō that of secretary.

It is with the utmost pain that I again call the attention of the reader to a circumstance, which, in the midst of our sufferings, harassed my feelings, and the recollection of which is, even now, attended by the most distressing sensations—I allude to the conduct of Mur. If I unfold his errors, it is not that I wish to dwell on the description of the horrors into which he plunged me and my unfortunate companions. No: may his example prove a warning to all young men whom fate may hereafter overwhelm with misfortunes such as we were doomed to endure. May it serve to convince them, that no wretch is visited by remorse so insufferable as he who renounces his faith and his country. If, like the unhappy Mur, whose history is as instructive as memorable, he has previously been a man of rectitude and extreme sensibility, how dreadful must be his torments when he returns to the paths of virtue, and looks back upon his past conduct. I entreat the reader not to condemn this unfortunate officer. If he accompanies me to the end of my narrative, his indignation will be converted into pity, and he will, perhaps, shed a tear over the sad memory of this poor miserable youth.

After Mur was quartered along with us, he often discoursed with the guards like a person bereft of reason. For instance, he assured them that he heard the officers of their government calling to him from the roof of the house, and reproaching him with having drunk the blood of the Japanese and ate their rice; that the interpreters, moreover, called to him from the streets, and came during the night secretly to consult with me and Khlebnikov on the best means of getting rid of him.

At certain intervals he was perfectly collected, and then what he said always indicated that he had a particular object in view. On one occasion, he told Teisuke, that he had many fine books, charts, pictures, and other objects of curiosity on board the *Diana*, and that if the Japanese would grant him permission to go first on board, he would send valuable presents to the officers and interpreters. Teisuke replied, that the Japanese were not desirous of receiving presents, as in fact they stood in need of none, and that all they wanted was that our government should send them a satisfactory explanation respecting the proceedings of the Company's ships.

Another time Mur, in the presence of the interpreters and Nobuakira, said that his devotion to the Japanese would only tend to ruin him, since they had refused to take him into their service, and he dared not return to Russia. "How so?" inquired the interpreters. "Because," he replied, "I have offered to enter the Japanese service; nay, even to become a servant of the magistrate; this is known to my companions, and must, of course, become known to the Russian government; therefore, were I to return home, I should be condemned to the gallies."The interpreters, and Teisuke in particular, endeavored to set his mind at ease. They told him that his wish to enter the Japanese service was sufficiently excused by his situation. Teisuke added, that he had never mentioned to us Mur's proposal of entering the service of the magistrate, which he had now himself disclosed, but that he trusted we would communicate nothing to the Russian government that might tend to injure him.

We, on our part, assured him that he had no reason to fear returning to Russia: our government would not judge of his offense, if ever it came to their knowledge, with the severity which he anticipated. But Mur was far from being satisfied. Some secrets of which he had made a written disclosure to the Japanese weighed upon his mind. This was what he alluded to when he spoke of his devotion to the Japanese. He endeavored, by various means, to prove his attachment to Japan, and said, that if the Japanese could see what was passing within his heart, they would place greater confidence in him.

At length the interpreters informed him that even a Japanese who should live for any length of time in a foreign country would forfeit the confidence of his countrymen. "How then," said they, "can we venture to take a foreigner into our service, whatever degree of attachment he may profess towards our nation?" They further observed, that though a thousand Russians had been made prisoners by the Japanese, their fate would depend on two alternatives. If our declarations were confirmed by the Russian government we should all be liberated; even such amongst us who might be unwilling to return would be forcibly carried on board our ships: but in case the expected confirmation should not be received, we must remain in confinement without being permitted to enter into the Japanese service, or even to follow any kind of employment.

The interpreters added, that if Mur had reason to dread the consequences of returning to Russia, the Japanese must sympathize in his fate, but that their laws could not be violated in his favor.

On our informing the interpreters that the apprehensions expressed by Mur were totally unfounded, they represented to him that his fears arose merely out of the disordered state of his mind. But Mur declared himself to be perfectly collected and observed that the laws of Japan were severe and barbarous. The interpreters replied that he might, indeed, think them so, but that the Japanese considered them extremely lenient and good.

On this occasion they explained to us the grounds on which their laws prohibit them from reposing any trust in Japanese subjects who have lived in foreign countries. The great mass of mankind, said they, resemble children; they soon become weary of what they possess, and willingly give up everything for the sake of novelty. When they hear of certain things being better in foreign countries than in their own, they immediately wish to possess them, without reflecting that they might, perhaps, prove useless, or even injurious to them.

With regard to Mur's conduct, he still continued either to discourse like a madman, or remained totally silent. He once told me, in a determined tone, that he saw only two courses he could take: we must either request that he and Alexei might first be permitted to go on board the Russian vessels, when he would take measures to ensure our safety; if not our refusal would compel him to adopt the only remaining alternative, which might, perhaps, prove fatal to us all, namely, he would inform the Japanese that the object of our voyage was to inspect their coasts, and that there was even a probability of the Russians declaring war against them. I replied that we were not to be intimidated by threats of this kind. We knew, from experience, the disposition of the Japanese; they would, of course, come to no speedy decision on his representation. In the meanwhile, communications might take place, and all would, probably, terminate favorably to us. The sailors, with tears, entreated that he would not act so dishonorably, assuring him, that on their return to Russia, they would never divulge a syllable that might operate to his disadvantage. "I know well," he replied, "what I have to expect. I recollect that when we were in the presence of the magistrate, Skajev, in a threatening tone, inquired whether I entertained thoughts of returning to Russia?" The words which Skajev uttered on that occasion had apparently made a deep impression on his mind; he frequently alluded to them.

On my asking him what would be his feelings, were he to succeed in convincing the Japanese of the truth of his assertions, and should thereby induce them to entrap our countrymen, he made me various incoherent answers. "Even allowing," continued I, "that the Japanese should capture our vessels, the truth may sooner or later come to light, and we be sent back to Russia, what then would become of you?"

"I should then only undergo the same punishment as I must, were I to return now," he replied.

I endeavored to console him, and observed, that he was not responsible for his conduct, as he was evidently laboring under derangement.

When I asked him what rendered him so impatient to go first on board the Russian vessels, he constantly varied in his answers. Sometimes he said he wished to be the instrument of reconciliation between two nations, and thus to expiate his faults. At other times he expressed a wish to warn our countrymen of the snares the Japanese had laid for them, or to persuade them to send from the ships some cannon and other things as pledges for the restoration of the articles of which Khvostov had robbed the Japanese. These singular answers sufficiently proved that he was occasionally under the influence of derangement.

Though Mur found that his menaces made no impression on us, he did not, on that account, cease to harass us. He sometimes told the interpreters what threats he had held out to us. They, however, paid no regard to this discourse, which was directly aimed at our ruin. They called him a madman. Instead of making replies consistent with his applications, they referred to a physician. After some time it was, indeed, found necessary to place him under the care of a physician. But no investigation was ever instituted, in order to ascertain whether he had been in his right senses at the time he uttered these expressions. This circumstance led Khlebnikov to believe that the Japanese were practising some artifice; that they pretended to believe Mur insane, in order to throw us off our guard, and to deceive the sailors, who were to be sent as messengers to our countrymen. But that their real design was to capture the Russian ships by some stratagem, after which they would probably inquire whether or not Mur had spoken truth. This suspicion, groundless as it appeared, induced me to write five notes, addressed to Captain Ricord, which the sailors and Alexei stitched within the lining of their jackets. As it was not known which might be sent off, it was necessary that each should have one in his possession. These notes I directed to be delivered to the commander, whoever he might be, of the Russian ships, on board of which any of our sailors might be put by the Japanese. The distrust Khlebnikov entertained of the sincerity of the Japanese was certainly pushed to the extreme of improbability. Still, it was proper to warn our countrymen, lest, by any imprudent confidence, they might have been plunged into a state of wretchedness similar to our own.

The five notes I wrote were all to the same purport, and contained an exhortation to Captain Ricord, or the Russian commanding officer, to observe the utmost caution in his communications with the Japanese, and not to suffer his boats to approach within gunshot of the garrison. I requested him not to take offense at the tardy proceedings of the Japanese, as their laws prohibited them from doing anything with precipitancy, and obliged them to submit every affair of importance to the consideration of their government. I moreover stated all that Mur had disclosed to the Japanese, in order that he might be prepared to answer all the questions that would, probably, be put to him in the course of his examination. In conclusion, I observed that there was every reason to hope for reconciliation with the Japanese, and that, in course of time, commercial relations might probably be established between them and Russia.

Finding that all his plans proved unsuccessful, Mur seemed lost in despair. On two or three occasions he attempted to put a period to his existence. But his designs were discovered by the guards, in time to prevent their execution. It sometimes struck me that these attempts were mere artifice; for had he really intended to commit suicide, he might easily have found an opportunity to carry his horrible design into execution without being observed. But whatever might be the fact, the Japanese began to watch him with the utmost strictness: even whilst he was asleep one always sat near him, to listen whether he continued to breathe. And if, for a moment, his respiration was not heard, the sentinel would strip down the quilt of his bed to ascertain he was still living. They likewise watched me with much attention. This caution may be readily accounted for. Had any of our party committed suicide, not merely the guards who were near us, but likewise our surviving companions, and the soldiers stationed on the outside of the house, who had no communication with us, would have been answerable for it. Such is the singular severity of the Japanese laws!

The precautions the Japanese had adopted having deprived Mur of all opportunity of putting an end to his existence, he made every possible endeavour to prevent any negotiation between the Russians and the Japanese. He advised the latter to demand, on the arrival of our ships, that their cannon, and arms of every kind, should be sent ashore as pledges, to remain in the hands of the Japanese until the property Khvostov had robbed them of was restored. They replied that if the Japanese emperor should be convinced that the Russian government had no connection with the proceedings of the Company's ships, he would regard the robbery as an act of private aggression. In that case, how could a great monarch require that another should indemnify his subjects for losses they may have sustained by robbery?—They besides added, that their emperor had long since compensated the individuals whose property was carried off by Khvostov for the loss they sustained.

Mur now appeared to be driven to the last extremity. He frequently refused to taste food for several days together, and all our endeavours to encourage and console him proved unavailing. For my own part, I now augured no good from all that was passing. The indifference with which the interpreters listened to the declarations of Mur was to me unaccountable. It in no way corresponded with the curiosity natural to the Japanese, who were accustomed to make the most minute and circumstantial inquiries respecting the merest trifles. I considered the matter in every point of view, without being able to come to any fixed opinion on the subject. Did the Japanese regard Mur as a madman, on whose declarations no reliance could be placed? Did the interpreters, after the supposed termination of the inquiry into our case, and after having been rewarded for their conduct, apprehend disagreeable consequences to themselves, if difficulties were now created by the disclosure of new and important circumstances? Or were Mur's words only apparently disregarded, in order that some more of our countrymen might be inveigled into a snare?

Though we could not believe Teisuke capable of so treacherously deceiving us, yet we recollected that he might, perhaps, be only doing what he considered his duty, in fulfilling the orders of his government, which, according to the representations of the Japanese themselves, was capable of almost any atrocity. In this state of doubt and perplexity we were doomed to await the unravelling of the mystery.

On the 10th of May, the note we had written, to be dispatched to the different harbors, and sent on board our vessels, was returned from the capital. The government had approved of its contents, and consequently not a single letter could be altered. Having made five copies, and affixed our signatures to each, they were dispatched on the same day to their several destinations. These notes were to the following effect:

> We are all, both officers and seamen, and the Ainu Alexei, alive, and reside in Matsumae.
> VASILII GOLOWNIN
> Feodor Mur
> May 10th, 1813

Khlebnikov was unable to sign the notes on account of severe illness.

The season had now returned when we daily expected to hear of the arrival of the Russian vessels. From Captain Ricord's letter, I concluded that he would sail straight to Matsumae. Every violent gale of wind made me tremble for the safety of our ships, on account of the fogs, which, in this quarter of the world, constantly accompany the east wind. Violent storms, accompanied by fogs and rain, frequently arise in these ports during the months of May, June, and July, which are precisely the periods when the whether is fair and the wind moderate in the northern hemisphere. Even when at sea, I never watched the state of the weather with more exactness than I did at this time. I marked down every variation however slight. The following memoranda may enable the reader to form some notion of a Japanese summer:

During the whole of the 30th and 31st of May, and 1st of June, a violent east wind blew without intermission, accompanied by fogs and rain.

On the 15th, 16th, 17th, and 18th of June, the same kind of weather prevailed, and for several succeeding days it likewise continued exceedingly stormy, the wind invariably blowing from the east.

In the expectation that we would be sent on board the Russian ships, the Japanese supplied us with materials for new suits of clothes, that we might make a decent appearance in the presence of our countrymen. Mur, Khlebnikov, and I, were provided with fine silken stuffs for our clothes and the lining. The sailors had the cotton cloth called *monba*, of which I have before spoken, delivered to them. The Japanese made for Alexei a dress after their own fashion.

At length, on the 19th of June, 1813, we were informed that a Japanese vessel, lying at anchor off a promontory in the Island of Kunashir, had observed a Russian three-masted ship sail round the cape, and enter Kunashir harbor. The Japanese vessel immediately weighed anchor, and brought infor-mation of this event to Hakodate.

On the 20th of June the arrival of the *Diana* in Kunashir was officially confirmed. But nothing more was said on the subject.

On the following day the interpreters, by order of their superiors, asked me which of the sailors I wished to send on board. That I might avoid showing any preference to one more than another, I determined that chance should decide the matter. And the lot happened to fall to Simanov. I requested that the magistrate would permit Alexei to accompany him. This he consented to, and they received orders to prepare for their departure. On the same day Mur and I were conducted to the castle, where the two deputy magistrates, in the presence of other officers, formally inquired whether we were perfectly satisfied that Alexei and Simanov should be sent on board the *Diana*. I replied in the affirmative. But Mur remained silent. Deputy magistrate Takahashi Shigekata then informed us, that he himself intended to depart for Kunashir, for the purpose of treating with Captain

Ricord. He, at the same time, promised to bring the affair to a conclusion, and assured us that Alexei and Simanov should experience every accommodation during their voyage. We were then dismissed.

Mur and I were again conducted to the castle on the 22nd of June, when the papers sent on shore by Captain Ricord were presented to us. They consisted of two letters, the one addressed to the commander of Kunashir, and the other to me. In the former he acquainted the Japanese of his arrival and friendly intentions, together with the return of their countryman, Takadaya Kahei, and two sailors whom he had carried off in the preceding year. Two Japanese and an Ainu had died in Kamchatka, though every endeavour had been made to save their lives. He, besides, described Takadaya Kahei[4] as an intelligent and good-principled man, who would, of course, convince the Japanese of the peaceable disposition of Russia, and would prevail on them to liberate us. But intimated that if they did not set us at liberty they might apprehend serious consequences. He concluded by saying that he trusted to the pacific character and generosity of the Japanese, and waited for an answer to this letter.

Ricord, in his letter to me, requested that I would return an answer, to acquaint him with the state of our health, and also what was our situation in other respects. It was evident that Ricord had written the letter before he received the papers dispatched to him. This circumstance surprised us not a little, for the Japanese had informed us that the orders issued by the government required that these papers should be conveyed by Ainu on board the first Russian ship that might appear on the coast. We were directed to take copies of both letters in presence of the officers, and in the evening we made translations of them. On the following day the originals, together with the translations, were sent off to the capital.

On the 24th of June, Takahashi Shigekata, Kumajirō, Simanov, and Alexei, sailed for Kunashir. I took every opportunity of instructing Simanov what to communicate to the officers of the *Diana* respecting the fortifications, military power, and tactics of the Japanese, and what would be the most

4 Takadaya Kahei (1769–1827) was a native of Awaji Island (in the Inland Sea) who earned his living as a sailor during his early years and later moved to Hakodate where he made his wealth in maritime trade and the fishing industry, contributing greatly to the towns economic growth.

advantageous mode of attacking them, in case such a proceeding should be found necessary. He seemed perfectly to understand my directions, and to be prepared to furnish his countrymen with much important information. I afterwards found I had formed an erroneous opinion of Simanov. Before he reached the *Diana*, he had forgotten nearly the whole of what I had stated, and could repeat only a few unconnected fragments of my instructions.

Previously to his departure, Simanov informed me that Mur had directed him to request Captain Ricord to send ashore the property he had left on board the *Diana* at the time he was made prisoner. I knew not what could be his object in making this application. I, however, ordered Simanov to deliver the message to Captain Ricord, and at the same time to request that he would not send the property on shore as, in doing so, he might involve us in fresh difficulties. Khlebnikov sent a note by Simanov, in which he warned Captain Ricord not to place too much confidence in the Japanese.

We heard no accounts from Kunashir until the 2nd of June, when a short letter was brought to us, addressed by Ricord to the magistrate of that island. It merely contained his thanks for the receipt of the note we had written, which, he observed, fully satisfied him with respect to our safety. We were required to translate this letter, and both original and translation were immediately dispatched to Edo.

On the 19th of July Mur and I were carried before the magistrate, and shown an official letter from Captain Ricord to Takahashi Shigekata, together with a letter to me, and one to Mur. In the first letter Captain Ricord thanked the Japanese government for their wish to correspond with the Russians, and promised immediately to sail back to Okhotsk, and to return in September, provided with the declaration required by the Japanese government. As he was unacquainted with the entrance of the harbor of Hakodate, he wished to put into the harbor, which had been visited by Captain Brougton, and requested that a skilful pilot might be sent thither to conduct the ship to Hakodate. Finally, he thanked Shigekata for having permitted Simanov to go on board the *Diana*. His letter to me commenced with the words we had agreed should be the token of his having received my note; he congratulated us on our approaching liberation, and promised to return without fail in September. He advised Mur to be patient, and not to give way to despair, observing that his countrymen at home had had no small share of distress, difficulty, and danger, to contend with.

The magistrate withdrew after having heard an explanation of these papers. We then took copies and prepared translations, which were immediately sent to Edo.

The Japanese informed us that the *Diana* left Kunashir immediately after these papers were sent ashore. According to our calculation this must have been on the 10th of July. A few days afterwards Shigekata, Kumajirō, and our two companions, returned to Matsumae. The reader may perhaps conjecture what were our feelings on again beholding them. It seemed as if missionaries, sent out by the dead, had returned from the land of the living. For two whole years we had heard no accounts from Russia or any other part of the world. We were even ignorant of the events which were passing in Japan. Our curiosity on the return of our companions, was unbounded. We hoped to be circumstantially informed of all that had taken place in Russia and other parts of Europe. But in this we were sadly disappointed. Simanov was one of those men to whom the term blockhead may be applied in its fullest acceptation. Turks and French were all one to him. He had never troubled himself with politics during the whole course of his life. All the information we could obtain from him was, that the French, together with the troops of three other nations, the names of which he did not know, had entered Russia; that they had been defeated in an engagement which took place about sixty kilometers from Smolensko, where several thousands of their troops were killed; that the remainder, under Bonaparte, had made a precipitate retreat. But how all this had taken place, who commanded the armies, and what was the actual state of the operations, he had totally forgotten. We consoled ourselves with the reflection that Simanov was not given to romancing, and that none of his news, as far as he was concerned, could be liable to the suspicion of fabrication. He had been told, on board the *Diana*, that his friend Fomka Mitrofanov was married, that Seniuschka Chlebalkin was dead, and a variety of other events of similar importance, and he gave as detailed a description of the wedding and funeral as if he had been present. His companions listened with the deepest interest to these accounts, which did not go beyond the narrow circle of their ideas.

It is of course unnecessary to detain the reader by a repetition of what

Simanov stated respecting the conferences between the Japanese and our countrymen. As Captain Ricord's narrative contains a full and accurate account of all that occurred in the negotiations, I shall therefore merely mention what the Japanese themselves disclosed on the subject. Kumajirō, who had been present with Sampei during the negotiations, gave us reason to hope for the most favorable result. The prospect he ascribed entirely to the ability and prudent conduct of Captain Ricord, who had so won the goodwill of Takadaya Kahei, and impressed him with so high an idea of the honor and rectitude of the Russians, that this Japanese declared himself willing to make oath, in the presence of the highest authorities, to his belief in all our statements. Kahei even accused Yoshisaemon, the Japanese who had returned from Russia, of falsehood; called him a dishonourable wretch. He protested that he would rather forfeit his life than recognise the opinion the Japanese government had hitherto entertained of the Russians as well founded. These words had such an influence over Takahashi Shigekata, that he refrained from urging certain conditions which he, at first, intended to insist on in his negociation with Captain Ricord. Among others, he departed from his original proposition for a complete restoration of all the Japanese arms that Khvostov had carried off, which he reduced to a demand for such only as could be collected in Okhotsk. In case none could be recovered, he observed that the Japanese would be satisfied with the assurance that the attack was not authorized by the Russian government. Kahei knew not how to bestow sufficient commendation on Captain Ricord, the officers of the *Diana*, and all the individuals he had known in Kamchatka.

He arrived at Matsumae in company with Sampei. But he was not permitted to pay us a visit, notwithstanding the infinite gratification it would have afforded both to him and ourselves. The Japanese laws required that he should have a guard set over him. His relations and friends were, indeed, allowed to see him, and to remain with him as long as they pleased, but a *bakufu* soldier was present the whole time of their visit.

Though Simanov could give us so little information concerning the political situation of Europe, it furnished a subject for the endless chattering of the Japanese. They informed us that two large Dutch ships, laden with East India goods, had arrived at Nagasaki, from Batavia. The Dutch assured the Japanese, that in consequence of a maritime war between England and

Holland, they had been unable to bring with them any European goods. But as the Dutch and English East India Companies had at that time concluded peace, and traded with each other, they were under the necessity of conveying Bengal goods to Japan. The Japanese now asked me whether this statement could, consistently with the practice of European warfare, be true. I frankly told them that there was some deception at the bottom of the statement. The fact, we told them, was, that the English had taken Batavia, and that the Dutch, it appeared, had fabricated this story, as they were apprehensive that the Japanese would not trade with them if they knew that their chief possession was in the hands of foreigners. I proposed that the Japanese should inform the Dutch who had arrived at Nagasaki, that they had learned in their negotiations with the Russians that Batavia was taken by the English, and to demand some explanation from them. The Japanese themselves concurred with me. At their request I drew up my advice in writing, and it was dispatched to Edo. What I stated in this instance was the more readily attended to, as I had, on a former occasion, communicated an important fact respecting Holland, which I afterwards had the opportunity of proving. It was as follows: The Dutchmen who lived in Nagasaki had declared to the Japanese, that their republican government had been converted into a kingdom, and that a brother of the French emperor had become their king. They did not, however, state that Holland had ceased to be an independent state, and had become a province of France. But of this circumstance they were probably ignorant, as no Dutch vessel had entered Nagasaki for several years. We frequently spoke to the interpreters on this subject. But they listened to us with indifference, and would not conceive it possible that Napoleon should so soon deprive his brother of the kingdom he had given him. Nothing appeared to the Japanese more improbable than this sudden manner in which kings and kingdoms were represented to be created and overthrown in Europe. At length, Mur looking over some Russian gazettes, which had been sent ashore along with the books from the *Diana*, accidentally found Napoleon's manifesto, in which Amsterdam was raised to the rank of third city of the French empire. Mur immediately showed this manifesto to the interpreters, who could, by this time, read Russian with tolerable facility, and they zealously commenced making a translation of it, which, when completed, was sent off to Edo.

When the Dutch residing in Nagasaki were questioned respecting this event, they replied, that they were totally ignorant of it: a circumstance which was by no means improbable.

I must here observe, that the Japanese do not entertain so favorable an opinion of the Dutch as they formerly did. Baba Sadayoshi told us that, during the last five years, no vessel belonging to Holland had entered Nagasaki, and that the Dutch, who lived there, had been exposed to the greatest privations, and even reduced to the necessity of selling the glass panes of their windows, in order to obtain the means of supporting their existence. On our inquiring why the Japanese government did not provide for their maintenance, as their expenses would afterwards be repaid, the interpreter replied, that the Japanese did not now think so well of the Dutch as they once had done, and that, as Holland had now become a French province, they certainly would break off all intercourse with them.

The most important intelligence the Dutch ships arrived at Nagasaki had brought, was an account of the taking of Moscow. We were told that the Russians, in a fit of despair, had abandoned and burnt their capital, and that the whole of Russia, as far as Moscow, was under the dominion of the French. We laughed at this story, and assured the Japanese that it could not possibly be true. We expressed our doubts on this subject, from real conviction, and not from any feeling of arrogance. We indeed believed it possible that the enemy might have concluded a peace on terms advantageous to himself. But as to the loss of Moscow, we looked upon that statement as an invention of the Dutch, and it never cost us a moment's uneasiness.

On the 21 st of August Kumajirō secretly informed us that in about five or six days we should be removed to a house that was being prepared for our reception. This turned out to be true. On the 26th we were conducted to the castle, where we found all the officers of the city in the great room, in which Arao Shigeaki used formerly to receive us. Adachi Nobuakira and Baba Sadayoshi were likewise there, seated near the officers, but on seats somewhat lower. The magistrate entered soon after our arrival. Having taken his seat, he drew a paper from his bosom, and with the assistance of the interpreter, intimated that it was an order relative to us, which had been transmitted to him from the capital. He read it, and desired the interpreter to translate it to us. It was to the following purport: That if the Russian vessel, according to the promise of Captain Ricord, should return that year to Hakodate, with the explanation required by the Japanese, and if the magistrate should look upon that explanation as satisfactory, the government authorized him to liberate us without delay. The magistrate informed us, that, in conformity with these orders, we must, in the course of a few days, depart for Hakodate, where he was likewise about to proceed, and that he would see us on his arrival there. He then took his leave, wishing us health and a safe journey.

When he had departed we also quitted the room. But previously to his retiring, we expressed our thanks for the kindness he had shown to us.

Mur declared he was unworthy of the favors the Japanese had conferred upon him. But to what particular acts of favor he alluded, or what he meant by this statement, we were unable to guess.

Release

From the castle we were conducted to the house we had formerly inhabited.
It had undergone a great change during our absence, and was now much
improved. The palisades, behind which armed soldiers were constantly stationed, gave it formerly the appearance of a prison. But these were now
removed, and our guards had neither muskets nor bows and arrows. A very
neat apartment was assigned to me, a separate one to Mur and Khlebnikov,
and a third to the sailors and Alexei. Our food was likewise superior in
quality to that which we had before been accustomed to. It was served up
to us in beautiful lackered vessels, by well-dressed attendants, who treated
us with every mark of respect.

We had no sooner arrived at our new residence, than several officers,
with their children, came to offer us their congratulations, and to bid us
farewell. Some of these men presented us with farewell cards in the Russian
language, which the interpreters had translated: they merely contained an
adieu, and a wish that we might have a safe voyage. Last of all came the head
of the Merchants' Company, or chief magistrate of the city, with his two
assistants, and presented us with a box of comfits. In the faces of all the
Japanese by whom we were visited we could read an unfeigned expression
of joy for our good fortune, and their kind behavior frequently caused us
to shed tears. Khlebnikov proposed that we should address a letter of thanks
to the magistrate, which I readily agreed to, and begged that he would
himself be the writer. The letter was accordingly written, translated into
Japanese, and forwarded to the magistrate, who, as our interpreters
informed us, received it with the strongest emotions of sensibility.

The Japanese now began to treat us like guests rather than prisoners. When our sailors sometimes showed an inclination to drink more spirits than was consistent with temperance, their attendants were directed not to serve it out to them without my consent, and only in such quantities as I should think fit to order. They were thus taught again to look upon me as their commander, which the Japanese never before required them to do.

As we were now convinced that the Japanese entertained the design of setting us at liberty, we wished to testify our gratitude to them as far as lay in our power. Khlebnikov presented and explained to the academician Adachi Nobuakira the tables he had prepared. I translated from the work of Antoine Libes everything relative to the latest discoveries in astronomy, and gave him the extracts, together with my own observations upon them. We wished to make presents of all our books and other property to those Japanese who had been most about us, and had manifested the greatest interest in our fate. They, however, said they could not accept them without the permission of their government, for which they promised to apply. After the magistrate had declared that it was the intention of the Japanese government to grant us our liberty, we remained in Matsumae for only three days, during which time we were liberally supplied with breakfast and dinner from the magistrate's kitchen, and the interpreters received orders to give us entertainments.

We departed on the morning of the 10th of August, and were conducted through the city with great ceremony. The people, who had assembled in vast multitudes in the streets, all pressed forward to bid us farewell. Notwithstanding that Khlebnikov complained of such pain in his feet, that he could with difficulty stand upright, yet the Japanese required him to proceed on foot through the streets. But when we got out of the city, they left it to our own choice either to walk or ride, as we pleased. Our escort consisted of an officer of the rank denominated *shitayaku* (assistant), our interpreter Teisuke, and his brother, eight common soldiers, our servants, together with a number of litter bearers, grooms for the horses, etc. who were occasionally relieved. The officer, who was a man of very agreeable manners, treated us with great attention. Whenever we stopped to rest, he seated himself beside us, gave us part of his own tobacco, and showed us many acts of kindness.

On arriving at the place where we passed the night, I observed to Teisuke that our departure from Matsumae had taken place on a day that is celebrated with great pomp in Russia; namely, the anniversary of the saint whose name our emperor bears. The Japanese, without any request on our part, immediately filled out some of their best *sake*, and we drank several glasses to the health of his imperial majesty. Our friends the Japanese followed our example, and repeated the words: "Long live the Emperor Alexander!" the meaning of which Teisuke explained to them.

In returning to Hakodate we took the same road by which we had travelled from that city to Matsumae, and we always halted in the same villages. But we now enjoyed greater freedom, and our food was of a superior quality. The Japanese kept a strict watch over Mur. They were apprehensive that distress of mind might tempt him to commit suicide, for, as we passed through the city, his face was bathed in tears, and he was observed to weep on several occasions during our journey. When the Japanese inquired the cause of his affliction when all were happy around him, he replied that he was unworthy of the kindness they had shown him, and that his tears were occasioned by remorse. To us, however, he declared that his uneasiness arose from the deceit and treachery of the Japanese; who, he assured us, were bent on our destruction. But all this was mere artifice. Though Mur's assertions were ludicrous in the extreme, yet the poor sailors placed implicit faith in them, and they manifested no slight degree of apprehension. The singular conduct of Mur was, and still remains, an enigma of which I can give no explanation.

On the 2nd of September, 1813, we entered Hakodate amidst a vast throng of spectators. The residence assigned to us was a *bakufu* building, in the vicinity of the garrison. Our apartment was separated by a gallery from a little garden. To the palisades of the gallery wooden shutters were fastened, which were close at the bottom, but open about three feet distant from the top of the gallery. The light therefore penetrated but faintly through these apertures, and no external objects were visible. In these respects our house bore some resemblance to a prison, though it was extremely clean, and very neatly furnished. In the course of a few days these shutters were at our request removed, and besides enjoying light, we had an unobstructed view of the garden. In addition to our usual repasts, we were now treated with desserts, consisting of apples, pears, and sweetmeats. And, according to the Japanese custom, these desserts were always served up one hour before dinner.

A short time after our arrival in Hakodate, we were visited by the commander of the city, the deputy magistrate Kōjimoto Hyōgorō. He inquired after our health, and observed that the house was much too small for our accommodation. But as a vast number of officers were at that time in the city, and as the magistrate was likewise expected, all the best houses had been engaged for them. He added that the Russian vessel would in all probability arrive, and we should be sent back to our native country. But that if, contrary to all expectation, it did not come to Hakodate, another house would be provided for our winter residence.

In the course of a few days, Kōjimoto Hyōgorō, Takahashi Shigekata, Adachi Nobuakira, Baba Sadayoshi, and Uebara Kumajirō, arrived at Hakodate by sea. The interpreter (Kumajirō) and the academician (Nobuakira) immediately paid us a visit. They afterwards spent the whole of their time in our society, remaining with us from morning till night, and they even gave orders that their meals should be sent to our house. They spared no pains to obtain all the information they could collect from us before the *Diana* should arrive. Sadayoshi transcribed several sheets of Wassili Nikititsch Tatischtschew's French and Russian dictionary, and he adopted the plan of translating the Russian significations of the French words into Japanese. He thus made himself acquainted with the peculiar meaning of each word better than he could have done by any other method. To us this occupation proved extremely tedious and troublesome. I shall merely state one example, by which the reader may form some notion of the difficulties we encountered.

Among the Russian words the Japanese had set down in the lexicon made at Matsumae was *dostoiny* (worthy), which we had translated to them by meritorious, respectable, etc. We never entered into critical illustrations of words, knowing that it would be no easy task to make our pupils comprehend them. When the Japanese came to the word *digne*, which, in the French-Russian dictionary, was unluckily exemplified by the phrase, "worthy of the gallows," they immediately concluded that the "gallows" must be some high office or distinguished reward. Notwithstanding all the pains we took to elucidate the meaning of the word gallows, the Japanese could not easily extricate themselves from the confusion of ideas in which they were involved by the different definitions. "A meritorious, respectable man, worthy of the gallows!" was an association they had formed in their minds, and which they repeated with amazement. We employed all our knowledge of the Japanese language, and summoned all our pantomimic powers, to facilitate our explanations to the interpreters. And we were obliged to quote a number of examples in which the word worthy corresponded in signification with the several translations given of it, and was made to apply to very different objects. When occurrences of this kind took place (and they were by no means unfrequent), the Japanese would hang their heads to one side, and exclaim, *Muzukashii kotoba! Nakanaka muzukashii kotoba!* (a difficult language! An extremely difficult language!)

Baba Sadayoshi also undertook to translate into Japanese a small Russian book on the subject of vaccine inoculation. The volume was brought to Japan by Nakagawa Yoshisaemon, who had received it as a present from a Russian physician. On the other hand, Adachi Nobuakira labored to collect all possible information from the *Physics* of Libes.

But the office which Teisuke performed was to us the most interesting and important of any. He told us, by order of the magistrate, that his government entertained doubts of Laxman and Resanov having fully understood the explanations that had been given in answer to their inquiries. For the embassy of Resanov appeared to be altogether inconsistent with the intimation made to Laxman by the Japanese government, that a Russian ship would be admitted into Nagasaki, to treat respecting commercial relations. Resanov had himself, on various occasions, manifested ill humor, or rather hatred, towards the Japanese, and they therefore suspected that he had not received a correct translation of the papers, and consequently could not be acquainted with the nature of their laws. Teisuke said his government now was fully convinced of the justice and philanthropy of the Emperor of Russia, who, besides watching over the welfare of his own subjects, ensured the happiness and prosperity of neighboring nations. And great anxiety was now manifested that such a monarch should not, through the misrepresentations of his ambassadors, imbibe an erroneous opinion of the Japanese. The government therefore wished that we, together with the interpreters, should make new translations into Russian of the original rescripts addressed to Laxman and Resanov. And that, on our arrival in Russia, we should transmit the translations to the government, or, if possible, to the emperor himself. For the same purpose, the Japanese requested that we would take copies of Khvostov's two documents to which I have before alluded.

In translating these papers our interpreters sought to adhere as closely as possible to the literal sense. We likewise were no less desirous of becoming acquainted with the peculiar idioms of the Japanese language, and of obtaining a correct translation of these interesting and important documents. We therefore paid no attention to elegance of style, and deviated as little from the original as the spirit of our own language would admit. On my return to Russia I laid these papers before the government.

Our interpreters, moreover, gave us a complete history of the negotiations between the Japanese and Laxman and Resanov. But I will not trespass on the patience of the reader, by detailing the particulars they stated. The rescript delivered to Laxman evidently proves that the Japanese were not very well satisfied with his conduct. Nevertheless, he succeeded in his mission, and obtained an authority for sending an envoy to Nagasaki, for the purpose of further communications. This permission shows, beyond a doubt, that the Japanese government was, at that time, willing to enter into a commercial intercourse with Russia.

With the assistance of the Japanese, we now proceeded to translate the paper that was to be delivered with us on board of Captain Ricord's ship. It was to the following purport:

From the deputy magistrates, the chief commanders next to the magistrate of Matsumae,

Twenty-two years ago a Russian vessel arrived at Matsumae, and eleven years ago another came to Nagasaki. Though the laws of our country were, on both these occasions, minutely explained, yet we are of opinion that we have not been clearly understood on your part, owing to the great dissimilarity between our language and writing. However, as we have now detained you, it will be a easy to give you an explanation of these matters. When you return to Russia, communicate to the commanders of the coasts of Kamchatka, Okhotsk, and others, the declaration of our magistrate, which will acquaint them with the nature of the Japanese laws with respect to the arrival of foreign ships, and prevent a repetition of similar transgressions on your part.

In our country the Christian religion is strictly prohibited, and European vessels are not suffered to enter any Japanese harbor except Nagasaki. This law does not extend to Russian vessels only. It has not this year been enforced in Kunashir, because we wished to communicate with your countrymen, and orders have been issued to prevent firing against the vessel that is expected. But all that may henceforth present themselves will be driven back by cannon-balls. Bear in mind this declaration, and you cannot complain, if at any future period you should experience a misfortune in consequence of your disregard of it.

Among us there exists this law: 'If any European, residing in Japan, shall attempt to teach our people the Christian faith, he shall undergo a severe punishment, and shall not be restored to his native country.' As you, however, have not attempted so to do, you will accordingly be permitted to return home. Think well on this.

About eight years ago, and three years previous to the arrival of the Russian vessel at our Kuril Islands, islanders from Rasshua were repeatedly sent from the islands under your dominion to inspect our islands. Although we were aware of their real intentions, yet we took pity on the islanders from Rasshua, who were compelled blindly to obey the commands of the Russians, and on two occasions we suffered them to depart. But should they again return, in defiance of our prohibition, they will be seized and condemned to undergo a legal chastisement. Bear this likewise in mind.

Our countrymen wish to carry on no commerce with foreign lands; for we know no want of unnecessary things. Though foreigners are permitted to trade to Nagasaki, even to that harbor only those are admitted with whom we have for a long period maintained relations, and we do not trade with them for the sake of gain, but for other important objects. From the repeated solicitations you have hitherto made to us, you evidently imagine that the customs of our country resemble those of your own. But you are very wrong in thinking so. In future, therefore, it will be better to say no more about a commercial connexion.

Takahashi Shigekata, (L. S.)
Kōjimoto Hyōgorō, (L. S.)
Bunka, the 26th day of the 9th month of the 10th year. [19 Oct. 1813]

When the translation was completed, Teisuke, by order of his superiors, observed to us that we must not, from the contents of this paper, infer that the Japanese entertained so great an abhorrence of the Christian faith as to regard all who acknowledged it as wicked and contemptible. On the contrary, added he, we know there are good and bad people in every country, and of all religions: the former are entitled to our love and respect, to what ever faith they may belong. But the latter we hate and despise. Teisuke, besides, reminded us that the strict prohibition of Christianity by the Japanese laws, was solely to be attributed to the mischievous civil wars that had arisen in Japan after its introduction.

The commissioner (*shirabeyaku*) Odachi Kōeki about this time arrived at Hakodate. He was commander of Kunashir during both the periods at which Captain Ricord visited that island. On his arrival, he immediately came to see us, and we observed a total change in his behavior. He now treated us with great civility and politeness, made inquiries respecting our health, and wished us a speedy and safe return to Russia. We were informed by Teisuke that the answer this officer gave to Captain Ricord in the preceding autumn, when he declared that we were all dead, was really contrived with a hostile view, but that, on the last arrival of the Russian vessel, Odachi Kōeki had endeavored to make amends for his former misconduct. It appeared that the fortress of Kunashir was garrisoned by troops belonging to the *daimyō* of Nambu. The commander of these troops, though a person of distinction, and an older man than Odachi Kōeki, was his inferior in command, because the latter governed the island on behalf of the *shōgun*. The intention of the Japanese government to treat with the Russians had been communicated to the Nambu chief, but he had received no instructions on the subject from his own *daimyō*. On the appearance of the *Diana* he therefore made preparations for firing upon her, in conformity with his former orders. This decree was, however, opposed by Odachi Kōeki, and the officer who was joined with him in the commission for treating with the Russians. They placed themselves before the cannon, and declared that if the Nambu chief had formed a determination to attack the Russians, he must first fire on them, and all the Japanese in the *bakufu* service; for that, as long as they lived, they would, at every hazard, prevent him from executing his purpose. The obstinate Nambu leader was thus brought to comply with the wishes of the *bakufu* government. We asked Teisuke how the emperor would regard this refractory conduct on the part of the commandant of the garrison. "The conduct of the commandant," he replied, "must be decided upon by the *daimyō* of Nambu. The emperor will merely inquire why his orders were not earlier dispatched."

The two first weeks of September passed away, and we heard no tidings of the *Diana*, We feared that her departure had been delayed, and that, during the late season of the year, she had encountered some accident in her dangerous passage. We therefore hoped that Captain Ricord had postponed his voyage until the following spring, and would willingly, on that account, have remained eight or nine months longer in captivity. But Captain Ricord's courage and indefatigable activity prompted him to use the utmost dispatch in a case that concerned the interests of the state. He was anxious to conclude, that very year, the correspondence that had been so happily begun, and to prove to the Japanese that the Russians knew how to keep a promise.

On the night of the 16th of September our interpreters surprised us with the agreeable tidings that a large European three-masted ship had been seen near Cape Ermio (Cape Anama), forming the western side of the bay on which is situated the harbor of Endermo (Hakodate), which Captain Ricord wished to enter, in order to obtain a pilot. We did not doubt it was the *Diana*. We had, however, to lament that continual western winds detained her at sea near these dangerous coasts. The interpreters further informed us that, on the *Diana* being observed, a courier had been sent off to the magistrate, who, it was expected, would immediately proceed to Hakodate.

We heard no more of the *Diana* until the evening of the 21st of September, when we were informed she had been seen that day at noon, near the east side of Vulcan's Bay, endeavoring to enter the harbor of Endermo.

In the meanwhile a vast nu'mber of officers and soldiers arrived from all places in the vicinity of Hakodate, and curiosity induced them continually to come and see us. On seeing so many strange visitors, and recollecting that, during our journey to Hakodate, we had observed new batteries and barracks erected along the bay and the coasts, I began to suspect that the Japanese intended by some stratagem to capture the *Diana*, in revenge for Captain Ricord having seized one of their vessels and several men, on which occasion nine of their countrymen were drowned. The Japanese, in the course of their communication with Captain Ricord, had never even mentioned this affair: a circumstance which served to strengthen my suspicions. I asked Teisuke for what reason so considerable a number of soldiers had assembled in Hakodate, and what was intended by the numerous preparations we had observed. He replied, that one of the Japanese laws required that measures of the strictest precaution should be adopted whenever they were visited by foreign vessels. "When Resanov was at Nagasaki," he said, "a far greater number of soldiers were assembled, and many more batteries erected: there are fewer troops here on account of the difficulty experienced in collecting them." He besides smiled at my suspicions, and assured me that we had nothing to fear on the part of the Japanese.

On the 24th of September the interpreters informed us that the *Diana* had arrived in Endermo. They showed us a letter addressed by Captain Ricord to the officers in that town (Hakodate), which had been written in the Japanese language by an interpreter named Kisselev, and the contents of which Teisuke explained to us. One of the Japanese sailors, whom Captain Ricord had conveyed home in the spring, had been sent to him as a pilot, and he requested in his letter that a more intelligent man—if possible, Takadaya Kahei, on whom he could place reliance—might be put on board the *Diana*. Captain Ricord informed the Japanese that he stood in need of a supply of fresh water, and begged that his letters might be answered in the common, and not in the high language, as the interpreter Kisselev could read only the former.

Teisuke and Kumajirō told us that orders had been immediately issued for supplying the *Diana* not only with water, but provisions of every kind, as far as they could be procured in Endermo. With regard to Captain Ricord's request that his letters might be answered in the common language, they observed that papers in that language could be signed only by inferior officers, and that, if the answers should contain anything important, they would require the signatures of individuals of higher rank; for, according to their laws, no person of distinction could sign official papers written in the vulgar tongue. Consequently his wish in this respect could not be complied with. As to his application for Takadaya Kahei, he could not be sent on board the *Diana* as a pilot without the consent of the magistrate, and some days must therefore elapse before the regular authorities for that purpose would be obtained. As, however, the Japanese authorities were well assured of the competency of the sailor who had been sent on board the *Diana*, Captain Ricord might safely rely on him until his ship came within sight of Hakodate, when Takadaya Kahei should be immediately sent on board. For this purpose regular signals were prepared, which communicated from a hill to the boat in which Kahei was to sail to the *Diana*. The Japanese wished that I should clearly explain to Captain Ricord all these arrangements. I agreed to do so and at the conclusion of my letter observed that I wrote to him in compliance with the request of the Japanese, as they wished me to assure him that he had no reason to apprehend danger on entering Hakodate. But this I could not resolve to do, lest I should become the instrument of the ruin of my countrymen, if the Japanese entertained any treacherous design. When I remarked that the Japanese might, by proceeding with candor and sincerity, convince Captain Ricord that he had nothing to fear, the interpreters made no observation on that subject, but expressed themselves satisfied with what I had written.

On the following day Deputy Magistrate Takahashi Shigekata came to visit us. He merely repeated what we had already heard from the interpreters, and informed us that my letter had been forwarded to Captain Ricord.

On the night of the 27th of September, a fire broke out in a magazine belonging to a merchant, at no great distance from the house in which we lived. A great alarm was excited in the city, the cause of which our attendants immediately explained to us, and they began to make preparations in case our removal should have been found necessary. The interpreter and Shigekata soon came to assure us that measures had been adopted to prevent the flames from communicating to our house. They then left us, and the fire was extinguished in the course of a few hours, but the magazine in which it first broke out was reduced to ashes.

On the morning of the 27th of September, the magistrate arrived, and in the evening the *Diana* approached the harbor. In fulfilment of the promise made by the Japanese, Takadaya Kahei was immediately sent on board, in company with the commander of the port, as the latter possessed a more intimate knowledge of the dangers of that part of the coast. Night having already set in, the *Diana* brought up in safe anchoring ground at the mouth of the harbor. This we learnt from the commander of the port, who returned on shore the same night.

Though the wind was unfavorable, the *Diana*, to the astonishment of the Japanese, came into the harbor on the following day. From the window of a little apartment in which our bath stood, we saw her working in. The bay was covered with boats, and every elevated spot in the city was crowded with spectators, who were filled with amazement on seeing so large a vessel making progress on every tack against the wind. The Japanese who were allowed access to us came every moment to express their wonder at the great number of the *Diana*'s sails, and the rapidity with which she advanced.

A few hours after the *Diana* had cast anchor, Teisuke, Kumajirō, Nobuakira, and Sadayoshi, appeared with a large paper, which Takadaya Kahei had received from Captain Ricord, and had conveyed ashore. This paper, which was by the magistrate's order brought to us for translation, was an answer from the commander of the Okhotsk district to the demand of the two officers next in rank to the magistrate. Minitzky clearly explained that the proceedings of Khvostov were quite unauthorized by our government, that the emperor of Russia had always been favorably disposed towards Japan, and that he had never entertained a design to injure the subjects of that empire. He accordingly advised the Japanese to prove, by our speedy liberation, their friendly disposition towards Russia, and their readiness to terminate differences that had arisen out of their own mistakes, and the reprehensible conduct of an obscure individual. He added, that every delay on their part must be attended with injurious consequences to the Japanese commerce and fisheries, as the inhabitants of the coasts would be severely harassed by the Russian vessels, in case further visits to Japan on account of this affair should be necessary.

The Japanese expressed themselves highly pleased with the contents of this letter, and intimated that the explanations it contained were sufficient to produce a thorough conviction that Khvostov had acted without the sanction of the Russian government. They therefore congratulated us on our speedy liberation and return to our native country.

With regret I must now recur to a melancholy subject. From the day on which the *Diana* had first been discovered off the coast of Japan, Mur had appeared unusually melancholy and thoughtful. As he had no longer any hope of remaining in Japan, he resolved, if possible, to prevent the communications that were about to take place. He began by observing that Minitzky's letter was rude and uncivil, and that it contained an insolent threat by declaring that the Russian vessels would injure the trade of Japan and the people who inhabited its coasts. He assured the Japanese that these were merely empty words. The interpreters, with some degree of dissatisfaction, replied, that the Japanese were not fools, but were well aware of the mischief that might be effected by Russian ships on their coasts, in case of war, and that they, moreover, thought Minitzky's letter extremely reasonable. We were much consoled by this declaration on a subject that was to us of such weighty importance. But all our prayers and entreaties made no impression on Mur.

I must not omit mentioning another praiseworthy trait in the Japanese character, which occurred at this time. Besides the official business to which Minitzky alluded to in his letter, he addressed an intercession to the magistrate in favor of Nakagawa Yoshisaemon, the Japanese who had been in Russia, and who, he was informed, had incurred the displeasure of the authorities. The interpreters assured us that the magistrate and all the officers were extremely pleased with the humane sympathy shown by Minitzky for the misfortunes of a foreigner, and the benevolent anxiety he had manifested for the bettering of his condition. Now, said they, the elders in the capital will be convinced of their error, and will learn that the Russians are not bears and barbarians, but a humane and feeling people.

On the same day the interpreters informed us that Captain Ricord was the bearer of a letter and several presents from the civil governor of Irkutzk to the magistrate of Matsumae, and that he had expressed a wish to deliver them with his own hands.

A day was to be appointed for Captain Ricord's coming ashore, as it was stated that the Japanese officers did not dare to meet him in boats, in order to communicate with him. This circumstance rendered some of my companions a little uneasy. What can the Japanese mean, said they, by wishing that another of our commanders should come ashore, when they have already made one the victim of their treachery.

We looked forward with anxiety and fear for the 30th of September, the day on which it was determined that Captain Ricord should deliver the letter and the presents for the magistrate.

When the 30th of September arrived, the Japanese brought us some wretchedly executed portraits of the Russian officers and sailors, which had been sketched as they came ashore. They observed that the interpreter had a Japanese face, and that he must certainly be a native of Japan in a Russian dress. We, on our part, knew nothing respecting Kisselev. When our interpreters explained to us Captain Ricord's letter from Endermo, which was written in Japanese by Kisselev, they inquired who he was. We conjectured that he was a native of Irkutzk, and that he had learnt the language from the Japanese who lived there.

When the conference was at an end, the interpreters came to inform us that we might, if we pleased, ascend to the second story of our house, to see Captain Ricord depart. We saw the magistrate's state boat sailing under three flags from the shore to the *Diana*. But owing to the great distance, we could not recognize the individuals on board.

We had no sooner returned to our apartments, than the Japanese brought a letter which had been delivered by Captain Ricord, and of which they wished us to make a translation. This letter had been written by the civil governor of Irkutzk, on Captain Ricord's first report, and consequently before he could have been made acquainted with the contents of the Japanese paper, which was afterwards sent on board the *Diana*. The magistrate began by representing the object of our voyage, and the treacherous conduct of the Japanese at Kunashir. He then declared that Chwostov had acted without the sanction of the Russian government, and entreated the magistrate of Matsumae to grant us our immediate freedom, or to negotiate on that subject with Captain Ricord, his plenipotentiary. If, however, neither of these requests could be complied with, without the consent of the Japanese government, he was requested to state when, and to what place the vessel should proceed, to obtain an answer. He mentioned the presents, consisting of a gold watch and some red Casimir cloth, which he sent to the magistrate of Matsumae as tokens of his neighborly friendship. He besides stated that Captain Ricord was the bearer of a letter of thanks, which he was directed to deliver whenever our freedom might be granted. Finally, he expressed his hope of obtaining an answer corresponding with his demand; on failure of which, he should be compelled reluctantly to conclude that Japan was hostilely disposed towards Russia, and must lay before his emperor a declaration to that effect. His imperial majesty would then consider himself bound to employ a force corresponding with his power, and to obtain satisfaction by an appeal to arms, though by such measures the empire of Japan might be shaken to its very foundation.

This letter was accompanied by translations in the Manchurian and Japanese languages. The Japanese said, however, that they had no Manchurian interpreter, and that several passages in the Japanese translation were quite unintellible. We were therefore obliged to make another translation, a task that kept us employed for more than two days. When the translation was finished, the interpreters carried it to the magistrate. But in a short time brought it back for the purpose of obtaining some explanations deemed necessary. They praised the general tenor of the letter, and expressed their dissatisfaction at two passages only. The Japanese were astonished the letter should speak of the faithless conduct practised towards us, and describe it as an arbitrary measure of the commandant of Kunashir, unsanctioned by the *shōgun* of Japan, since they had, by their communications, avowed that we were taken prisoners by order of the government. But their pride was chiefly wounded by the observation that Japan would be shaken to its foundation. They insisted on being made acquainted with the precise meaning of this sentence. I first wished to explain to them by examples what was meant by the employment of a force corresponding with a person's power. "Suppose," said I, "that I were to throw a feather at an individual with whom I was offended, I should not then use a force corresponding with my power, but if I threw a heavy stone with violence, I should then use a corresponding force. In the same manner, the two attacks made by Khvostov in no way correspond with the power of Russia, and his two ships, in comparison with our empire, are not equal to a feather in my hand." In order to make them understand the phrase "shaken to its foundation," I shook Teisuke several times by the shoulders.

At first the Japanese seemed offended at our entertaining so mean an opinion of the strength of their country, and asked, with haughtiness and ill humor, how our emperor could hope to shake Japan in that way. I replied, that the letter alluded to the people ot Japan, and not the territory. And you must surely be convinced, said I, that if Russia chose to declare war against Japan, and to fit out a force, she might easily effect the destruction of your empire.

I was well aware that the interpreters were merely the organs of the magistrate and the superior officers, and that often, in the course of apparently undesigned conversation, their language was purposely so framed as to inform us of all we wished to know. I therefore followed their example. And to set them at ease with regard to the threats that had so irritated them, observed, as it were accidentally, that the magistrate of Irkutzk had written his letter before he knew anyting of the papers left behind by Khvostov, the false declaration of the Ainu, or the wish of the Japanese government to correspond with Russia. I added that though their unaccountable proceedings towards our ship, in the preceding year, would have induced any other state to declare war against them, yet the humanity of our emperor would not permit him to resort to measures of violence, until he should receive a decisive letter of explanation.

The interpreters agreed with me in maintaining that the former situation of affairs justified the magistrate of Irkutzk in writing such a letter, though it was now unnecessary. I admitted the justice of this observation, and assured them that the magistrate would not have so expressed himself had he been convinced of the readiness of the Japanese to adjust all their past differences with Russia. They seemed fully satisfied with this answer.

I am sorry that I am, on this occasion, again obliged to speak of Mur's conduct. He declared, that the letter of the magistrate of Irkutzk was couched in arrogant and insulting terms, and that the presents he had sent were almost too insignificant to be offered to the meanest officer. Fortunately the Japanese had some time previously conveyed these presents 'on shore. The watch was shown to us: it contained a curious piece of mechanism, which excited the astonishment of the Japanese, and they were totally unable to comprehend it. On touching a particular spring, a horse appeared drinking in an artificial stream of water, and occasionally raising and lowering his head. On seeing it, Mur himself confessed that the present was not so trifling as he had supposed. The Japanese declared that they had never before heard of so wonderful a work of art.

When we had explained the magistrate's letter, the interpreters proposed that I should write to Captain Ricord, and request that he would send ashore the letter of thanks entrusted to him. I stated that this could not possibly be done, as Captain Ricord had been directed not to deliver the letter until our liberation should take place. The interpreters acknowledged the justice of this objection, and said nothing more on the subject.

In the meanwhile Takadaya Kahei, who had been sent to communicate personally with Captain Ricord, brought to his countrymen the intelligence of the French having taken Moscow, and burnt it to ashes, and that they had afterwards precipitately retreated from Russia with a prodigious loss. This news greatly astonished us, and we felt very anxious to know every particular relating to these events. With the consent of the Japanese, I wrote a note to Captain Ricord, to request that he would send me all the newspapers that might happen to be on board the sloop. On the following day the interpreter brought to me the *Military Gazette*, and several letters from my friends and relations in Russia. I immediately declined breaking open any of the letters, which were addressed to me, and requested Teisuke to enclose them in a packet, and send them back to the *Diana*. The interpreter praised my determination, and promised to make known my wish to the magistrate. I was well aware that had I broken open these letters, I must immediately have made copies and translations of them, to be forwarded to the capital. The interpreter soon after informed me that the letters could not be sent back to the *Diana* until we were set at liberty. But that they had sealed them up in a packet, which they would deliver to me, and which I might carry on board with me at my departure. I readily agreed to this proposal.

We perused the journals with the utmost impatience. They contained an account of all the events that had taken place from the enemy's invasion of Russia to the death of the prince of Smolensk, Mikhail Illarionovich Golenishchev-Kutuzov. The Japanese were almost as anxious as we to know by what means affairs had taken so surprising a turn in so short a period. And they requested that we would give them a translated narrative of the most remarkable events of the campaign. When we informed them that the French had been obliged to fight their way out of Moscow, in which they were blocked up, and that almost their whole army had been destroyed in Russia, they clapped their hands, and declared that the Prince of Smolensk had maneuvered in the true Japanese style; for one of their principal maxims of war was to allure the enemy as much as possible into the interior of their country, and then to surround him on every side with powerful armies. We smiled at this comparison, and jokingly observed to each other, that the presumption of the Japanese might perhaps induce them to believe that our immortal Kutuzov had studied tactics in the very books of which Khvostov had plundered them.

On the 3rd of October, Takadaya Kahei was permitted to visit us for the first time. He came, accompanied by the interpreters, on his return from the *Diana*. This venerable old man was unable to express himself in the Russian language. But with the assistance of the interpreters he succeeded in making us understand him in Japanese. He spoke in terms of the highest praise and gratitude of Captain Ricord, the officers and crew of the *Diana*, and of all the Russians whom he had known in Kamchatka. We asked him many questions concerning Russia, but he could not satisfy our curiosity, as he was ignorant of the subjects that most excited our interest. On taking leave of us, he requested that I would write to inform Captain Ricord that we had seen him. I readily agreed to do so, and he promised that he would himself forward the letter.

At length the interpreters received orders to inform us that the magistrate considered the paper brought by Captain Ricord perfectly satisfactory, and that he had resolved to set us at liberty. Before my departure, he wished that I should hold a conference with Captain Ricord on shore, in order that, as I was acquainted with the Japanese laws, knew the strictness with which they were enforced, and was in some measure familiar with the customs of the country, I might personally make the following communication to my friend. First, That, though the Japanese did not cherish the least hatred towards the Russians, yet the magistrate of Matsumae could not accept of the presents that had been sent to him. If he accepted them, he would be bound to make some recompence for them. But intercourse of that kind was wholly prohibited by the laws of Japan. The Japanese, therefore, hoped that we would not take offense at the presents being returned. Secondly, That the letter from the commandant of the circle of Okhotsk was a satisfactory answer to the demand for explanation transmitted that year by Captain Ricord, therefore the said letter would be the only paper mentioned in the written declaration the magistrate intended should be delivered to Captain Ricord. Thirdly, That as affairs doubtless stood in the state in which it was represented in the letter of the commandant of Okhotsk, the magistrate of Matsumae could not answer the magistrate of Irkutzk, as the latter was ignorant of many circumstances relative to Khvostov, and had not been apprised of the intention of the Japanese government to correspond with Russia on that subject. Fourthly, The Japanese requested that Ricord would address a letter to the two officers next in command to the magistrate, to assure them that the magistrate of Irkutzk knew nothing of the documents left behind by Khvostov, the false statements of the Ainu, nor the intentions of the Japanese government at the time he wrote his letter. Fifthly and lastly, that Captain Ricord should pledge himself to a perfect understanding of the Russian translation of the declaration to be delivered in the name of the magistrate of Matsumae, and promise to lay it before our government on his return. And, to enable him to give this pledge, I was to be furnished with a copy of the declaration, which I was to show to him on our conference.

The 5th of October was the day appointed for my interview with Captain Ricord. The Japanese proposed that Mur should be present. But this, to their astonishment, he declined. Khlebnikov wished to enjoy the satisfaction of seeing his countrymen and companions, but the Japanese were of opinion that, considering Mur's disordered state of mind, it would not be prudent to leave him alone.

On the morning of the 5th one of the interpreters brought my hat, and the other my sword, which they presented to me with demonstrations of great respect, whilst they, at the same time, sincerely congratulated me. In compliance with the wish of the Japanese, I dressed myself in a rich silken jacket and loose trowsers, which had been made in Hakodate for the occasion. The sword and cocked hat was calculated to add to the singularity of this dress in the eyes of Europeans. But this was an object of indifference to the Japanese. As the restoration of our swords indicated that the Japanese no longer looked upon us as prisoners, I readily acceded to their wishes, and resolved to appear before my companions in a dress in which, had they not been prepared for the meeting, they might have found it difficult to recognize me. In addition, my hair was far from being cut in the Russian style and, had I not recently shaved my long beard, my appearance would have been altogether extremely ludicrous.

The place fixed upon for my interview with Captain Ricord was an apartment in the customhouse, which was situated near the shore. The three interpreters, the academician Adachi Nobuakira, and a few of the inferior officers, were ordered to be present as witnesses. At midday I was conducted to the custom house, round which a number of troops were drawn up in parade. I proceeded along with the interpreters to the conference chamber. The Japanese, according to custom, seated themselves upon the floor, but a seat was handed to me. Captain Ricord soon arrived in the magistrate's barge, accompanied by Saveljev, one of his officers, the interpreter Kisselev, and a few sailors. The latter were stationed in an open place in front of the house, and Captain Ricord, Saveljev, and Kisselev, entered the apartment in which I was waiting to receive them—I leave the reader to imagine the transport of our meeting.

A seat was immediately placed for Captain Ricord. And the interpreters having intimated that we might converse together as long as we pleased, they stepped aside, and paid no attention to what we said. The joy, astonishment, and curiosity with which our questions and answers succeeded each other, may easily be conceived. Captain Ricord wished to know all that had occurred to us during our imprisonment. And I, in my turn, inquired after the affairs of Russia, and thus we proceeded from one subject to another. At length I explained the object of our interview, and the wish of the Japanese. And he acquainted me with the instructions he had received from the civil governor of Irkutzk, respecting a determination of boundaries, and a treaty of friendship between the two empires. On taking into consideration the whole business, it appeared to us that the propositions of the Japanese were reasonable, and that, consequently, we ought to comply with them. But that, for the following reasons, it would not be advisable at that time to negotiate for the fixing of boundaries and an alliance.

From the documents we had translated, we knew the conditions on which the Japanese government had authorized the magistrate to liberate us, and likewise what declaration he had to communicate. Consequently, he could have returned no answer to any new proposal on our part without receiving instructions from the capital. The vessel must, besides, have wintered in Hakodate. And this would have been placing ourselves completely in the power of the Japanese; for though the harbor seldom freezes, yet the winter is severe, and of long duration. The crew on board the *Diana* would also have been exposed to considerable danger, and the vessel might even have been rendered unfit to perform the voyage home; for the violent storms that occur during winter on the coast of Japan, might have parted her from her anchors, and driven her ashore. To have requested permission for the seamen to disembark and live on shore, and to have the ship unrigged in a safe place, would have been to subject ourselves to the same conditions which Resanov and his suite had submitted to at Nagasaki, namely, to resign the vessel entirely to the Japanese. And this at a time when we ought to have asserted our claim to three islands, which, in our opinion, they had unjustly occupied.

Besides, it had, at various times, been intimated to me by the interpreter, (who always voiced the sentiments of the magistrate), that notwithstanding the unfavorable answer of the Japanese government, they did not entirely despair of seeing a friendly alliance established between Russia and Japan, but that to accomplish it would require prudent management on our part. The interpreters suggested one method to us, but I shall pass it over, in order that I may not farther interrupt the thread of my narrative.

When everything was arranged between Captain Ricord and me, the Japanese produced the translated declaration of the magistrate of Matsumae. Captain Ricord, in return, delivered in the document required by the Japanese, which Teisuke translated, showed to the officers present, and then informed us that they were perfectly satisfied with it. The Japanese did not evince the least sign of impatience at the length of this interview, and at the end of our conference presented us with tea and sweetmeats. At length Captain Ricord departed. I accompanied him to the boat in which he embarked to go on board the *Diana*, and then returned to our house.

My companions awaited my return with the utmost anxiety. I acquainted them with all I had heard from Ricord respecting the political affairs of Europe, the entrance of the French into Russia, and every particular relative to our families and friends. Two circumstances, however, I was under the necessity of concealing; namely, that Takadaya Kahei had communicated to the Japanese the instructions given to Ricord respecting the settling of the boundaries, and that the interpreter Kisselev was a Japanese by birth. These facts I did not choose to disclose, in order to avoid giving uneasiness to my distrustful fellow prisoners, who to the last moment doubted the sincerity of the Japanese.

It will appear from Captain Ricord's account of his expedition to Hokkaido how much we were indebted to him, and to his excellency the civil magistrate of Irkutzk. I must also with a feeling of gratitude mention that Captain Ricord's bold decision to land, and hold a conference in the town, contributed not a little to the favorable conclusion of the negotiation; for the interpreters had previously assured us, that if Captain Ricord did not come on shore great difficulties would arise, the end of which could not be foreseen.

On the 6th of October, in the morning, the interpreters delivered to Khlebnikov and Mur their swords and hats in the most respectful manner, and stated that we were on that day to be presented to the magistrate, who would in person notify our liberation. He advised us to put on our best clothes, and to wear our swords when we appeared before the magistrate. To this proposal we gladly assented. At noon we were conducted to the house of the magistrate of the town where the magistrate resided. We three officers were shown into a very neat apartment, and the sailors and Alexei were desired to remain in another. In a few hours Khlebnikov, Mur, and I, were requested to enter a spacious hall, in which the officers, the academician, and the interpreters, were assembled. They were more than twenty in number, and were seated in rows on each side of the hall. The magistrate soon entered with his retinue and took his seat. The officers made their obedience to him, we bowed in the European way, and he returned our salutation—all the old ceremonies were repeated, except that the sword-bearer, instead of laying the sword by the side of the magistrate as formerly, held it perpendicularly in both hands, with the hilt upwards. The magistrate then drew a large sheet of paper from his bosom, and holding it up said: "This contains the orders of the government."

The interpreters immediately translated these words; while the officers sat with their eyes cast down, as if they had been deprived of all animation. The magistrate then unfolded the paper, and read its contents aloud. It was the document, a copy of which has already been giving, stating that Khvostov's misconduct had been the occasion of our imprisonment. But that, as the magistrate was convinced that the said Khvostov had acted without the sanction of the Russian government, he was authorized to grant us our liberty, and that we should embark on the following day.

The interpreters having translated this paper, and assured the magistrate that we understood it, one of the senior officers was dispatched in company with Kumajirō to communicate its contents to the sailors. In the meanwhile, the magistrate produced another paper, which he likewise read aloud, and afterwards desired Teisuke to translate and to hand it to me. It was a congratulation from the magistrate to the following effect:

> You have now lived three years in a Japanese frontier town, and in a foreign climate, but you are now about to return to your native country. This affords me great pleasure. You, Captain V. Golownin, as the chief of your companions, must have endured most anxiety of mind, and I sincerely rejoice that you have attained your happy object. You have, in some measure, become acquainted with the laws of our country, which prohibit us from maintaining any commerce with the people of foreign nations, and require that we should drive all foreign

vessels from our coasts. Explain this to your countrymen on your return home. It has been our wish whilst you remained in Japan to treat you with all possible kindness. But, before you became acquainted with our customs, our behavior may have appeared to you the very opposite of what we intended. Each nation has its peculiar customs, but good conduct will everywhere be esteemed as such. On your return to Russia, inform your countrymen of this likewise. I wish you all a safe voyage.

We thanked the magistrate for his condescension. Having listened to our acknowledgments, he withdrew, and we were requested to return to our house.

Throughout the whole of these proceedings, not the slightest indication of joy was observable on Mur's face: he merely repeated, that he was unworthy of the acts of kindness the Japanese conferred upon him.

On our return home, a number of officers, soldiers, and other individuals, came to wish us joy. The three officers next in rank to the magistrate also presented to me a written congratulation, which they requested I would preserve, as a memorial of our friendship. The following is a translation of this paper:

From the deputy magistrate.

You have all lived for a long period in Japan, "but you are now to return to your native country by order of the magistrate. The period of your departure is fast approaching. During your long residence here such an intimacy has arisen between us, that we cannot help regretting the necessity of our separation. The distance between the Island of Hokkaido and our eastern capital is very considerable, and in this frontier town there are many deficiencies. You have, however, been u accustomed to heat, cold, and other variations of weather, and are now prepared for your happy u voyage home. Your own joy must be extreme; we, on our part, rejoice at the happy issue of the affair. May God protect you on your voyage!—for that we pray to him. We write this as a farewell letter.

The joy of the Japanese was, indeed, unfeigned. We understood from the interpreters that in consequence of an application from the high priest of the city, the magistrate had issued orders that prayers for our safe voyage should be offered up in all the temples for the space of five days.

On the 6th of October, one of the officers, accompanied by Kumajirō, was sent on board the *Diana*, to inform Captain Ricord that the orders for our liberation had been officially announced by the magistrate. At their request, I wrote a letter to this effect to Ricord. In the evening, by the magistrate's order, a supper was laid out for us in the upper apartment of our house. This supper consisted of ten different dishes, containing fish, game, ducks, and geese, cooked in various ways. After supper, some of the best Japanese *sake* was served out to us. Several boxes, containing lackered vessels, were afterwards brought in as presents from the interpreters, in return for the books which, with the consent of the government, they had received from us. But they had been ordered to accept of nothing more. We were, however, very well assured that these presents were sent to us at the expense of the government.

On the following day, the 7th of October, we put on our best clothes. The servants and guards packed up our other clothes in boxes, without omitting the least trifle, and placed them in the portico of the house. At midday we were conducted to the shore. Our clothes, the presents we had received, and the provisions for our voyage, were carried behind us by a number of attendants. On reaching the harbor, we entered a building near the custom house, where Mur, Khlebnikov, and I, were shown into one apartment, and the sailors into another. We had been only a few moments in this place, when Captain Ricord came ashore, accompanied by Saveljev, Kisselev, the interpreter, and some other individuals. He and his two companions were conducted to the same apartment in which, a few days before, my interview with him had taken place, and which Khlebnikov, Mur, and I, were immediately requested to enter. Takahashi Shigekata and Kōjimoto Hyōgorō were among the officers whom we found assembled. They sat together on the place that had formerly been occupied by the magistrate. The former desired one of the inferior officers to present to Captain Ricord a salver, on which was a box, containing the declaration of the magistrate of Matsumae, folded up in silken cloth. The officer, with much ceremony and respect, advanced towards Captain Ricord, who, at the request of the Japanese, read the translation of the document from beginning to end.

The next ceremony was the delivery to me of the paper, entitled "A notification from the two officers next in rank to the magistrate of Matsumae." It was inclosed in a box and wrapt in silk, but it was not presented on a salver, nor by the same officer who had handed the other document to Captain Ricord. Though I knew perfectly well the contents of the paper, for the sake of formality, I was requested to read it. The presents sent by the governor of Irkutzk were then returned to us, and we received a list of the provisions provided for our voyage. The Japanese having wished us a happy voyage to Russia, took leave of us, and withdrew.

When everything was in readiness for our departure, we were conducted to the magistrate's barge, on board of which we embarked, accompanied by Takadaya Kahei. Our clothes, provisions, and the presents, were placed in separate boats. On our way from the custom house to the boats, all the Japanese, not only those with whom we were acquainted, but the strangers who were looking on, bade us *adieu*, and wished us a safe voyage.

The officers and seamen on board the *Diana* received us with a degree of joy, or rather enthusiasm, that can only be felt by brothers or intimate friends after a long absence, and a series of similar adventures. With regard to ourselves, I can only say that after an imprisonment of two years, two months, and twenty-six days, on finding ourselves again in an imperial Russian ship, surrounded by our countrymen, with whom we had, for five or six years, served in remote, dangerous, and laborious voyages, we felt what men are capable of feeling, but cannot be described.

Tragedy

My narrative should conclude with the preceding chapter. But the events here related are so closely interwoven with those that occurred during my captivity in Japan, that I feel confident the reader will not regard the addition as superfluous.

On our reaching the *Diana*, the magistrate's boat immediately put back, by Captain Ricord's orders, with a Japanese, who, on account of illness, had been left behind at Okhotsk. Ricord wished to have landed him at the harbor of Endermo, but there, as well as at Hakodate, the Japanese officers would not suffer him to go ashore, and they now, for the first time, consented to receive him.

In the afternoon we were visited by our interpreters, the academician, and several officers, whose rank was three or four degree beneath that of the magistrate. Teisuke and Kumajirō brought presents for Captain Ricord and me, consisting of silk, Japanese tea, and their best *sake* and sweetmeats. In return, we entertained our guests with tea, sweet brandy, and cordials. They drank so copiously that they soon became extremely cheerful and talkative. Captain Ricord delivered to the interpreters the letter of thanks from the governor of Irkutzk, and, as there was a copy at hand, they immediately, with our assistance, translated it into their own language. The Japanese now expressed a wish to see the signature of the emperor of Russia. Among my papers on board the vessel, I happened to have an imperial rescript, which I had received on being invested with the order of St. Vladimir. I immediately laid the paper on the table, and pointed to the signature of the emperor, upon which the Japanese all bowed their heads towards the table, and in that position remained for several minutes. They then inspected the signature with demonstrations of the highest respect, and having kept their eyes fixed upon it for some time, they again repeated the ceremony of bowing their heads to the table.

When our friends, the Japanese, were preparing to take their leave, we gave to each a present of more or less value, according to the degree of friendship that subsisted between us. They endeavored to accept them unobserved by each other, and concealed whatever we gave them in their loose sleeves, which occasionally answer the purpose of pockets. If we offered them anything of a large size, they declined accepting it. But they received books, maps, and copperplate prints, without the least reserve. We gave them an atlas of Captain Adam Johann von Krusenstern, several maps from the atlas of La Perouse, some books, and various other charts. The prints they accepted of, but returned the frames and glasses. Ricord gave them engraved portraits of Count Mikhail Fedotovich Kamensky, Prince Pyotr Bagration, and a drawing of Prince Mikhail Illarionovich Golenishchev-Kutuzov, beautifully executed in crayons, by a son of the magistrate of Irkutzk. When we related to the Japanese the achievements of Prince Kutuzov, they received his portrait with enthusiasm and gratitude. We could not, however, prevail upon them to take the frame and glass, though we represented to them that the former was merely a piece of gilt wood, of little or no value. We observed that the portrait of Kutuzov might be injured without a glass. But they replied, that they would adopt measures for preserving the gem when they went ashore.

Whilst the Japanese officers were entertained in the cabin, the deck of the *Diana* was covered with visitors. Soldiers, and even females, had come on board to see the interior of the ship, and when the officers departed, they all descended into the cabin.

We readily granted them the satisfaction of viewing the curiosities and ornaments of the cabin, which Captain Ricord had fitted up in a very tasteful style. As tokens of remembrance, Captain Ricord gave to each of the Japanese a piece of fine red cloth, for making a tobacco bag, and two pieces of cut glass belonging to a chandelier. They regarded the latter as great curiosities. To the children we gave pieces of sugar. But these little presents were immediately taken possession of by their parents, and carefully wrapped up in pieces of cloth. Our guests remained with us till evening, when, for the first time, we enjoyed tranquillity, and an opportunity of conversing together respecting our native country, and the adventures we had encountered.

On the following day, the 8th of October, we opened, out of curiosity, a box that had been sent on board in one of the boats. To our great astonishment this box contained every article belonging to us, such as clothes, linen, money, etc. in short, everything down to the last piece of rag. On every article was marked the name of the individual to whom it belonged. Among the things Captain Ricord sent on shore at Kunashir was a razor case, containing a looking glass, an article, the manufacture of which is totally unknown to the Japanese. On its removal from Kunashir to Hakodate, the looking glass had accidentally been broken, and we now found the pieces collected in a box, with a note, apologizing for the accident, which, it was observed, had arisen in consequence of the Japanese not knowing how to convey so brittle an article.

Takadaya Kahei was this day our first visitor. He informed us that our request to have a formal audience of the magistrate, for the purpose of thanking him in person, was not approved by the Japanese officers. He, therefore, advised us to set sail without delay, adding, that the ship would be furnished with a supply of water. Several boats soon after came alongside for our water casks, which were speedily filled, and sent on board.

On the following day everything was in readiness for our departure, but the wind proved unfavorable. On the 10th of October we unmoored, and proceeded to work out of the bay. Teisuke, Kumajirō, and Kahei, accompanied us in boats destined to give us assistance, if necessary. The shore was crowded with spectators to witness our departure. When we had completely left the harbor, our Japanese friends warmly repeated their wishes for our safe return home, and took their last farewell. With considerable difficulty we prevailed on them to accept a few presents: they assured us that we had already given them more than enough. As they left the ship, our repeated adieus were accompanied by ardent wishes that a friendly alliance might speedily be established between Russia and Japan. We separated with reciprocal cheers, and the Japanese continued their salutes as long as we remained within sight of each other. But our sails were soon filled by a brisk and favorable breeze, and the *Diana* rapidly removed us from a land in which we had endured much suffering, but had also experienced the generosity of a pacific people, whom some Europeans, perhaps less civilized, regard as barbarians.

And here I must take the liberty of offering a remark on the opinion of those who attribute our liberation, and the ultimate good conduct of the Japanese, to the cowardice of that people, and their dread of the vengeance of Russia. For my own part, I am persuaded that, generally speaking, they acted from feelings of humanity, not merely because I am always inclined to regard good effects as springing from good causes, but because I can support my assertion by proof. Had fear operated on the minds of the Japanese, they would, at an earlier period, have come to a reconciliation with us. But, on the contrary, they had determined to resort to force, and had ordered Captain Ricord to be informed that we were dead at a time when they were using every precaution for the preservation of our health. Fear might, indeed, be supposed to have had some effect upon them, were the eastern provinces of Russia in a state corresponding with those of the West. But the Japanese were well aware of the very important difference between the two divisions of our empire. In my narrative the motives and the proceedings of both parties are presented to the consideration of the reader, who is thus afforded an opportunity of forming a judgment for himself.

The only circumstance worthy of observation, which occurred during our voyage from Hakodate to the harbor of Petropaulowska, was a storm of extraordinary violence, which we encountered one night off the eastern coast of the island of Hokkaido. It even exceeded in fury and danger the most dreadful tempest I ever experienced, either in the autumn off Cape Horn, or during the winter in my voyage from the Cape of Good hope to New Holland. It would be superfluous to particularize all the precautions we found it necessary to adopt to save the ship, for they included all that may be found minutely described in any book of voyages to which the reader may resort for an account of a storm.

We cast anchor in Avacha Bay on the 3rd of November. Though at that season scarcely habitable, Kamchatka, with its snow-topped mountains, volcanoes, and impenetrable forests, seemed a paradise, for it was a portion of our dear native land. The individuals who first came to meet us were Lieutenant Jakuschkin, who had served with me on board the *Diana*, and Lieutenant Volkov, of the garrison artillery. On beholding me they were as much astonished as though I had risen from the dead. Lieutenants Narmanskoy and Poduschkin next came on board. In company with these officers I went on shore at Petropaulowska at ten in the evening.

I turn once more to my unhappy companion Mur, whose severe repentance had extinguished all recollection of his errors. The sad fate of that officer cannot fail to excite sympathy in every feeling heart, whilst, at the same time, it will serve as a dreadful example of the consequences of similar misconduct.

When we embarked on board the *Diana* at Hakodate, the officers eagerly thronged round us. Mur, however, stood motionless, and apparently insensible to all that was passing. We all resolved among ourselves never, in his presence, to converse on the affairs of Japan, or to mention any circumstance that might remind him of his former conduct. We made every possible endeavour to amuse his mind, by discoursing on subjects relative to Russia. But all was in vain. He dressed himself in a way unbecoming his rank, and seldom spoke, even to the sailors, among whom he was principally to be found. When we remonstrated with him on this mode of proceeding, he usually replied, "I am unworthy to associate with gentlemen; it is even too much if the sailors condescend to keep company with me." Even when we prevailed on him to come into the cabin, he remained buried in thought. For some days after we left Hakodate he joined the rest of the officers at dinner, supper, and tea. But this he soon discontinued, and confined himself entirely to his own cabin. Sometimes, after fasting for the space of three days, he would devour food in great quantities with the utmost voracity. It appeared as if he wished by this irregular mode of living to bring on himself some fatal disorder. Such was his behavior until we arrived at Kamchatka.

Lieutenant Rudakov, Mur's old shipmate and friend, was now commandant of the harbor of Petropaulowska. He had a short time before married a beautiful and accomplished young lady, and resided in a spacious house. We thought that if they could be prevailed on to receive Mur into their house, that the society of a sensible and sprightly woman might have the effect of removing the despondency under which he labored. We accordingly made the proposal to Rudakov, and he readily acceded to it. But our hopes were quickly disappointed, for no difference whatever was produced on Mur. He frequently withdrew to some retired place, where he wept aloud, and deprecated his unhappy fate. On one occasion he so greatly alarmed Madame Rudakov, that she considered him a madman, with whom it was unsafe to live under the same roof. We then removed him to the house of a priest, with whom he had resided before our captivity. Religion and spiritual discourse might indeed have had a beneficial effect upon Mur's mind, had the priest been possessed of any conversational talent. But, unfortunately, such was not the case with Father Alexander. He could celebrate mass and repeat the litany without blundering. But his dissertations on heaven and religion were not calculated to produce any deep impression on the mind of our unhappy friend.

After we were made prisoners in Kunashir, Mur's effects had been sold by auction, and he was now entitled to the sum of 8000 roubles. We advised him to provide himself with new clothes and various other articles, but he replied that he neither wanted money or anything else. His dress consisted of an old Kamchatka parka, made of reindeer skin. He at length said that his conscience obliged him to address a report to me, in which he styled himself a traitor and an outcast, and declared that he felt himself called upon by all that he regarded as sacred to make this confession. This report was so unconnected, and contained so many extravagant expressions, that not a doubt could longer remain of Mur having lost his senses. I immediately wrote a letter of consolation to my unhappy companion, to assure him that his error was not so enormous as he himself accounted it; that we all wished to forget what was passed, and that, as he was young, he would have many opportunities of making amends for a fault into which he had been driven by despair. I added, that his future good conduct would not fail to remove all the remorse that agitated his mind. I requested that Lieutenant Rudakov would be the bearer of this letter, and that he would use every endeavour to tranquillize his distressed friend. I afterwards visited him myself, accompanied by Captain Ricord, on which occasion we, in some measure, succeeded in cheering his spirits. He discoursed reasonably, thanked me for my letter, and observed that he was unworthy of so much kindness. He afterwards occasionally conversed with our officers, and devoted a portion of his money to the purchase of clothes. In the course of a few days he expressed a wish to take up his abode in a Kamchatka village, where, he observed, he could live more at his ease, as the sight of the Russians, whom he daily met with in Petropaulowska constantly reminded him of his misconduct. It seemed advisable that, in this particular, he should follow his own inclination, and we hoped that time would heal the wounds that, in his present situation, every circumstance tended to widen. Mur having obtained permission to remove, he began to make preparations for his departure, and purchased everything he thought would be necessary for his country life. The individuals whom for his safety it had been judged necessary to appoint as his guards were as overjoyed as we, as they concluded that their duty of watching would, in a certain degree, be diminished.

Mur was exceedingly fond of shooting, and when he went abroad to enjoy that diversion, one of the guards was directed to carry his musket, and to hand it to him when he wished to fire, but never to leave him for a moment. One day, as he was out shooting on the shore of Avacha Bay, he desired the soldier who accompanied him to return home to dinner. "You need not fear," he said, laughing, "for if I wished to put an end to my life, I could do so at home with a knife or a sword." The soldier obeyed. As Mur did not return at his usual time, the man went in search of him, and with horror beheld his bloody and lifeless corpse on the shore of the bay. His clothes were hanging on a post, and the musket lay by his side, with a stick on the cock. He had apparently fired it with his foot. His body was opened, and in the breast were found two pieces of lead, with which, instead of balls, he had loaded the musket.

He had left on a table in his apartment a paper containing the following singular expression: That life had become insupportable to him, and that, at certain times, he could even fancy he had swallowed the sun. It cannot be doubted that he was occasionally subject to fits of insanity, and that the fatal act was committed in one of these paroxysms.

This unfortunate officer terminated his life on the 22nd of November, 1813, in the thirtieth year of his age. At our own expense we erected a monument over his grave, on which were inscribed the following lines:

HERE REST THE ASHES OF
LIEUTENANT FEODOR MOOR,
WHO TERMINATED HIS CAREER IN THE HARBOUR OF
PETROPAULOWSKA, ON THE 22ND OF NOVEMBER, 1813,
IN THE FLOWER OF HIS AGE.
IN JAPAN
HE WAS ABANDONED BY THE PROTECTING SPIRIT,
WHICH HAD HITHERTO BEEN HIS GUIDE.
DESPAIR PRECIPITATED HIM INTO ERROR;
BUT HIS FAULTS WERE EXPIATED BY BITTER REPENTANCE
AND DEATH.
FROM THE FEELING HEART HIS FATE CLAIMS
A TEAR!

TO HIS MEMORY
THE OFFICERS OF THE DIANA DEDICATE
THIS MONUMENT.

Mur was an officer of great merit and accomplishments. In addition to the knowledge requisite for his profession, he was conversant with several languages, and was an admirable draftsman. He loved the service to which he had devoted his life, and was zealous and indefatigable in the discharge of his duty. In company he was extremely entertaining. I had served on board the same ship with him for five years previous to the unfortunate catastrophe that befell us at Kunashir. Had not fate rendered me an eye witness of his faults, I never could have believed him capable of such a change as his conduct in Japan exhibited.

Homeward Bound

On the second of December Captain Ricord and I departed from Petropaulowska, drawn by dogs. The new year, 1814, commenced whilst we were in that extensive and uninhabitable steep, called the Parapolsk Valley, which comprehends a space of three hundred kilometers, and where travellers so frequently fall victims to storms and drifts of snow. After surmounting many dangers, we entered, in the middle of February, the town of Inschiginsk, where the public service required that we should part. And Captain Ricord, without hesitation, undertook the task of retracing his journey. I continued my progress, and reached Okhotsk on the 11th of March, having travelled with dogs a distance of more than 3000 kilometers. On quitting Okhotsk, I first travelled with dogs, and afterwards with reindeer, or horses, and when at a distance of 200 kilometers from Irkutzk, I proceeded in post carriages (*kibitka*).

I arrived at Irkutzk, by the winter road, at the latter end of April. In the middle of May I left Irkutzk, and reached St. Petersburg on the 22nd of July. Soon after my arrival, I learned that his Imperial Majesty had promoted me to the rank of captain of the second guard. I felt this unexpected favor the more, as I had, about three years before, been invested with the order of St. Vladimir, on account of my successful voyage from Kronstadt to Kamchatka, and the attention I had devoted to the health of the crew placed under my command.

His Imperial Majesty afterwards rewarded the officers of the *Diana* in the following manner: to me and Captain Ricord (who had likewise been appointed a captain of the second rank) he granted an annual pension of fifteen hundred roubles each, and gave orders that our narratives should be printed at the the expense of the government. Lieutenants Jakuschkin and Filatov were each invested with the Order of St. Vladimir of the fourth class. Khlebnikov, who was a pilot of the ninth class, Nowitzky and Sredney, pilots of the twelfth class, and Popyrin, the master at arms, received pensions to the amount of their full yearly pay. To Saveljev the clerk of the fourteenth class, was granted a pension; to the commissary's assistant, Natschpinsky, the rank of the twelfth class; to the master's mate, Labutin, the rank of the fourteenth class; to the inferior officers, pensions amounting to a full year's pay. And to the inferior officers, who had been drafted from Okhotsk, a gratuity of one year's pay. The sailors, who had been prisoners in Japan, received permission to retire from the service, and were allowed annual pensions amounting to their full yearly pay. The Ainu Alexei, as a reward for his good conduct, was presented with a hanger, and received, instead of a pension, twenty pounds of powder, and forty pounds of shot.

Glossary

bakufu:	Military, lit. "tent"government or shogunate.
bugyōsho:	Miagistrate office.
daimyō:	Feudal lord.
kanjō:	Officer.
kanjō kumigashira:	Commander of officers.
miso:	Paste made of fermented soy beans.
monpa:	Padded garment.
ri:	Japanese leage; about 2.5 miles.
sakana:	Fish.
sake:	Rice wine.
shirabeyaku:	Commissioner.
shitayaku:	Assistant.
shōgun:	Hereditary military ruler during Japan's feudal era
tōfu:	Soy bean curd.
toion:	Ainu chief.
tsume-ginmiyaku:	Deputy magistrate.
unaya:	Prison cage.

TOYO PRess: Explore Dream Discover

Editorial supervision: William de Lange. Book and cover design: Chōkei Studios. Printing and binding: IngramSpark. The typefaces used are Perpetua, Prescript, and Herculanum.